CALL ME LUCKY

CALL ME LUCKY

by

Bing Crosby

AS TOLD TO PETE MARTIN

New introduction by Gary Giddins

DA CAPO PRESS • NEW YORK

Library of Congress Cataloging in Publication Data

Crosby, Bing, 1904-1977
    Call me lucky / by Bing Crosby as told to Pete Martin; new introduc-
tion by Gary Giddins.
        p.   cm.
    Originally published: New York : Simon and Schuster, 1953.
    ISBN 0-306-80504-9
    1. Crosby, Bing, 1904-1977. 2. Singers — United States — Biography 3.
Motion picture actors and actresses — United States — Biography.
    I. Martin, Pete, 1901-. II. Title.
    ML420.C93A3 1993   92-46437
    782.42164'092 — dc20   CIP
    [B]   MN

First Da Capo Press edition 1993

This Da Capo Press paperback edition of *Call Me Lucky* is an unabridged
republication of the edition first published in New York in 1953, with the
addition of a new introduction by Gary Giddins. It is reprinted
by arrangement with HLC Properties Ltd.

Published by Da Capo Press, Inc.
A Subsidiary of Plenum Publishing Corporation
233 Spring Street, New York, N.Y. 10013

◇◇◇◇◇◇◇◇◇◇◇◇◇◇ *Introduction* ◇◇◇◇◇◇◇◇◇◇◇◇◇◇◇

BING CROSBY AND Pete Martin's *Call Me Lucky* was a sensation even before it was published by Simon and Schuster in June of 1953. When the *Saturday Evening Post* serialized half the material a few months earlier, the weekly's sales reached an all-time high: the February issue containing the first of eight installments sold 4,800,000 copies alone. By the time the book contract was announced, *Variety* predicted it would eclipse Tallulah Bankhead's autobiography as "the biggest literary enterprise by a show biz personality." Crosby's memoir was brought out in simultaneous cloth ($3.50) and paperback ($1) editions, and received almost uniformly favorable reviews. It was an immediate best-seller here and in England. A year later, *Reader's Digest* condensed it, Pocket Books issued a mass-market version (35 cents), and Parker Brothers Inc. produced a *Call Me Lucky* board game.

How long ago that was — if we measure time by the vagaries of popular culture. Yet in order to understand the impact of *Call Me Lucky* and the appeal it continues to hold, one must remember that Bing Crosby was something more than a megastar; no one in the era of Madonna and Michael Jackson has quite the same station as the much treasured crooner. As Whitney Balliett wrote in his *Saturday Review* notice of this book, Crosby was a member of "the American royalty," in a characteristic way: "He has emerged as a figure that is often affectionately regarded as the ideal American male . . . [If] the bigger-than-life common man is a new figure to the world and is the century's hero, Bing may also be one of the first of the Universal Common Men." In 1953, Crosby was without doubt the most popular and beloved (hardly the same thing) entertainer in the

United States, possibly the world. Like Charlie Chaplin's Little Tramp and Mickey Mouse, with whom he shared the trademark of oversized ears, Crosby was known internationally through variations on a distinct moniker—El Bingo, Le Bing, Der Bingle, Bing Kuo Shi Bi. Beyond his mastery of the vocal art and of light comedy, Crosby personified something profoundly and unalterably American. Through fifteen years of Depression and war, he became our voice, manner, and disposition.

The appearance of *Call Me Lucky* came midpoint in his career and at a rocky point in his life. His wife, the former Dixie Lee, had passed away the previous year, and the music world was undergoing momentous changes. Within a very short time, he would be less a dominant figure than an elder statesman, dear to the generation that grew up with him, but remote from its children. And yet the book seemed to kick off a series of typical Crosby triumphs. In 1954, he enjoyed his final season as the nation's number one box office star, with the success of the film *White Christmas* (inspired by the Irving Berlin song he had introduced in *Holiday Inn*, in 1942). In that same year, after two decades as an exclusive recording star with Decca Records, he embarked as a free agent, and finally took a long-delayed starring bow on television.

Numerous successes would follow over the years, among them a number-three hit record ("True Love"); a third Oscar nomination (*The Country Girl*); many top-rated TV specials; a seasonal association with Christmas—second, among primarily secular figures, only to that of Santa Claus; and a stirring tour of theatrical appearances in the two years preceding his death. No less remarkably, he would also remarry—the former Katherine Grandstaff, in 1957—and raise a new family, producing his fifth and sixth sons and only daughter. But by 1957, rock and roll had upended the entertainment industry, and to a generation born to relative affluence and severed by the stalemate of a cold war, Der Bingle was an old man from the planet Adultworld. Relaxation, warmth, and security were no longer perceived as basic criteria in music.

Neither were they for Crosby once upon a time. When Bing and

Al Rinker traveled down from their hometown of Spokane, Washington in a flivver vividly described in *Call Me Lucky*, they were hot to put their mark on the most exciting music of the day. In time, Crosby created a wholly individual style informed by the improvisational power of Louis Armstrong, the theatrical charisma of Al Jolson, and the nuance and diligent enunciation of Mildred Bailey and Ethel Waters. One major bandleader of the 1930s called him "the first hip white person in the United States." At a time when prissy tenors were the norm among male pop vocalists, Crosby was a virile baritone with a cry in his throat and an ability to expound any lyric as though it had a story to tell. His two-beat jazz interpretations had fire and feeling and surprise; his ballads were dramatic — even fervent — without being maudlin.

Crosby could sing anything and make you believe him. He was singularly influential in popularizing cowboy songs and bringing country music into the mainstream. He was no less closely associated with Hawaiian songs, especially after he starred in *Waikiki Wedding* (1937), in which he introduced "Blue Hawaii," as well as "Sweet Leilani," his first official million-seller. He recorded albums in French and Spanish, both of which he spoke fluently; and his mellifluous speaking voice, always a songful instrument, proved ideal for several narrations, including Walt Disney's animation of "The Legend of Sleepy Hollow" (*Ichabod*) and a recording of Oscar Wilde's "The Little Prince," directed by Orson Welles. As a film actor, he usually played variants on himself — a cocky, independent sort who'd suffer a comeuppance or two and get the girl in the end. When the action stopped long enough for him to emote "Going Hollywood" (in the movie of the same name) or "May I" (in *We're Not Dressing*), his voice could rattle the balcony — and still does.

In the 1940s, wartime, Crosby's personality took on a more resolute quality. Immensely likable, he was widely publicized for his love of horses (he was an owner of the racetrack at Del Mar), golf (he was a near-scratch player, and his annual tournament at Pebble Beach was a sporting legend), baseball (part owner of the Pittsburgh Pirates), and ranching (the Crosby ranch at Elko, Nevada was no resort, as he duly reports in his memoir). His participation in the war effort was celebrated here and abroad, especially when he traveled to London. The military dubbed him Uncle Sam without Whiskers. His place at the top of the entertainment world was uncontested, and he was surely no less admired by the readers of the fan magazines for his ideal marriage to the beautiful Dixie, herself once a budding actress, and their clamorous sons — Gary, the twins Dennis and Philip, and Lindsay.

The marriage, we now know, was deeply troubled; Dixie and her sons all fought alcoholism, and Bing himself overcame overindulgence in alcohol early in his career. When Gary, in a widely misunderstood account of his own life, *Going My Own Way* (1983), reported on his father's use of corporal punishment, the tabloids swooped down to decimate the once pristine image. When two of his sons took their own lives, attempts were made to blame Bing, despite repeated denials by their families; indeed, Lindsay was a manic depressive with an abiding and demonstrated love for his father. In any case, the belated shock — the outrage that Crosby was not a saint, a role he never claimed for himself — was ludicrously overplayed. He candidly addresses the issue of child-rearing himself in *Call Me Lucky*. Yet despite his approving reference to the Italian proverb, "Never kiss a baby unless he's asleep"; his admission that "friends think I'm too tough a disciplinarian"; his boast, "I'll bet [my sons] remember the spankings they got when they were younger"; and intimations of cruelty suggested in the way he points up the boys' failings rather than achievements, the reviewers emphasized Crosby's love for his children as manifested in the book. No one *wanted* to see beyond the myth of perfection.

In several interviews of the 1950s and after, Crosby publicly questioned his own wisdom in over-disciplining his sons, and recalled that he too was brought up with a raised hand. Moreover, he learned from his mistakes, as Gary himself acknowledges. The children of his second marriage — Harry, Mary Frances, Nathaniel, all successful in their chosen fields — have no such complaints. As Gary and scores of other relations, friends, and associates also underscore, the

Crosby persona was no less real for the PR gloss of his private life. The accessible grace of his artistry, the loyalty to friends, the generosity to many causes, the extraordinary professionalism, and the fundamental decency of the man were all genuine. No one fools all the people all the time for half a century.

Bing died on October 14, 1977, after completing a round of golf on a course in Spain. If the intervening years have not always been kind or fair to his memory, a new and unmistakable appreciation for Crosby's art has emerged. At this writing, more than sixty Crosby CDs are available, and his films — especially the romantic comedies of the 1930s and the Road pictures with Bob Hope — are enjoying renewed favor. The republication of *Call Me Lucky*, which so successfully sustains the casual, upright, anecdotal voice once familiar to millions from the more than thirty years he appeared on radio, is part of a long overdue rediscovery of one of the most extraordinary figures in entertainment history.

Call Me Lucky belongs to the genre of as-told-to books, a tradition probably as old as autobiographical accounts by non-literary celebrities. Not the least lucky thing about it is the man to whom it was told, Pete Martin, an editor and writer with the *Saturday Evening Post*, who became nationally famous for his celebrity interviews. Born in Virginia in 1901, and educated at the University of Virginia, Martin served a two-year stint with *College Humor* before moving to the *Post* in 1926. Two decades later, he began a widely noted series of Q&A interviews called, "I Call On . . ." The series continued until 1963, when he left the magazine, and was so popular that a record album was released of excerpts from his taped visits. Two best-selling books also resulted: Bob Hope's *Have Tux, Will Travel* (1954), as well as its predecessor, *Call Me Lucky* — each topped 100,000 sales. The writer died three years after Crosby (almost to the day, on October 13, 1980), at 79, in Pennsylvania.

Martin's work with Crosby resulted in one of the first as-told-to's done on tape, which was entirely appropriate, as Crosby was greatly responsible for introducing tape into American life. He helped finance the first tape recorders ever manufactured, and he was the first singer to install them in his studio as well as the first radio star to tape his shows in advance, a procedure strenuously resisted by networks and sponsors for a short while. Throughout the book, Martin manages to capture and sustain the breezy Crosby lingo made famous on radio — a medium Bing adored and stayed with from 1931 until 1963, by which time just about everyone else had long since left the field to disc jockeys and newscasters. If the book's first half, in its conventional autobiographical form, is most intriguing for its historical details, the loosely compiled anecdotes of the second half are possibly more revealing of the Crosby personality. Note, for example, that Chapter Eleven, the longest by far, is devoted to golf, and that the often jocular episodes about that pastime and other leisurely pursuits account for nearly a third of the work.

Crosby took a hands-on role in every aspect of his career, and you can bet he was fully involved in the final form of *Call Me Lucky.* The book is by no means entirely upbeat or free from self-criticism, and it surely represents the way he wanted to be known to his public and in all likelihood to himself — as a man's man, suspicious of people who analyze themselves, utterly lacking in vanity about his appearance (he is wonderfully funny on Hollywood's attempt to remodel him with toupees, corsets, and spirit gum to hold down his ears) or his talent, which he attributes to dumb luck. In this respect, he was modest to a fault: Bing worked hard to build his career and his business empire. He was nothing if not a craftsman, always the first on the set or in the studio, and always prepared — though he was also the first to leave, especially when the sun was shining and the first tee beckoned. Yet part of the nature of his art was to perfect the illusion of pure insouciance, and it would be a mistake to underestimate the significance of that illusion among his gifts to the public. He made everyone feel he or she could sing, act, mug, and dance as well as *he* could; he envied no one and, miraculously, no one appeared to envy him.

On one issue, however, he was determinedly less than candid. Crosby always insisted, even to his friends, that he was born May 2,

Introduction

1904. In truth, he was born a year earlier, in 1903, in the early hours of May 3rd in his parents' home in Tacoma, Washington, as he well knew — his brother Larry even had a professional genealogy service produce a family history with the correct date. Why shave a year? Actually, Paramount Pictures did it for him, in 1933, when he was signed to a contract. Someone in public relations decided a matinee idol ought to be in his twenties, and *voilà!* — the first release went out with the 1904 birthdate. Bing eventually dispensed with spirit gum and corsets, and he never wore a toupee when he wasn't performing. But he held fast to his official movie age. As he explained to a business associate, "In this business, youth is everything." Perhaps only in that regard did he undervalue the devotion of his countless fans.

— GARY GIDDINS

December 1992

Gary Giddins, a prize-winning columnist for the Village Voice, *is the author of* Faces in the Crowd. *His long-awaited biography of Bing Crosby is slated for publication by William Morrow in the fall of 1995.*

✧✧✧✧✧✧✧✧✧✧ *Table of Contents* ✧✧✧✧✧✧✧✧✧✧

ILLUSTRATION SECTION   1-32

CHAPTER ONE   33
A memorable party—Leo's system—Father Sharp—
"Just hovering"—Pops Whiteman

CHAPTER TWO   45
Dixie Lee—No sacrifice—I haven't worked very hard
—Prayer is a potent thing

CHAPTER THREE   52
Mother and Dad—"It'll do him good."—Uncle George
—I become Bing—Bim Crosland—A small knight—A
few with a yardstick—Early jobs—The Sholderers

CHAPTER FOUR   68
Earliest theatrical experiences—Ou est le Jug?—The
faculty and the tongs—The Musicaladers—Bailey's
Music Company—I gave up law—Boo-boo-boo—The
Morrisey Music Hall Revue

CHAPTER FIVE   83
Debut with Whiteman—Bell-belting—Bix—Bix's crowd
—A real handy fellow—Happy days are here again—
The act goes sour—On to Hollywood—Narrow escape
—Into durance vile

CHAPTER SIX   103

The Montmartre—The Coconut Grove—End of The Rhythm Boys—"The wrong Crosby"—Snafu—At the Paramount—More movies

CHAPTER SEVEN   116

"The Old Ox Road"—Jack Oakie—Life with Marion— My ears stay put—Cake make-up—Carole—"Now, where were we?"—Bear facts

CHAPTER EIGHT   130

Blessed events—Lament for privacy—The Crosby building—Leo Lynn—Doc Stevens—Jack Kapp—The skolinest cat—The pluggers—"In the morning you'll be jealous as hell again."—How to get behind an eight-ball—Self-criticism—Chaliapin—Everybody's taping

CHAPTER NINE   155

Bill Fields—Our first Road picture—"Tsk-tsk"—Little Frankenstein—Johnny Burke—Rib—"Wolf, wolf."— "What's new?"—The Doctor

CHAPTER TEN   172

The Birth of the Blues—*Wingy*—Rhythm on the River —*Jimmy Cottrell—Trouble in Morocco—Working with Capra—France—Great lady—Life with Father—Tribute to McCarey*

CHAPTER ELEVEN   190

Relaxed and casual—Look at them birdies!—Fun at Pebble Beach—Whistler—Exhibitions—Joker—Special booking—The doubter—Jock McLean—Hole in one— Quick change—Menace to mice—Fanny and elbows— Nose bleed — Harvey — Rug-cutter — The "Bandit" — Ringer—Republican postmaster—Sixty-five per cent dive—London

Table of Contents

CHAPTER TWELVE   231

Lucky, indeed—Black Forest—Help from Hope—Jocky Club—Seabiscuit and Ligaroti—The route to insolvency—Dreamboat—The "leaky roof" circuit—Christmas spirit—Parlay—I'm offered a job

CHAPTER THIRTEEN   253

John O'Melveny—Joe Venuti—"I was going great."— "I feel it coming on."—Skull music—John Scott Trotter —Yates, the Eater—Scotch scarcity—Loss leader—To Morrow—Little man who wasn't there—Society Kid Hogan—Historical note—The Taxi Driver's Revenge

CHAPTER FOURTEEN   281

Couple of loggers—In the hands of the gendarmes— Drop-ins—Pants, too long—The twins—Trip overseas —The Stytion Mawster—Visit with General Bradley

CHAPTER FIFTEEN   298

Gary at Stanford—My fuddy-duddy notions—I haven't licked them lately—Ensembles—Our principal knotheads—Hard money—Ranch stuff—The neighbors— Fatherly pride—Party line—Miss Sleeping Bag

CHAPTER SIXTEEN   321

She was that way always—"What a lady!"—Last reunion—Just as she'd always been

CHAPTER SEVENTEEN   328

TV and me—High spots—Aloha

INDEX   335

PENGUIN

Age 4

Age 16—I was nicknamed Bing (see page 57)

Baseball was my game, I am and always was nutty about it

The Rhythm Boys: Harry Barris, Al Rinker, and I (see page 92)

Bix Beiderbecke *(right)* and the Wolverines (see page 87)

Dixie Lee *(left)* and starlets

Paul Whiteman and The Rhythm Boys at a recent reunion

In the Mack Sennett Keystone Comedy days (see page 105)

With Marion Davies in *Going Hollywood* (see page 118)

With Margie "Babe" Kane in *Billboard Girl*

Five shows a day at the Paramount for twenty-nine weeks (see page 112)

PENGUIN

The Studio had large, glittering plans for Dixie until we were married (see page 45)

PENGUIN

Gary, Philip, Dennis, and a man adding up the cost of baby shoes

Carole Lombard in *We're Not Dressing* (see page 125)

With Carole and Ethel Merman, who was also featured *(below)*

Mississippi, with one of my idols,
W. C. Fields—(see page 155)

With Joan Bennett *(right)*

(left) With Leo Lynn, my stand-in (see page 135)

With Fred MacMurray and Gary Cooper — we named our first son after Gary

With America's sweetheart, Mary Pickford

With Louis Armstrong—Louis has been my friend for twenty years (see page 140)

(left) Gary and the twins, visiting the *Star Maker* set

In *Road to Zanzibar*, with friend

Dorothy Lamour, a friend, and I in the *Roads to Singapore* . . .

. . . *Bali* . . .

. . . and *Utopia*

The Westwood Marching and Chowder Club

With Wingy Manone in *Birth of the Blues* (see page 172)

With my radio writer, Bill Morrow (see page 266)

The Firehouse Five plus Two on the Kraft Music Hall

With Irving Berlin

With Joe Venuti, the unpredictable violinist (see page 255)

During the construction of our Del Mar race track (see page 237)

Losing *(right)*, and winning *(below)* at Santa Anita

The challenge of golf is just as rewarding whether I practice on the set *(above)*, play with my son Linny *(below)*, or give exhibitions with a friend *(right)*

Going My Way—with director Leo McCarey (see page 35)

With Risë Stevens in a scene from the picture

PARAMOUNT

The picture won a flock of Academy Awards: Leo was given the director's and screenplay award, Barry Fitzgerald the supporting Oscar, and I won the male actor award (see page 38)

PARAMOUNT

With Ethel Barrymore, one of my favorite dolls . . .

. . . and one of my favorite guys, Groucho Marx

On the set of *The Bells of St. Mary's*

Preparing to go overseas with Fred Astaire

Doing a charity show with a friend

Singing at the Hollywood Canteen

Hunting, fishing . . .

. . . riding and working on our Elko, Nevada, ranch

Breakfast with the boys

Guitarist Perry Botkin at a party   Linny watching a good shot

Basketball *(above)* and family portrait *(below)*

GENE LESTER

. . . and with Cindy

THE AUTOBIOGRAPHICAL KICK is a new caper for me. Starting the story of my life makes my memory feel like an out-of-kilter juke box. When I drop a nickel into it, I'm not sure which story it will play back.

I might push a nickel in and have the story of my grandmother, Katie, come out. Katie married an Irishman named Dennis Harrigan. When she was on her deathbed, Dennis sat near by watching her for some sign of recognition.

Just before the end, her eyes opened and she said, "Give me your hand, Dinnis."

He put his hand in hers and said, "Katie, it's a hand that was never raised against ye."

Her eyes opened wider. "And it's a domn good thing for ye it wasn't!" she said. Then she died. She must have been a very spirited woman.

I might shove in another nickel and my memory juke box would play the story of the oddly assorted crowd which attended a New Year's Eve party given by Win Rockefeller at the Pocantico Hills estate which had once belonged to his grandfather, John D.

I was having lunch with Win in New York, where business had taken me in 1946, just after Christmas. "You know what we ought to do this New Year's Eve?" he asked. "Instead of going to a café and letting people throw confetti at us and blow horns in our ears, and stomp on our toes and push us around, we ought to throw our own party."

He warmed up to the notion as he talked about it. "We can go up to my grandfather's estate, open the house and get in some servants. You bring your gang from show business and I'll bring my friends. We'll have a band and we'll hire some entertainers. I'll supply the drinks and food. It should be fun."

"Hmm," I said doubtfully. "But your gang has probably never been exposed to my kind of a gang."

"I don't care," he said. "Bring anybody you want to. We'll meet in front of the Sherry-Netherland about four or five New Year's Eve afternoon. I'll have a chartered bus there with a bar installed in it, and I'll stock it with sandwiches and we'll drive out. We'll be out there in time for a swim in the indoor pool. Then we'll have drinks, dinner, a big New Year's Eve dance, spend the next day and come home in the evening."

I talked some of my pals in show business into going. Among them were such blue-blood Back Bay types as Phil Silvers; the song writers Johnny Burke and Jimmy Van Heusen; Barney Dean, an ex-vaudeville knockabout comedian; Jack Clark, a song plugger; and Rags Ragland, a *magna cum laude* graduate from burlesque.

Some of the married fellows brought their wives and there were some extra unattached lovelies, too. I held a meeting with my group before the take-off and begged them not to get gassed or start any fights or make flip observations about the clothing or mannerisms of our host or his friends.

They promised solemnly that they wouldn't, and they did pretty well in the bus. After reaching Tarrytown we drove through a vast stone gateway and a succession of parks, then more gates and more parks and more gates, with watchmen at each gate. Finally we pulled up before a tremendous pile of brick and masonry, and I heard a whispered question from one of my pals, "Is this the rumpus room?" I silenced him with a reproachful glare. Then we got out of the bus and started up the fifty or sixty stone steps leading to the main entrance.

We were halfway up when Barney Dean stopped and said, "Wait."

"What's the matter?" Win Rockefeller asked.

"I can't go in," Barney replied.

I asked, "Why not?" I should have known better.

"I forgot my library card," Barney said.

I gave him a dirty look. I had a feeling my gang was getting out of control.

The head butler assigned us to rooms and told us that we could do anything we wanted to do; we could swim or play table tennis or indoor tennis on a regulation-sized court. There was everything anyone could want for recreation or amusement. We opened one door and there before our bugged eyes were long, gleaming bowling alleys with pin boys waiting, their arms folded across their chests. We opened another door, and there was Dorothy Shay, the Park Avenue Hillbilly, singing songs to entertain us. Behind another door a band was holding sway, thumping and blaring.

We were watching a tennis game from the gallery above the indoor tennis court when one of Win Rockefeller's dowager friends popped her head in and asked, "Has anyone seen Millicent?"

We stared at each other blankly. Then Barney Dean said helpfully, "Maybe she's upstairs playing polo."

After that the atmosphere grew a little tense, but following a highball or two, the chill thawed. We played the piano and sang and danced, and everyone became bosom friends. All in all, it was a memorable party.

A third nickel in my memory juke box might spring loose a disk of me reciting the story of making the movie *Going My Way* in 1944. Leo McCarey, a top director and also an old golf-course, football-game and Del Mar-Race-Track friend of mine, was always threatening to use me in one of his pictures.

"I'll get an idea for you, and when I do, I'll let you know," he said. It became a running gag. Every time I saw him, even if he was three or four fairways away, I'd holler, "Now?"

He'd give a slow, negative shake of his head and yell, "No."

That went on for years. Then one day I saw him at a football game, and when I asked "Now?" he said, "Now!"

I said, "Come over to the house."

When he came over, he told me, "After you hear the idea I have for you, maybe you'll think it isn't 'now.' I want you to play a priest."

"Now what kind of a priest could I play?" I asked. "I'd be unbelievable, and besides, the Church won't like that kind of casting."

"I think it would," he said. "I've talked to some pretty wise priests in this diocese and they think you can handle the character I described."

I said, "Let's hear it."

So he gave me the story—or, at any rate, such story fragments as he had then for *Going My Way.*

Leo is of the old school of directors. His roots go back deep into the silent days when a director never put anything down on paper. In Leo's fledgling days, directors had to be accomplished actors and great mimics. When they told a story they had to put it over so effectively that the producer suffered an acute attack of enthusiasm and said, "Okay. Here's five hundred thousand dollars. Make it."

Leo told me a terrific story. It wasn't the story he eventually used, but when he was through, there wasn't a dry eye in the house—his or mine. In his preliminary take-out of his idea, I played a priest all right, but from there on it wasn't much like *Going My Way.* Looking back, I don't think he had a story at all. He just made one up as he went along. Nevertheless, he had me transfixed. When he finished, I was sold. I said, "I'll be ready in the morning."

But first he had to see those good, gray, elder statesmen, Paramount's top brass. Probably he told them an entirely different story, but at least it had a priest in it, for the higher-ups back East who controlled the studio's purse strings blew a gasket when they heard that I was to wear a long, black, buttoned-down robe. One or two of them suggested that it might be a good idea to have Leo committed for observation. However, Paramount's production head, Buddy DeSylva, believed in Leo. He was willing to go along with him on his Crosby-as-a-priest notion. Eventually, Buddy sold it to the people in the East.

Leo had his own movie-making system. I don't think that even when we started Leo had a final story mapped out. He began with a few scenes to establish the locale and to give an idea what kind of priests Barry Fitzgerald, Frank McHugh, and I were. After that, we never knew what we'd be doing from morning to afternoon. We'd come on the set about nine, have coffee and doughnuts, and Leo would go over to a piano and play for a while, while the rest of us sang a little barbershop. Then he'd wander around and think. He might even take a walk down the street and come back, while we waited. About eleven o'clock, he'd say, "Well, let's get going."

We'd run through the scene he'd described to us the previous night. Then he'd say, "We're not going to do that. Take a two-hour lunch break. I'll whip something up and we'll shoot it after lunch." When he came back, what he'd whipped up might change the whole direction of the story. We shot it anyhow.

Leo is no Fancy Dan, Mittel-European technician who tosses close-ups, medium shots, montages, angle shots and camera tricks around. Most of his shots are old-fashioned, no-nonsense, full-figure shots. One of the scenes in the picture was a checker game which involved Fitzgerald, Frank McHugh, and me. We ad-libbed it right on the set under Leo's direction. He shot it from just one angle, and then he said, "Print it."

"What, no close-ups?" we asked.

"It looked good to me from that angle," he said, and that was that.

The picture won a flock of Academy Awards. Leo was given the director's award and the award for writing the screen play. Barry Fitzgerald won the supporting Oscar. I got lucky and wound up with the award for the best male movie actor of 1944.

My memory of the award-giving at Grauman's Chinese Theater is not too clear. I'd heard there was a chance I'd get an award, but I was sure that it would go to someone who was recognized as an able actor rather than a crooner. So I didn't take it too seriously until shortly before the ceremony, when it began to look as if I had a chance. After that I took it seriously enough to put on a dinner jacket, which is unusual for me. I'm not a great lad for getting into a dinner jacket in which to attend functions of a semi-official character.

Gary Cooper was chosen to hand me the award. I don't remember what he said, but when he managed to put the idea over to me that I had won the award, a great warm feeling came over me. I stumbled up on the stage like a zombie. Neither Coop nor I said much.

I asked, "Are you talking about me?"

And he said, "Yup."

My memory juke box might decide to give out next the story of Father Sharp, one of the most beloved men who ever taught at Gonzaga University. Father Sharp came from Butte, Montana. Butte is not a panty-waist community today, and in those days it was even less so. Father Sharp went into the Jesuit order, then came to Gonzaga to teach. He was a stern disciplinarian, but a fair Joe. If you were innocent and could prove it, you were free and clear.

He had a leather strap made up. The out-of-line younger students in the high school operated by Gonzaga caught it across their behinds. The older students got it on the hands. When some of the older students who fancied themselves with their dukes demanded fistic satisfaction after such punishment,

Father Sharp removed his collar and put on the gloves with them. He never blew a decision either, as I recall it.

In the mid 1930's Gonzaga held a Home-coming Week. Part of that celebration was a football game with the University of San Francisco. I was asked to revisit the campus and do a radio show to raise money for the college library. I was also asked to take part in the ceremonies at the football game.

It was a three- or four-day affair, with functions each evening. The night before the game one of these functions kept me up late and, what with the conviviality born of seeing so many of my old classmates, I woke up feeling rocky and with a case of the whips and jingles. I went out to the college for a late breakfast and afterward repaired to the locker room to wish the coach luck. As a restorative, I had with me a flagon of spirits, but since it had only a scanty drink left in it, I planned to save it until just before game time.

When the team ran out onto the field, I stepped into a little office off the locker room for a final belt at the bottle. Just as I lifted it to my lips, I saw Father Sharp coming down the corridor, and with an instinctive return to the habits of my student years, I stashed the flagon under a desk, hoping he hadn't seen me do it.

The game was about to start, and since I'd been asked to say a few words at midfield before the kick-off, I was growing restive. But Father Sharp showed no disposition to leave. Finally I decided to abandon the bottle, but just as we got to the door, he went back, reached under the desk, fetched the bottle out and took a swig which emptied it. "It wouldn't be right to let a soldier die without a priest," he said, his eyes twinkling.

No wonder we loved him at Gonzaga. It wasn't hard to love a fellow like that.

That Home-coming Week was a big week for me in more ways than one. I gave the football team a gadget they nicknamed Bing's Bucket. It was a sort of portable fountain brought out onto the field during times out to give the players a drink. It was painted blue and white and it had rubber wheels. It moved faster than the old-fashioned bucket and water didn't slosh from it. And it had a hose attached to it so the team could drink out of the hose.

During that week there were a number of festivities to raise money for the athletic fund. All the old grads I'd gone to school with when we were kids were there. One of them had grown up to become a Spokane judge. He presided and made a speech. I made a speech too and sang a song.

The undergraduates were all on hand and the glee club sang. Then someone, inspired by a burst of local pride, decided to confer a degree on me. They gave me a Ph.D., but after I'd gone back to Los Angeles, they found that nothing I'd ever done entitled me to such a degree, so I was sent a substitute certificate. The wording was changed to Doctor of Music.

But if I'm to get on with my story, I'll have to rid myself of the feeling that my memories are a busted juke box and get them organized so they'll begin somewhere and end somewhere. In the assortment will certainly be the letter my youngest son, Linny, wrote to me when he was nine or ten and I was back East.

In his letter he gave me a detailed account of the sporting news from the Pacific Coast. I forgot whether football or baseball was in season, but I remember he closed: "Your *friend*, Lin." That made me feel happier than an actor over a rave notice from George Jean Nathan. Father *and* friend.

In another scene featuring Linny, there was some preliminary footage involving a Hollywood director who's a bigger ham than any actor I've ever known on stage, screen, radio, or TV. He owns the traditional wardrobe: the camel's-hair coat, white, buttoned, pleated, and belted; the spats; the cane; the soft gray hat turned down on one side à la Jimmy Walker. He has the sonorous, directorial voice larded with Barrymore intonations. When he calls "Camera" or "Cut," his delivery is dramatic in the extreme. He has a swagger and a flair which reek of the boards.

He's a frustrated actor if I've ever seen one, endowed with a full portion of well-smoked Smithfield characteristics.

One evening when a fellow director who occupied studio space next to his entered his office after work, he noticed a gaunt shadow stalking to and fro in the dusk behind the building. Investigating, he discovered that the shadow was the ham-bone director.

"What's the trouble?" he asked the stalker.

"My dear David, haven't you heard?" the Hamlet of the megaphone asked in sepulchral tones.

"No," David replied.

"It's my wife! She underwent surgery today."

"How's she feeling?" David asked anxiously.

The hammy one held out a hand, palm down, thumb extended, and wavered it like an airplane signaling with its wings. "Hovering," he said dramatically, "just hovering." Then he added, "By the way, do you have an extra seat for the fights tonight?"

I told this story around the house, and my boys got quite a jar out of it. A year or two went by and I forgot about it.

In the summer of 1946, when we were at our ranch in Elko County, Nevada, Lindsay, who was about nine, came down with a mysterious attack of fever. Twenty-four hours passed and he showed no improvement. In fact his temperature rose, so I had Ralph Scott, a bush pilot who operates out of Elko, fly Dr. Les Morin out. When the doctor examined Linny, his diagnosis confirmed the suspicions which were already lurking in my mind. He had Rocky Mountain spotted fever, induced by a tick bite.

His fever increased and he became delirious. The doctor advised against moving him to a hospital, but he promised to fly out twice a day to care for him. For several days and nights the fever raged. During all that time Linny was unconscious. On the fifth day, in the small hours of the morning, he broke into a drenching sweat and his temperature fell. For a while he dozed, then he opened his eyes and looked inquiringly around the room.

"How do you feel, Lin?" I asked anxiously.

He grinned feebly and stuck his hand out, palm down, thumb extended, wavered it from side to side, and said in a quavering voice, "Hovering. Just hovering."

There are other memories of me telling my sons bedtime stories when they were very little. I tried to give those tales modern overtones and put things in them my sons knew about. In that way I hoped they'd be more vivid and would hold their attention. I had Little Red Riding Hood riding a scooter through the woods at Pebble Beach, where we had a house. Her basket was filled with chocolate bars and she was on her way to see her grandma, who was living at the Pine Inn Hotel. The wolf was tall, dark, and sinister, wore a high silk hat and was passing through in a fancy car on his way to Nevada. In my version of *Don Quixote,* Don was a taller and thinner edition of my sons' friend, Gary Cooper. His groom, Sancho Panza, was so dopey you wouldn't let him fool around your stable if you were in your right mind.

Still another of my most vivid recollections is of my first meeting with Paul Whiteman, known as America's greatest band leader. This meeting took place before Harry Barris teamed with Al Rinker and me as a team known as the Rhythm Boys. Rinker and I had left our homes in Spokane in a beat-up jalopy with twenty dollars in our pockets and had chugged and spluttered southward to Los Angeles.

In 1927 we were playing the Metropolitan Theater there in an act we'd worked up when Whiteman came to town with his orchestra and occupied the Million Dollar Theater down the street a piece from us. Al and I went down to catch Whiteman's band several times. I thought it tremendous. But the main attraction to me was a Whiteman singer named "Skin" Young. He had a sensational singing style, and he'd come out of a little jazz group called the Mason-Dixon Orchestra. Skin had a tremendous range. He could go very high and very low. He could not only sing things like "The Road to Mandalay," he could sing blues songs and fast rhythm songs and he could make sounds as uninhibited as a pre-Cab Calloway.

Whiteman didn't catch Rinker and me doing our routine, but some of the members of his band heard us and told him about us. He sent for us and we went to see him.

He had a little piano in his dressing room, and we did a few numbers for him there. During our audition he sat on an ottoman, fragrant with toilet water and wearing a silk dressing gown which must have cost *beaucoup* bob. He weighed three hundred and ten pounds and was eating caviar from a bowl which held a pound of those little gray eggs. And he had a silver-plated cooler of champagne beside him.

These, I thought, are the habiliments of success. This fellow is really there. When you can eat a pound of caviar and drink champagne from a cooler in your dressing room in the middle of the day, you've reached the pinnacle. He asked us if we'd join his organization at the Tivoli Theater in Chicago when we'd completed our contract in Los Angeles, which had a couple of weeks to run.

Rinker and I hit a small pinnacle of our own when we joined the Whiteman band in Chicago. But as we rolled east, our routine began to seem countrified to us, and we began to wonder how we were going to put it over in a theater in a big city like Chicago, with a "sophisticated Midwestern audience." At that point we weren't looking far enough into the future to give thought to how "sophisticated" New York audiences could be.

When we reached Chicago we were definitely chicken, and Pops Whiteman gave us a fight talk before our first show to cure us of our shakes. We'd learned to call him Pops or Fatso Whiteman by this time. The rest of his band did too. Behind his back we employed more disrespectful words, such as "the Fat Fiddler."

"Music's the same all over," Pops said. "They liked you in Los Angeles and they'll like you here. You've nothing to worry about. Just do your stuff the way you've already done it."

We listened, and when we walked out there to face our first matinee audience, we were cocky on the outside, but inside the butterflies were fluttering restlessly.

Pops introduced us by telling the crowd, "I want you to meet a couple of boys I found in an ice-cream parlor in Walla Walla." Afterward he told us he'd picked Walla Walla because its name sounded funny to him. Funny or not, it struck exactly the right note. We went out there, did our stuff, and if I do say it, we were very big. I'm confident that oldsters who attended the Tivoli Theater on Chicago's South Side in those days will bear me out in this.

But after being very big in Chicago and on the road, Rinker and I laid an egg in New York of sufficient size to make a soufflé for Paul Bunyan. What a thud!

THE FIRST TIME I ever heard the name "Dixie Lee" was in 1929. I rolled it on my tongue like honey. Dixie's real name was Wilma Winifred Wyatt. She came from Harriman, Tennessee. She was raised in New Orleans, then her folks moved to Chicago. When she was a seventeen-year-old Chicago high-school girl, she won a Ruth Etting contest. Ruth Etting was one of the popular women singers of the 1920's. The contest selected the Chicago girl "who sang most like Ruth Etting." Dixie's prize was a two-week singing engagement at the College Inn, café-restaurant-night club in the Sherman Hotel.

She was working at the old Fox Studio and I was one of Whiteman's Rhythm Boys singing at the Montmartre in Los Angeles. She came to the Montmartre on a date with Frankie Albertson, and Frankie introduced us. She came back several times after that. I couldn't tell whether she came back to hear the band or me. I wasn't sure. But I knew what I hoped.

The head man at Dixie's studio had fine, large, glittering plans for her. He told her that if she married me, it would interfere with those plans. That didn't influence her. She married me anyhow. One of the things they told Dixie was that if she threw in her lot with me, she'd have to support me for the rest of her life. She did support me for the rest of her life, but not in the way they meant. I was able to do somewhat better for her financially than the doubting Thomases predicted, but the kind of support Dixie gave me and her sons was more important than money. She was an understanding and loyal wife, a wise and loving

45

mother. We could always count on her for the truth about ourselves, and that's a rare and helpful commodity in Hollywood.

Not only was there opposition from her studio, whose big wheels told her I was nobody going no place and she was somebody going big places, but also her father took a dim view of me as a son-in-law. He thought, and with just cause, that rated on past performance I was a useless, good-for-nothing type. I hadn't been too industrious. I hadn't put out too much in the way of work. I'd played golf and had a good time. I couldn't seem to be serious about anything.

Our marriage was regarded as newsworthy by the press, but it was because of Dixie, not me. It was a case of Miss Big marrying Mr. Little. The papers knew so little about me that they fouled up the spelling of my name. WELL-KNOWN FOX MOVIE STAR MARRIES BING CROVENY, the headlines read. Croveny, yet!

When my name became better known, I could count on Dixie to keep my head from getting too big. Like any wise wife, whenever she thought my ego was getting out of hand, she had her methods for shrinking me to proper size. She'd say, "Listen to the Romantic Singer of the Songs-You-Love-to-Hear Blues." Or she'd call me "The Bumptious Baritone," or "Ole Gravel Throat." Or, when I'd try ineffectually to lecture the kids, she'd say, "You're foolin' the people, but you can't fool them, eh?"

Jack Oakie, who's always been one of my favorite comedians, had another way of deflating me. In one movie, *Mississippi*, I was so pudgy I had to wear a girdle to pull my stomach in. Jack took a look at my two-way stretch; he thought of the hours Paramount's make-up men had spent gluing my jug ears back against my head, and attaching a toupee to my scalp to supplant my thinning thatch, and he nicknamed me the Robot of Romance. But even such barbs as Oakie's couldn't cut me down to size like Dixie's wifely needling.

What Dixie's studio and her fans didn't know was that she didn't want to go big places. She didn't like show business and the hokum that goes with it, and the necessity of being nice to people you don't enjoy being nice to. She never could bring herself to con people or butter them up, the way a girl breaking into pictures is asked to do to advance herself.

For this reason, it was no sacrifice for her to leave show business. She had a very good agent who did a terrific job for her after she came to Hollywood, but she hated the things he wanted her to do. As a part of pushing her career, he asked her to give out interviews, or go to benefits, or make radio broadcasts to exploit pictures. Then there was the business of being sweet to writers and producers and directors and other studio executives who, her instinct told her, didn't rate sweetness or even civility. She tried to do these things, but she died inside as she did them.

Although she was very frank and outspoken, she was also diffident and shy. She had little self-confidence. She never did think she was good in show business. I've known all of the others, and when it came to singing a song, Dixie had no equal. But it was a matter of life and death to persuade her to sing.

When we were going together before we were married, she did a guest-soloist spot with Ben Bernie on his radio show. She was almost in a state of shock when she finally stood before the microphone to do her number. She wasn't ashamed of the fact that facing people or working in public was an ordeal for her. She admitted it to her friends, but the public has never known this.

She cut a couple of records with me, but no one will ever know the ordeal I went through persuading her to make those records. Building the Pyramids would have been easier. She thought of scores of reasons why she didn't want to do them— all of them sprang from her shyness. She was an only daughter; she had been very close to her parents, and they'd sheltered her as much as possible. As a result, she'd never been before the public much prior to leaving home, and she never got over disliking it. She went into show business because she'd won that contest in Chicago for which a chum of hers entered her name without telling her about it. She followed through with it so as not to let her chum down.

She talked to our four sons as if they were her own age. Even when they were small, she didn't like it if they acted like babies. She always wanted them to have an adult point of view. I think the reason for this was that she didn't want them ever to be diffident, as she was.

She never got over her dislike of any interference with her private life or anyone prying into it. After she stopped being an actress and a singer, she gave only a few interviews to personal friends in the newspaper or magazine business. If a stranger tried to interview her, she was scared to death. She didn't want any part of the limelight. She just wanted to have her family and her home and her friends.

Even if she hadn't married me, she wouldn't have stayed in pictures. If she had married someone else, she would have quit movie-making just as surely and just as soon.

On the other hand, she was keen about show business from an audience point of view. She liked to go to movies and liked to hear about what I was doing professionally. She listened to all my programs and was the hottest record fan I had. I gave up listening to my records years ago, but Dixie had a standing order for every new one of mine released. She kept them all and played them. I've come home unexpectedly to find her playing records, and mine were generally included.

As far as my work was concerned, she was my most honest and intelligent critic. By the same token, she was the most helpful. It was Dixie who told me that I sing too loud of late, that I've lost the intimate quality I had. She played some of my old records back to me to prove her point.

She was right. I've fallen into the habit of trying to "deliver" a song too much, instead of "saying" the words the way I once did. For this reason my records haven't been too successful lately. I listen to my own voice too much when I record. When a singer of popular songs begins to listen to his own voice, nobody else will listen to him. He's lost his sincerity, his ability to create an image or a mood, and he's had it.

I've had a lot of advice from a lot of different people about how to go about telling this tale. I've been told, "You want to keep in mind that the way the world is today, yours is a story that could happen only in this country."

There may be some truth in that notion. I couldn't sing my songs in Russia. They have no ideological significance. If I started to boo-boo-boo, I'd have to clear each boo with the Kremlin. Here, if I want to croon, I find an unattended microphone somewhere and croon. I'm either accepted or stoned by the public. I'm not put through an MVD chopper.

I've also been told, "Take a boy like yourself who started from humble beginnings and has achieved success—why it's nothing short of inspirational."

This idea sounds strictly out of the popper to me. In this country we like to tell our youngsters that the way to succeed is by hard work and self-sacrifice. If you read my story, it'll be obvious to you—it's obvious to me—that I haven't worked very hard. The things I've done are the things I've wanted to do. Doing them was no great sacrifice. And I've been heavily paid for having fun while I did them. Singing or movie acting has never been drudgery for me. So I don't know that my story contains an inspirational point of view. However, it is certainly shot full of another American commodity—luck.

As I've gone along, I've come to a lot of crossroads and intersections. Everybody comes to them. If you turn this way or that, something happens or doesn't happen in your life. Suppose I'd learned to do a good roll on the drums in high school instead of one you could throw a dog through, and to play the xylophone and the vibraphone, the way all good timpani players do? I'd probably be playing percussion instruments in the Spokane

Symphony Orchestra right now or drums in a dance band somewhere around the country. I might have had lots of fun doing it, but I don't suppose there's the income in that that there's been in crooning.

Also, I was lucky in knowing the great jazz and blues singer Mildred Bailey so early in life. I learned a lot from her. She made records which are still vocal classics, and she taught me much about singing and about interpreting popular songs. She was called the Rockin' Chair Lady because her first big hit was a wonderful song, "Rockin' Chair." She used it for her theme signature when she had her own radio program. And I was lucky in having part-time jobs in Spokane theaters so that I got to see great performers like Al Jolson, Eddie Cantor, Savoy and Brennan, and the Avon Comedy Four. They gave me something to emulate.

Even having Whiteman find out that I existed was luck. It might be argued that since Al Rinker and I were doing all right with our song presentations when he first saw us, having him employ us was not so much luck as good judgment on his part. But it was luck that he happened to be in Los Angeles just when we were there. Suppose he hadn't booked Los Angeles that week. Suppose he'd played San Francisco instead. We wouldn't have had a chance to audition for him and we wouldn't have had the opportunity to join his band.

Perhaps meeting Whiteman was the luckiest corner I turned in my road. If I have any ability as a song stylist or have made out musically, it's largely because of the associations I formed while I was with his band. I lapped up the opportunity to work with such masters of their trade as Bix Beiderbecke, Joe Venuti, the Dorsey boys, Max Farley, Harry Perella, Roy Bargy, Mike Pingatore and all the other fine, progressive musicians in that organization. I hung around them day and night. I listened to them talk. I picked up ideas. Although I wasn't a musician— I'm still not one—I learned to appreciate good things when I heard them and to recognize bad things and avoid them.

Prayer is a potent thing

When my mother hears me say that luck has had a powerful influence on my life, she pooh-poohs such talk. She says, "Your luck has been my prayers and the prayers I've asked the Poor Clare nuns to offer up for you." The Poor Clares are a community of semi-cloistered nuns in Spokane. My mother has visited them ever since she came to that city as a young married woman.

She attributes any success I've had to the efficacy of prayer. I'm not scoffing at this theory. I think prayer is a potent thing to have working on your side. Some of my friends have noted the fact that when I pass a chapel of a church, I'm apt to say, "I guess I'll go in and bow a pious knee." It seems a good idea for me to go in, say a prayer and meditate for a little while upon what an oaf and lout I've been—as who hasn't?

A LTHOUGH MY MOTHER takes a poor view of luck, the luckiest thing that ever happened to me was being born to the mother and father I was born to, and inheriting the characteristics I inherited from them. My dad was relaxed and casual and believed in living in the present and having a good time. He had a full life and enjoyed himself no matter what happened. In his youth, Dad had sung in amateur Gilbert-and-Sullivan productions. My mother had a sweet, clear voice. Their shared love of singing helped bring them together.

Dad was quite a lad when it came to plinking the mandolin. It was the big instrument of his day. You weren't a gay blade unless you could accompany yourself with it when you sang. Dad had a variety of songs on tap. One of his favorites was called "Keemo Kimo." I heard Nat King Cole sing it not long ago on one of his broadcasts. But Nat's version was different from the way Dad sang it. Dad played a little guitar, too—an accompanying guitar, just a four-string instrument, not a solo guitar.

Mother was the level-headed one of our family, its business manager, the stretcher-outer of Dad's modest salary. She was also our family disciplinarian. The small Crosbys got a healthy amount of corporal punishment dealt out with a hair-brush or a strap. But Dad let Mother do it. He could never get angry enough. When a licking was coming up, he ducked out of the house and didn't come back until he was sure it was over. My mother loved us as much as any mother loves her children, but that love included doing the things that were good for our souls, even if doing them hurt her.

"It'll do him good."

While I was in grade school, I had a certain amount of trouble with the truant officers. If they caught a teen-ager around town during school hours, they'd assume that he was playing hooky, take him to the juvenile-detention ward and call his parents.

During one hooky session I had with some of my pals, we became involved in a rhubarb with Jesmer's Bakery, near our house. We waited until Jesmer's delivery wagon came back from taking pastries around to different stores and brought back what wasn't sold. When the driver went inside to hand in his slips, he left his wagon unprotected. This was an invitation to hollow-legged urchins, and we ran away with a couple of pies apiece, as well as bags of cinnamon buns. We ate all of them we could hold, but cinnamon buns are filling, so we had a number of them left.

We were down on Mission Boulevard pegging buns at motorists when one of the cars we pelted proved to be a car full of policemen going home from work. Its occupants tossed us into the pokey and called our mothers.

"Keep him there overnight," my mother said firmly. "It'll do him good." She didn't relent. I cooled my heels in that juvenile-detention ward all night.

I guess I'm a blend of my father and mother, although as far as characteristics go, theirs must have got twisted somewhere along the way. Rated by my father's ancestors, he should have been the reverse of the easy-going, generous, good-time type he was. Judging by my mother's effervescent and volatile forebears, it seems incongruous that she was so level-headed, such a thrifty manager, so inflexible in training us in the right direction.

My father's family stemmed from a rock-ribbed, tough-minded Plymouth elder, Edmund Brewster, who settled in Massachusetts in the 1600's. His descendants lived in Massachusetts and other parts of New England for several generations. Most of them took to the sea, including my father's grandfather, Captain Nathaniel Crosby. Nathaniel captained a ship for John Jacob Astor. More than once he sailed around the Horn to California, Oregon, Washington, and China. Finally, leaving Astor, he bought his own ship. In addition, he entered into partnership with another man to buy and operate a ship-chandlery store. It was located in what is now the center of Portland, Oregon.

Captain Nathaniel made frequent trips to China. Each trip kept him away for a year or two. Returning from one trip, he found that his partner had sold the store, the property on which it stood, and all the equipment, and had skipped. Captain Nathaniel could obtain no redress and had to start anew. Several years ago my brothers went to Portland to reopen the case and see if anything could be done about it. The property, in the heart of a big city, had achieved a fantastic value. But it was impossible to revive the case.

I have a picture of Captain Nathaniel's ship, *The Kingfisher*, taken from a painting done by an itinerant artist many years ago. Because of his many trips to China, Nathaniel had Chinese servants, as did his son—my father's father. Having been raised by Chinese servants, my father spoke fluent Chinese and could even sing a few Chinese songs. I remember him singing them as he twanged his mandolin.

My mother's parents, Dennis and Katherine Harrigan, came from Ireland. When they were very young they settled in Ontario, Canada. They moved to Stillwater, Minnesota, where my mother was born. When she was still a young girl they headed west and settled in Tacoma, where my Grandfather Harrigan became a building contractor.

He raised a large family, including my mother, her sister Annie, and five sons: George, Frank, Will, Ambrose and Ed. Mother's brother, George Harrigan, was my boyhood idol. She had five brothers, but Uncle George was the stand-out. He was a very talented entertainer. As an Exalted Ruler of the Elks in Tacoma, he took part in theatricals around Seattle and in the

Tacoma area. He picked up the song "Harrigan, That's Me," and audiences all over the state of Washington insisted that he sing it wherever he appeared. He had a powerful Irish-tenor voice. It wasn't a lyric tenor like John McCormack's or Dennis Day's, but a powerful Irish tenor. Uncle George could shatter the crockery when he took dead aim at a high note.

He was a genius when it came to telling dialect stories. He could do French-Canadian stories, he'd picked up a store of Swedish stories from the loggers around Puget Sound, and he was wonderful at Italian dialect. At Irish-dialect stories he was nothing short of magical.

When he came to town the Crosby kids never left the house; we hung around and listened to Uncle George tell stories and sing songs. If he'd gone into show business he'd have been a hit. He was a handsome man with a shock of black hair, freckles, blue eyes, and a colorful Irish personality. But he was a court reporter, he had a large family to support, and although he worked hard, he could never get enough cash together to have a fling at breaking into show business.

Uncle George kept my father company, diverted him with his best stories, and raised a comforting glass with him when I was born on May 2, 1904, in Tacoma, Washington. I've seen several dates listed for my birth in various publications, among them 1901, 1903, and 1906. I'd like to take 1906, but 1904 is the one I was stuck with.

In 1906 my family moved to Spokane. My father had accepted a job as a bookkeeper with the Inland Brewery. Spokane has always been a growing community but in 1906 it was busting out the seams of a new pair of work pants every week. It was the center of a mining and logging area. It was the axis of the rich Palouse country, which was becoming one of the greatest wheat centers of the world. Since then it has become just that. In short, Spokane was a booming community. Those who live there don't care who you are, what you've been, or what your reputation was before they met you. It's how you handle yourself after you arrive there that counts. Dad thought it would be a fine place for a man to raise his family. He couldn't have been righter.

My earliest memories of Spokane are the tales I overheard, jug-eared and bug-eyed, about the local gambling halls. Being a mining community, it was a lusty town. There were some big gambling places in Spokane in those days. Dad wasn't really a gambling man. He could ill-afford to gamble with his salary from the brewery—but he took an occasional flutter at the wheels of chance, hoping that a dazzling stroke of luck might increase his funds.

My mother tells that when we moved to Spokane we arrived on very short funds, rented a house, and ran up a sizable grocery bill as well as a large tab for fuel and other household necessities. But when Mother plagued Dad about the bills he was never seriously concerned. He merely opened his newspaper, put his feet up, lit his pipe and said, "Don't bother, Kate. It'll work out all right." It always did.

We small Crosbys took our cue from Dad. Whether inherited or not, his ability to relax has helped me in a life which has had its share of pressure. I don't worry seriously about anything. I do the best I can about a situation. If I can't improve it, I drop it. I don't feel there's any point in going farther than that. All a man can do is his best. If he can't handle it that way, what's the use of driving himself crazy?

Dad spent part of his first month's pay check from the brewery on a phonograph. I remember that extravagance of his well. It had a big morning-glory horn. Some of the records it played were "Cohen at the Telephone"; songs by Henry Burr and by a baritone named Denis O'Sullivan; some by Oscar Seagle; marches by Sousa; others featuring old-time concert artists; and songs from *The Mikado* sung by a light-opera group.

At first we had no piano, but Dad wanted us to have everything musical, and he went into hock to buy us one. Both my sisters "took" piano, but although we boys had our chance to "take," too, we couldn't find time.

One of my schoolmates, who is now Dr. Joseph Lynch, a famous neuro-surgeon in the Northwest, has told me since that everybody in Spokane knew when I was coming because they could hear me singing or whistling. I suppose that was because of having a dad who was always bringing a new tune into the house on sheet music or on a record—I had a constant succession of them in my head. And I had to whistle or sing to get them out.

I was named Harry for my father. My mother called me Harry. She still does.

It was while I was seven or eight years old and at Webster School in Spokane that I stopped being Harry Crosby and became Bing. There are two stories about how I got the name, but the real story is this. We lived next to the Hobart family. One of the boys in that family was Valentine Hobart. Valentine and I both liked a comic feature called the "Bingville Bugle." It was edited by a man named Newton Newkirk, and in it was a character named Bingo. The *o* was later deleted.

So I became Bing. It's been my name ever since.

There's another story that I pointed my finger or a wooden gun at things and said, "Bing-bing!" I don't think there's anything to that yarn. I never heard it until I grew up.

To me, my name seems simple and easy to pronounce—as simple as Jones or Smith. But there have been those who have as hard a time wrapping their tongue around it as if it were Cholmondeley.

Time was when I was quite a tennis enthusiast. I played the game in a sweat shirt over a rubber shirt. Tennis served not only to give me exercise, but also helped me take off weight. One day, when I was living in a home in the San Fernando Valley on Camarillo Street, I made an early-morning phone call to a friend, Mr. Polesie, for a tennis match. When I called, Mr. Polesie was pounding his pillow. But Mr. Polesie's Japanese house boy was awake and was preparing breakfast when my call came in. He put down the phone and knocked on the bedroom door.

"What is it, Togo?" asked the sleepy Mr. Polesie.

"There is a Mr. Crost on tel—ee—phone."

"I don't know any Mr. Crost," Mr. Polesie said. "Take the message." But I was determined to get through and sent the Japanese Garcia back to the bedroom door again, this time with a message I thought would identify. It did. Togo rapped once more.

"Yes, Togo?" the sleepy one asked.

"It's Mr. Crost still on tel—ee—phone."

"I told you I don't know him, Togo."

"He say you do. He say he short, fat fellow, sing on radio—name B-I-N-G!"

That did it.

These were not the only humbling experiences I've had with someone fumbling my name. Another happened when Dixie and I were going East one time. We generally took the Union Pacific's *City of Los Angeles,* the Santa Fe's *Super Chief* or the *Chief.* But on this excursion we tried another route. We took a train which goes through Phoenix, then goes on to El Paso and so up to Kansas City.

The road had a rule that its brakemen must change every three hundred miles. There was a rear brakeman and a front brakeman. The rear brakeman sat in the observation car.

There was trouble up the road ahead and our train stopped to wait for it to be cleared up. It was ten o'clock at night. We were told there'd be a wait, so Dixie and I got out and walked up and down the track behind the train. We weren't the only ones doing it. The rear brakeman, a little, hard-bitten, sunburned Texan, was walking up and down too, swinging his lantern.

He came up to us and said, "They tell me that rascal Bim Crosland's aboard."

"Who?" I asked.

"Bim Crosland," he repeated. "He's on the train. I'd certainly like to get a look at that lil 'ol scoundrel. They tell me that he's quite a singer. I haven't heard him much. But as far as I'm concerned, Larry Ross could run him in a gopher hole."

Dixie and I agreed with him and thought no more of it. A few minutes later the engineer gave a couple of toots. Everybody climbed back into the observation car and Dixie and I went to our stateroom and retired.

In the morning there came a knock on our door. When we opened it there was our little brakeman friend. He eyed me with a twinkle in his eye and said, "You hoaxed me, didn't you?"

"How do you mean?" I asked.

"You're Bim Crosland yourself!" he said. "Just for that you've got to sign my book."

So I signed it, Bim Crosland.

Of course, there are compensating episodes, too. A fellow can't always be tearing himself down. He needs to give himself a little complimentary nudge every once in a while.

Like the time I bumped into the very nice gentleman in the lobby of the Vancouver Hotel who introduced himself as Colonel Carter. And he told me he had been on that part of the Canadian armed forces staff which participated in the Japanese surrender ceremonies on the battleship "Missouri" at the conclusion of the Second World War. He said at the conclusion of the whole procedure General George Kenny leaned over toward him and said with all sincerity, "Well, now, if we just had Bing Crosby here to sing a couple of songs it'd be perfect." Naturally, I was immensely flattered but I do think this would have been rubbing salt in the already gaping wounds of the prostrate Japanese.

But that came later on. I had to grow up before that happened. For one thing, I had to grow up a little before I got over minding singing for an audience. One of my first memories is of a group of moppets from Webster School, including me, in some kind of musical production. In it we were all supposed to be blocks jumping up and down.

Then there was a Christmas pageant in which I was dressed like a girl. I can't remember anything else about it except my hot shame at wearing such a costume. Other than that, having to sing in public embarrassed me until I'd almost finished high school—especially the non-popular kind of songs which teachers usually forced upon kids. My mother once took me to a singing "professor" for a couple of lessons, and the professor took my popular stuff away from me and told me to practice breathing and tone production in a certain way. As a result, I lost interest in public singing for a long, long time.

Before I removed the professor from my life, I did make one appearance at a neighborhood function. I sang "One Fleeting Hour." I didn't like it very much and I certainly didn't sing it well. It evoked only an apathetic response from the audience. That cured me of singing publicly until I began to fool around with drums and singing with a band. Then I liked it.

But there never was a time when I didn't love athletics. Webster grade school, where I took my early educational hurdles, was a block and a half from Gonzaga University. Gonzaga had fine football teams. When I wasn't at Webster, I hung around the Gonzaga stadium. I was so interested that when I went to high school I played baseball, basketball, handball, and football. In high school I played center and we had a good football team. But when I reached college I weighed only one hundred and forty-five or fifty pounds. With that trifling amount of beef on my bones, no one took me seriously as college-football material; I wasn't big enough for center, and I wasn't fast enough for the backfield.

Baseball was really my game. I was and am nutty about it. When I thought I wasn't appreciated around home, I used to say that I was going to run away to play baseball. But it was merely a youthful threat. I took it out in playing semi-professional baseball with the Spokane Ideal Laundry team.

While I was in Webster grade school my athletics were confined to a personal contest or two. One of my sisters, Mary Rose,
was a little on the chubby side, or, to be honest about it, tubby.
However, I resented any reference to her roundness by anyone
except members of my family. One of the kids in the eighth
grade at Webster school drew a picture on the blackboard of a
big fat girl. Under it he wrote "Mary Rose."

I met him after school and questioned him. "Yeah," he said.
"I did it. What are you going to do about it?" I told him I'd see
him later. I got my gang together and he got his gang together,
and we met in an alley back of his house. Eighty or a hundred
kids gathered to see the battle, and a few truck drivers who
came by formed them into a circle.

The other kid was strong, but he knew nothing about boxing.
Since I knew how to box a little, I cut his eye and gave him a
bloody nose. Every time he rushed me I stuck out my left and
he ran into it. Then I'd throw my right. I couldn't miss. I'd
learned that much about boxing from my uncle, George Harrigan, who was quite an amateur boxer. I took in all of the local
boxing matches, so I knew something about using my dukes.
My opponent didn't. He was older and bigger, and if he'd known
even the rudiments of self-defense, he could have killed me.

Funny, the memories that stick to the inside of the skull. I
remember that during that fight I wore a gray flannel shirt. Before a couple of the truck drivers finally separated us, the fight
became pretty gory. I hit my sister's traducer in the nose and
must have torn a cartilage, for blood spurted and got all over
my gray flannel shirt until it was more red than gray. When I
went home my mother thought the blood was mine. I had a hard
time convincing her it was the other fellow's, but when some of
the kids who'd seen the battle backed me up, she believed me.

It's one of my mother's favorite stories about me, I suppose
because in her eyes it made me seem chivalrous and gallant—
a small knight in gray flannel armor protecting defenseless
womanhood from abuse. I'm loath to have her tell it, because,

as mothers do, she builds me up in it. But I'm not so loath as if I'd lost.

The insulting one was on the muscle, flexing it all the time. So not long after that a pal of mine, Jimmy Cottrell, had a fight with the boy who'd poked fun at my sister's poundage. The bout was held back of a grocery store. Jimmy won. Jimmy was with the Logan Avenue gang and I was with the Boone Avenue gang. So the logical thing would have been a match between us for the short-pants championship of Spokane. Luckily for me, it never happened. If it had, Cottrell would have torn my head off, for he was a very good fighter. He wound up Northwest middleweight champion. Then he came to Los Angeles and fought such fighters as Mushy Callahan and other main-eventers there.

While still small fry, I got into another row over a dame. This time the cause of the trouble was not one of my sisters, but a girl named Gladys Lemmon. I'd taken Gladys bobsledding on Ligerwood Hill a few times. She was a real doll with long, fluttery eyelashes. I'd hook my bobsled rope on the steps of a coal wagon. The coal wagon would take us up the hill and we'd slide down while Gladys squealed with entrancing shrillness and clasped her arms around my middle.

It was all very idyllic until my brother Larry needled me about her at the dinner table one night. "Where've you been?" he asked. "Out squeezin' that Lemmon again?"

The family laughed uproariously and I saw red; I picked up a leg of lamb and let my tormentor have it, gravy and all. The laughter stopped and a scuffle began, but my mother quelled it. The lamb was retrieved, refurbished, and repaired in the kitchen, and we attacked it instead of each other.

Another story my mother tells about me has to do with a personal contest I lost to Webster's principal, C. J. Boyington. He was affable and amiable, but he could be firm when he had need to. One day I brought a note home from school. It read: "If Harry doesn't behave better, the principal will have to deal with him." Several days later, when I came home, I said I'd been called to the principal's office. "What happened?" my mother asked.

"He dealt with me," I told her. He had "dealt" with me by bending me over a chair and letting me have a few with a yardstick.

Leaving Webster in 1917, I entered Gonzaga High School. Gonzaga High is run by the Jesuit fathers of Gonzaga College in preparation for Gonzaga itself. When I went there it was a rugged school. Certainly it was not dressy. One pair of corduroy pants lasted all year, although my pair got a little gamy, especially in spring and summer. Once they've been broken in, corduroy pants are, as they say around a gym, very high.

My dad's wages as bookkeeper at the Inland Brewery were not munificent, so it was necessary for us Crosby boys to work at odd jobs after school or in the mornings to help out. Mother and Dad told us, "We'll provide a place in which you can live and we'll feed you, but you'll have to earn your own money for your clothes and athletic equipment and recreation."

The jobs I've held down were legion. I don't blame anyone who eyes me skeptically as I list them. My own kids give me a guffaw when I tell them what I've done. *That's Dad for you,* that guffaw seems to say, *romancing about his youth again.*

I did work at a slew of jobs, although most of them were part-time and some of them petered out after a few weeks. While I was in grade school and high school, I had a morning-paper route for the *Spokesman-Review.* This meant that I got up at four o'clock each morning and went out to the intersection of Nora and Addison Avenues to wait for the paper car. It was an area dotted with old cars discarded by the street-car company. We stripped them for firewood, built a big bonfire, and awaited the first car of the morning, the paper car. When it came, we folded the papers into throwable shapes by the comfortable warmth of the blaze we'd started.

There were several ways of folding papers: the three-cornered, the dog-ear, and the boomerang. My favorite was the boomerang. It had a tight twist in the middle which made it hug a porch when it hit. But I'm afraid my best shots were on the roof, under the porch, and in the bushes.

One summer I thinned apples near Wenatchee and Yakima. For two summers I worked in a logging camp.

Another summer I worked at a topography job—as a member of a party locating new logging roads and sluices—for another cousin, Lloyd Crosby, who was a big wheel with the Weyerhaeuser Timber Company. I didn't last very long there—only two or three weeks. I laid my right knee open with an axe and when I got well, I cut my other knee. I remember my cousin saying, "We'd better get this kid the hell out of here before he kills himself."

One whole winter I gave up the paper route in favor of a job as a janitor in a place called Everyman's Club. Everyman's was in the workingmen's district and was a club for the loggers and miners in town, as well as other workingmen. It had a reading room, showers, and bathroom facilities. I arrived there at five-thirty in the morning, after walking from our house, about a mile and a half away, and went to work cleaning up the joint. It was generally full of empty soup cans and snoose cans.

Snoose is powdered tobacco put under the lower lip. There were also canned-heat cans. Some of the loggers used to get canned heat, take it into the washroom and put a match under it to liquefy it, since it came in a pasty or semi-solid form. Then they drank it. It had a high alcoholic content. It also had a high blindness-and-madness content. If those who drank it didn't end up sightless, they were likely to fight six policemen and wind up in jail. My job involved a lot of hard work, but I stuck it out for a winter. What with that job and the paper route and going to six-thirty Mass at Gonzaga, I formed the habit of getting up at the crack of dawn. I've never got over it.

Things got underway early at Gonzaga. Not only was Mass

at six-thirty, but we had to be in class at eight-thirty. After having to get up at four-thirty in the summertime to meet the paper car and at five-thirty to tidy up the Everyman's Club, it was a relief to get up at six o'clock in the winter for six-thirty Mass.

The part-time job I liked best was assistant or flunky in the prop department of the Auditorium Theater. Spokane's big opera house, the Auditorium, was the place where most of the touring theatricals played. They'd stay for maybe a matinee and a night, then go on to Seattle and Portland. It was there, I guess, that the first priming coat of show business rubbed off on me.

I remember Savoy and Brennan playing there. I saw George White's *Scandals*, and Willie and Eugene Howard's shows, and Al Jolson in *Sinbad* and *Bombo*. Although Jolson was the star of those shows, he spent most of his time when he wasn't on stage rushing out to the box office and counting the take. The star of a show that penetrated that far into the hinterland had to be a businessman as well as a performer.

Later, when I got to know and work with Al, he remembered how industrious he'd been on those hegiras so far from Broadway, and we laughed at it. He didn't remember the lop-eared lad named Crosby who watched his every move, but I remembered him vividly.

For a while I tried to sing like Al. Since Dad saw to it that we kept abreast of the times musically at home, I had all of Jolson's records. I think we had one of the first radio sets in Spokane. My brother Ted had a mechanical turn of mind and around 1917 or '18 he built a crystal set with the help of Father Gilmartin, the physics professor at Gonzaga University. Ted and the Father built the thing out of old wire and left-overs salvaged from the Gonzaga chemistry and physics lab.

I've omitted to say that for a while I worked at the brewery where my dad kept the books. I had a wonderful time working there. The braumeister was an elderly German, Otto Held. I'd go up into the great rooms in the brauhaus where the giant vats, twenty feet across, were installed. On a hot summer day it was cool up there. I'd visit with Otto and enjoy myself immensely. He smoked a long German pipe with a porcelain bowl with roses on it, and he wore big hip boots. He spoke broken English with a heavy German accent. In fact, all the older fellows who worked there were Germans from the old country, with genuine musical-comedy German accents. But they were solid men with great pride in their profession.

Otto reminisced about his youth and groaned about how tough it was to make the prohibition-type near beer fit for anyone to drink, and how he prayed for the return of the real stuff. To him the frustrating thing was that he had to make real beer first and then pasteurize it until it was the sissified prohibition stuff.

Another of my early memories is of the Sholderers, a big, hearty German family who lived down the street from us. They were very friendly and neighborly to my mother and father when they first arrived in Spokane. There were seven young ladies in the family and one boy, named Walter.

At first we Crosbys lived on Sinto Avenue, about a block from the Sholderers. Later on we moved to Sharp Avenue, about six blocks away. There was always wonderful cooking to be had at the Sholderers. Their latch-string was always out and there was always something simmering on the back of their stove. We Crosby boys were a good deal younger than the Sholderer girls, so much so that they seemed grown-up young ladies to us, although they were only teen-age girls. My mother had so many children so close together that the Sholderers helped take care of us for my mother when she was otherwise occupied.

Looking back, I'd say we spent about as much time in the Sholderers' home as we did in our own. In addition to the good food there were big, playful dogs roaming the house to wrestle with. Papa Sholderer smoked one of those old-fashioned German pipes, shaped like a question mark, and Mrs. Sholderer was big-hearted and generous.

Her German pancakes and Sauerbraten and Hasenpfeffer

and pumpernickel were mouth-watering and she had wonderful draught beer, and bock beer in season.

Only two of the seven Sholderer girls got married. The rest of them still live together and when I go back to Spokane, I can still count on a good meal with them.

A year or two ago I brought them some venison from my ranch at Elko, Nevada. I'd killed a nice big yearling buck who'd been coming down in the evenings, raiding our grain fields and getting fat on our wheat and oats. Before fetching him north, I'd hung him for about a week. The Sholderer girls took that haunch of venison and put it in brine in their basement for about a week. The brine they use is their own pet mixture. Among other things, it's composed of salt and onions and thyme and rosemary and cloves and garlic. They marinated the venison in it, then they brought it upstairs and cooked it as a kind of pot roast with potato pancakes. The result was immortal.

MY EARLIEST THEATRICAL EXPERIENCES which amounted to anything were the elocution contests in which I took part in my last year of grammar school and all through high school. Elocution, oratorical contests, and debating societies are very important in Jesuit schools. I remember reciting "Whisperin' Jim," and "The Dukite Snake," which was a grim story of an Australian family that carved a homestead out of the Australian bush. The father of the family killed a snake in the bush, and the snake's mate followed him home and did away with the entire family. It was a gruesome little number.

I recited many of Robert W. Service's things, such as "The Spell of the Yukon" and "The Shooting of Dan McGrew." I remember sinking my teeth into "Horatius at the Bridge" and "Spartacus to the Gladiators," classic pieces that seemed obligatory for all youthful elocutionists. I won a couple of awards with "Horatius" and "Spartacus." I took those eloquent lines in my teeth and shook them as a terrier shakes a bone. I can't remember whether I carried off the first or second prize, but I was in the money. I did fairly well in oratorical contests too. I also belonged to the debating society, but the elocution contests were the big events. They were held in the parish hall and everybody in the parish came.

My teachers at Gonzaga never knew it, but I once had a chance to put their public-speaking course to practical use. It happened that I was on my way home one summer evening from the Mission Park swimming pool. En route I passed a political meeting. I stopped to listen and heard the speaker, who was haranguing the crowd, giving them a rabid anti-Catholic speech. His theme was "Go to the polls and defeat the Pope." I asked him if I could speak. He said, "Go ahead." I got up on the podium and we had quite a debate. I remembered some of the things I'd learned from the Jesuits at Gonzaga and I don't think I finished a bad second. I got a good hand when I was through.

The education which seeped into my pores at Gonzaga—or maybe it was pounded through my skull—has paid off all through my life—sometimes in unexpected ways. In the film, *The Road to Morocco,* the plot called for Bob Hope and me to have trouble with a gendarme.

Hope asked me, "Can you talk French?"

"Certainly I can talk French," I said. Since the *Road* pictures are shot for the most part off the cuff or out of our heads, neither Hope's question nor my response were in the script. Nor was the long French spiel I ripped off.

It was the tale of Monsieur Corbeau—French for Mr. Crow—and the piece of cheese. Mr. Crow was holding a piece of cheese in his beak, and a fox came along and tried to slicker him out of it. Many French students will remember this fable. At all events, I did. It had been used in my second- or third-year high-school French classes for pronunciation, memory work, and vocabulary.

Hope was tremendously impressed by the glibness with which I launched into a foreign tongue. To this day he thinks I speak French fluently. He's visited France two or three times, but I don't think he knows how to say much more than *"Oui, monsieur"* or *"Oui, mademoiselle"*—especially the latter.

It seems to amuse my friends nowadays when they discover that I spent a lot of my time at Gonzaga in The Jug. I suppose that their amusement stems from the fact that later on, when I'd left Gonzaga, being inside another kind of jug presided over by a turnkey and guarded by men in blue, was an experience not unknown to me. But The Jug at Gonzaga wasn't a jail. It was a room where students who weren't behaving or who had broken some rule were sent to do penance. We were given something from Ovid or Virgil or Caesar's *Gallic Wars* to memorize or to write. But if the offense was grievous, we had to memorize it backwards. That was not easy. But easy or not, we memorized it just the same.

Part of my time in The Jug resulted from the fact that mathematics was my blind spot. Although I went through algebra, geometry, and calculus and studied the slide rule, I still can't do long division. If I have to multiply more than two digits, I retire to my den and work it out where no one can witness my struggles. Occasionally we had to write essays on subjects selected by ourselves. Once I chose as my subject: "Why Algebra and Geometry are Unnecessary in the Modern High School Curriculum." I don't think I proved anything, but I put a great deal of heart into the piece.

We had some wonderful priests at Gonzaga—men like Father Kennelly, the prefect of discipline. He weighed in at two-eighty and we called him Big Jim. He stood in front of his office as we went by on our way to class. If we misbehaved, he brought his "discipliner" into play. He had a key chain ten or twelve feet long, with a bunch of keys on it. He kept this weapon coiled up under his cassock, and if we got out of line or were mischievous, he flicked out that chain and made contact on our anatomy where we'd feel it most. He delivered his shots with the accuracy and speed of a professional fly-caster. Knowing this, when we passed his office we generally were doing what we should do, maintaining strict silence and watching our deportment. He was no sadist. He just tried to do his job conscientiously. He was always ready to tuck his cassock under his belt and play baseball or football with anybody who wanted him to.

When we small Crosbys got to be about fourteen or fifteen, our punishment at home became less muscular and took the form of confinement. We were told that we couldn't go out for a few nights after supper, or we'd have to chop wood or haul coal or (if it was summertime) mow the lawn or hoe and weed the garden. In other words, we had to do chores we didn't like much, which was as bad as getting a licking.

But to get back to the Gonzaga faculty: there was a Father Gilmore, the chemistry professor, another physical giant, who prided himself on his strength and always kept himself in shape. He invented a hair restorer and tried to get me to use it. Even then my hair was showing signs of becoming somewhat less than bushy. Out of courtesy, I promised Father Gilmore I'd use his invention, but I didn't. He'd be happy, I'm sure, to know that I've never used anybody else's, either. To anyone who's seen me on the screen or in person, that's belaboring the obvious.

Our English teacher, Father O'Brien, had a mop of iron-gray hair wiry as steel filings, and a powerful physique. He had been a sailor in the British Navy when he decided to study for the priesthood. We called him Wild Bill O'Brien—but not to his face.

I think it was in my third year of high school that two organizations, The Dirty Six and The Bolsheviks, burgeoned into being. The matter of who was to grab off our class-officer jobs seemed terribly important to us, and the factions in our class divided into rival tongs or parties. It was our first experience with the two-party system of politics. As I remember it, The Dirty Six was made up of Joe Lynch, Bob Porter, Mike Derham, Pinky Callahan, myself, and one other whose name escapes me. We headed a sizable following. The Dirty Six and The Bolsheviks waged a red hot, ding dong political campaign, complete with speeches and placards. We indulged in some pretty outrageous skulduggery and juvenile character-assassination, and only stopped short at kidnapping.

Wild Bill O'Brien grew alarmed at our use of the Godless word "Bolsheviks," and gave us a serious lecture about belonging to an organization that was opposed to religion. Apparently his devoutness and his English sense of humor had him confused,

71

for he said we'd be "cleansed" if we stopped using the name. Obviously our violent political habits would be O.K. under some other label.

But while under such men I learned virility and devoutness, mixed with the habit of facing whatever fate set in my path, squarely, with a cold blue eye, I didn't have to learn a feeling for music and for rhythm. I was born with that. If I wasn't, there was a lot of it at home for me to sop up. Inevitably I tried to make it contribute a few dollars to the money I made from odd jobs. Although it probably would have become the dominating force in my life if it had brought me no money at all.

In 1921, toward the end of my first year in the University, I joined a group called the Musicaladers, a six-piece combo made up of Spokane boys, most of whom hadn't gone to Gonzaga High School but had gone to other schools, like North Central High. I'd been part of an earlier one-hundred per cent Gonzaga musical group called the Juicy Seven, but the Musicaladers were more sophisticated and professional. We were Bob and Clare Pritchard; Jimmy Heaton, now a trumpet player at the Goldwyn Studios and on the musical staff there; Miles Rinker and his brother, Al, later one of Paul Whiteman's Rhythm Boys; and me.

I'd been playing the drums a little and singing around Gonzaga High with the Juicy Seven when I discovered that Al was a genius at listening to phonograph records, absorbing their arrangements and committing them to memory by ear. For that matter, all the Musicaladers worked by ear. None of us could read music. But we gave our own interpretation to arrangements which had been originated by the Memphis Five, McKinney's Cotton Pickers, Vic Meyers' band from Seattle, the original Dixieland Jazz Band, Jack Chapman's Hotel Drake Orchestra, and other great bands. Since the only other bands around town were playing stock arrangements sent out by publishing houses, we were a novelty for Spokane. Ragged, but novel. We weren't good musicians, but our technique was modern and advanced.

72

The other musicians could read notes, but they couldn't play stuff the way we played it. Young folks liked us and two or three nights a week we got dates to play high-school dances and private parties. We made trips to places as far away as Washington State College at Pullman. We also got dates at Lareida's Dance Pavilion at Dishman, eight or ten miles outside Spokane. We played there three times a week. That was our first steady job. We pulled down three dollars apiece for a night's work. Our uniforms featured bright blazers.

We had only a small repertoire, but we stretched it by playing the same tunes in different ways. We'd change their tempo; we'd take a waltz and make a fox trot out of it. Or we'd learn a popular song, and if it was a big hit, we'd do it several times during an evening. Since most of the things we played were taken from records made by Dixieland-type orchestras, we specialized in instrumental numbers, for these Dixieland bands never had vocals. They went in for novelty effects—shufflin' sounds, steamboat whistles, and paddle wheels chunkin'.

I don't suppose we Musicaladers ever had more than thirty numbers on tap. But the people we played for had never heard those thirty anywhere else, unless they'd heard the records we'd borrowed them from, and not many folks in Spokane had. I did any singing that was done, and played the drums. My vocals were stuff like "Pretty Little Blue-Eyed Sally" and "The End of the Road," lifted from Fred Waring's records.

Early in my association with the Musicaladers, before I had any drums, I'd borrowed those belonging to the Gonzaga music department. The department kept a nice set of drums in the basement of one of the college buildings. The Musicaladers had an engagement to play for a dance at the public library. It was a non-denominational dance and when I asked permission to use the Gonzaga drums, the priest-moderator in charge of the music department said the drums could be used only at Gonzaga functions.

After all, that was merely his opinion. To me, it seemed much more important that a Gonzaga boy who'd made an engagement should keep it. So I decided to spirit those instruments out of a basement window with a rope. We Musicaladers hauled them through a window, so we wouldn't be seen carrying them through the halls. We got them back the same way. However, the whole thing was a lesson to me. I saved up a little money, wrote to a mail-order house and bought my own set, a beauty. The bass drum was decorated with a Japanese sunset and was illuminated inside. It had spikes in it to make it stick to the floor when I was making it thump. Even with spikes, it was a highly ambulatory case. At the beginning of each number, when I'd begin to beat the foot pedal the vibration made the drum gradually inch forward. I hitched my chair along after it until I was well out in front of the band. Then I'd have to move back to start the next number. I never did learn a professional drumming technique. I faked rolls with a wire fly-swatter or I frim-frammed the cymbals with the swatter or a stick instead of rolling, which was one way of sounding like an accomplished drummer in spite of a lack of technical ability.

Regardless of our lack of expertness, whatever else we were, we were different, and when Roy Boomer, manager of the Clemmer Theater in Spokane, decided to put stage shows ahead of the pictures, he thought of us. Boomer was a progressive type, for stage shows were pioneer stuff then. We tried to do songs which would fit the pictures he'd booked. If the film featured the great outdoors or the Northwest, we sang "By the Waters of Minnetonka," or "Indian Summer," or "Pale Moon." If it was laid in New Orleans, we sang blues songs. In short, we tried to give a prologue. Later on, Boomer decided he didn't want the whole band, so he cut it down to Al Rinker and me, and we did our songs in the pit.

For three or four months the Musicaladers had a job playing twice a week in a Chinese restaurant on Riverside Avenue. It had a dubious reputation, but The Pekin was a favorite Friday and Saturday night hangout for high-school kids. There were rumors that alcohol was available to teen-agers there, and my mother was purse-lipped about it. But the pay was more than I'd ever taken home before, and I was able to allay some of my mother's doubts about the restaurant's respectability by pointing to its most respectable financial rewards.

Bailey's Music Company was the town's leading record store, and Al Rinker and I haunted it. Mildred Rinker, known professionally as Mildred Bailey, was Rinker's sister. She was not related to the family who owned the music company, but it may be that's where she got the idea for the name under which she sang. Mildred and Al's father had Dutch blood, and when I first heard the name it made me think of *Hans Brinker and the Silver Skates*. Mildred, the area's outstanding singing star, was singing in a Spokane cabaret—Charlie Dale's—a fancy semi-speak-easy spot. Before long she was one of the country's outstanding singing stars, too. She specialized in sultry, throaty renditions with a high concentrate of Southern accent, such as "Louisville Lou," and "Hard-Hearted Hannah."

Bailey's Music Company was big about letting us spend all the time we wanted to in one of its listening rooms. We'd take a couple of records in and play them, and Al would memorize the piano chords while I remembered the soloist's style and vocal tricks. Then we'd rush home or to Al's house and practice before we forgot them. When a band came through Spokane we hung around them while they rehearsed, and we sneaked into their playing engagements and soaked up every note that they played. Spike Johnson's orchestra from Portland helped us a lot, both with new material and new songs, and showed us better ways to handle our instruments. I think I saw every vaudeville act involving a piano and singer that played Spokane. I couldn't afford those shows; money was short, but I got in one way or another.

Back in the 1920's, lads—or even grown men—who sang with bands did so at the risk of having their manhood suspected. It was a time when tennis players or men who wore wrist watches were given the hand-on-hip and the burlesque falsetto-voice routine. I had a little trouble like that myself at Lareida's Dance Pavilion. A girl on whom I had a case was brought to Lareida's by a rival. They spent almost the entire evening dancing in front of my drums, while he poured out a steady stream of ridicule about the effeminacy of characters who sang the kind of songs I was singing. When the Musicaladers took a break, I invited him outside and I asked him to repeat his innuendoes, which he did with frightening alacrity. I took a swing at him and he took a poke at me, but friends intervened before either of us was really hurt.

Gradually the Musicaladers disintegrated. Jimmy Heaton, our cornet player, went to California. The Pritchard boys entered Washington State and took up veterinary medicine. Only Al Rinker, his brother Miles, and I were left. Miles was a happy-go-lucky fellow who didn't care for the effort and trouble of trying to get together another sextet. That left Al and me working our singing act at the Clemmer Theater.

In my third year of college I shifted to studying law, and worked part-time in the law office of Colonel Charles S. Albert, a legal counsel for the Great Northern Railway. My chief assignment was handling garnishments. That's another way of saying I was handling attachments placed on the wages of employees of the Great Northern Railway Company. It wasn't up to me to serve them personally, but when a garnishment came in, I had to make a record of it. I was also supposed to inform the paymaster at Hillyard, where a unit of the Great Northern shops is located, that a garnishment had been filed against the salary of so-and-so and that he wasn't to be paid any more until judgment was satisfied.

Some of my friends worked at the Great Northern shops. If any of them drew a garnishment, I'd let them know first and give them an opportunity to draw their pay in advance, before I called the paymaster. I'd tell them if they owed the debt they ought to make an effort to pay it, but in the meantime I suggested that they draw out a little. This caper of mine was not strictly legal, but I was never caught at it. They were all young guys making small salaries, and I didn't want to work them a hardship.

Then, too, I used to type out briefs for Colonel Albert. But it began to dawn on me that I was making as much money on the side, singing and playing the drums, as Colonel Albert was paying his assistant attorney. This gave me to think: what was I doing pursuing the law when singing offered fatter financial possibilities? I talked it over with Al Rinker, and we decided to light out and head south.

My mother had just about given up on me as a law student. She faced the fact that I had a bug to go into show business. She knew that I'd be unhappy and restless unless I had a whirl at it, and while she didn't say so, I think she was confident I'd soon be home looking for three squares again. So she offered no adamant objections. By then Rinker's sister, Mildred Bailey, had moved to Los Angeles and we figured we could stay with her when we arrived there. And my big brother, Everett, was down there selling trucks. Mother was happy that we would have a place to stay instead of just being a couple of youngsters on the bum.

After all, I wasn't a child any more. She had a big family of daughters and sons, and I wasn't her only chick. Everett and Larry had been away to war, and I had been in and out of town on summer jobs at ranches and logging camps, so this wasn't the first leave-taking. It was in 1925 when Al and I took off in a jalopy which had belonged to the Musicaladers. It had cost the Musicaladers twenty-four dollars, but it was kind of beat up. It was terrible looking. It had no top, just a chassis. The top had disappeared long before. So we bought it for eight dollars. We were to change many a tire with clincher rims between Spokane and Los Angeles, which was quite a chore, and the inner tubes were almost entirely patches when we got there. But painted on that flivver was: "Eight million miles and still enthusiastic."

When we started we had twenty dollars in our pockets and my drums in the back seat. The nice thing about Al's instrument was that he didn't have to take it with him. He could find a piano anywhere he went. Our first stop was Seattle. We wanted to hear Jackie Souders' band at the Butler Hotel. We'd heard him on the radio and we'd met him when he played in Spokane. He gave us an audition and then he put us on at the Butler over a week end when the place was filled with University of Washington kids. The songs and arrangements we did were mostly fast-rhythm songs and I sang a couple of solos. We also tossed some of Irving Berlin's waltzes into the hopper: the early ones—"When I Lost You," "All Alone"—things like that. We got a good reception and we could have stayed there for a while, working a night or two a week, but we had heading south on our minds. We couldn't get it off.

It took us a week or more to drive from Seattle to Los Angeles. We hit Medford, Portland, Klamath Falls, and San Francisco on the way. I've read stories about how our flivver stuttered and back-fired, and that the stuttering and back-firing gave me the idea of boo-boo-booing. I don't remember that. Could have been, though. I've heard my own kids sing to the rhythm of our washing machine. Anything that gave a steady beat made them want to keep time with it.

I imagine my boo-boo-boo stuff started with humming. I'd have to do two choruses, and it seemed a good idea to do something at the first part of the second chorus to make it a little different from the first chorus, such as humming or whistling. I tried to vary my humming by imitating the kind of saxophone solo Rudy Wiedoeft or Ross Gorman produced when they played their ballad-type numbers. My notion was to make a sound which resembled the human voice with a bubble in it.

By the time we hit Bakersfield, California, our jalopy was held together almost entirely by youthful optimism. Leaving Bakers-field, we climbed a fifteen-mile grade till we reached Wheeler Ridge, the entrance to the Ridge Route. From there on it's about eighty miles into Los Angeles. When we reached Wheeler Ridge our flivver blew up. She started to fume and smoke and wheeze, and when she blew, she blew good. We just walked away and left her. But first we lifted out my drums. We thumbed a ride on a vegetable truck, threw the drums on, and when we got to the Padre Hotel on the highway leading into Hollywood, we called Mildred Bailey in downtown Los Angeles. She came and got us. She was married to a man named Stafford then. I stored the drums in their basement.

In Los Angeles she sang at a place called The Swede's and we sneaked over to The Swede's once in a while to hear her. The Swede's was much frequented by film actors and actresses who were in the chips. It also featured a singing duo called Varian and Mayer. Ray Mayer was afterwards in vaudeville and in movies, including *The Cowboy and the Lady*. Those two guys had a wonderful comedy delivery. They were good friends of Mildred's. They used to drop in at her house during the day and they taught us a few songs.

Mildred took us to see Mike Lyman, Abe Lyman's brother, at his café, The Tent. He liked us, but said he had no spot for us, adding, however, that if we'd come back a night or two later, he'd have Marco come and see us.

It was a lucky thing I had a big brother in Los Angeles, too. Everett let me use his shirt and studs for that audition with Mike Lyman at The Tent Café. I had a tuxedo but none of the usual accouterments to go with it.

Marco was head of the Fanchon and Marco circuit and was putting on stage presentations in thirty-five or forty Coast and Northwest theaters. We did our routine for him. Rinker sat at the piano and I stood beside him, and we did two or three numbers like "San," "China Boy," and "Copenhagen"; then comedy songs like "Paddlin' Madeleine Home" and "Row, Row, Row," and "Get Out and Get Under." He booked us into the Boulevard Theater in Los Angeles.

Even at this point I'd worked up a way of singing that people were calling "individual." At times I used a kazoo, sticking it into a tin can and moving it in and out to get a trombone effect in a trick I lifted from the Mound City Blues Blowers. It gave out a wah-wahing sound I thought jazzy. At the end, Al and I popped a few jokes—I use the term loosely—but at least they had catch lines.

The Boulevard Theater, where we went to work for Marco, was near the University of Southern California campus, and our audiences were mostly students. The type of work we did seemed particularly appealing to them. I don't think they knew what we were doing, and it was probably better that way. We couldn't have analyzed it ourselves, but what with my kazoo and the coffee can and our scatty way of singing and the new songs we'd worked up, they thought us something fresh and different.

Marco decided we had a pretty good act and booked us over the rest of his circuit. The shows included a chorus line and an animal act or gymnastics, or an acrobatic act or trampolin act. Then there was us singing, and there'd be a girl dance team. The whole thing added up to a forty-minute presentation. We went around the circuit two or three times for Marco, then signed for a show Arthur Freed was doing with Will Morrisey, called *The Morrisey Music Hall Revue*. Freed wrote the songs and put up the money. Morrisey produced the show.

Marco had been paying us from two hundred fifty to three hundred dollars a week as a team. We got the same from Morrisey. *The Morrisey Music Hall Revue* played ten or twelve weeks at Los Angeles' Majestic Theater, although Freed and Morrisey renamed it the Orange Grove Theater for the occasion, thinking that tag would give it more verve. Finally, feeling they'd exhausted the Los Angeles field, they took their show to San Francisco, where we played the Capitol Theater. In addition to our regular performances, we put on midnight shows to

which the students from the University of California flocked
from Berkeley across the bay. In the *Morrisey Music Hall Revue*
I worked with Al Rinker in the pit. The spotlight picked us up
there and we'd do our songs. We had a couple of songs we
hoped were risqué, such as "Where'd Ya Stay Last Night?" but
compared with the material used by some of our café performers
today, they were pretty pallid.

During the eight or ten weeks we stayed in San Francisco, I
became quite buddy-buddy with a group of boys from one of
the fraternities at the University of California, who came over
to catch our midnight shows. The idea was conceived that it
would be quite a lark if we brought the show over by ferry
some afternoon to meet the other members of the fraternity,
have lunch and put on an impromptu performance. Not
only Rinker and I were included in the invitation but the whole
show, chorus girls and all. The chorus girls were very decent
kids. Most of them were in their teens, and had come out of high
schools and dancing schools around Los Angeles.

We went over in one of the ferries, were met by our collegiate
hosts and were taken to their Greek hogan for lunch. The fraternity brothers felt that the consumption of a little punch would
break down any barriers of reserve which might rear themselves between gown and mortarboard and sock and buskin.
They had a washtub filled with gin, a big block of ice and a soli-
tary orange floating dejectedly about in it. It was punchy, all
right. Unhappily, the chorus girls thought they *were* drinking
punch and they sipped several saucers of the brew. By two
o'clock everybody was feeling good, and about two-thirty, when
a large group of other students had gathered, we put on a show.
We chose a secluded spot for our performance—or so we thought
—in front of the famed Campanile, not realizing that it was the
hub of the campus. Our show bordered on the—shall we say
outré?—and some of the faculty who had got wind of it and who
had hurried down to catch it remained to tongue-cluck and
head-shake. This frightened some of the saner minds in the tong,

who stopped the entertainment and spirited us back onto the San Francisco ferry.

Our gay doings were treated as if they had been an orgy, a far more sensational term than they deserved. It had all been outdoors in broad daylight and there wasn't anything orgiastic about it. But an investigation was launched on the campus, some of the boys were suspended, and the fraternity chapter almost lost its national charter.

The show closed shortly afterward. I don't know whether our frolicking at Berkeley had anything to do with its closing, but the authorities at Berkeley had issued a ukase that no U. of C. students could attend our midnight matinee. *Morrisey's Music Hall Revue* played one more date at the Lobero Theater in Santa Barbara, but there its sins and inadequacies caught up with it and the show expired on the old Camino Real, once traversed by decidedly different itinerants, the old dons and padres. Al and I were picked up by Paramount-Publix. Jack Partington, who was putting on stage presentations for them, booked us into what is now the Paramount Theater in Los Angeles, only it was then called the Metropolitan. We were at the Metropolitan when Paul Whiteman heard about us, asked us to audition for him, and placed us under contract as a singing-and-piano novelty act with his band.

To AL RINKER and me it seemed incredible that Paul Whiteman—a man who in 1927 stood out above other American
band leaders as Mount Everest stands out above other mountains—thought us good enough to ask us to appear with his
band. We were to join Whiteman in Chicago when we'd finished playing our own route, so we decided to break the jump
by playing a week at a Spokane theater and seeing our folks
once more.

By this time we had made a recording with the Don Clarke
band, a group which played at the Biltmore Hotel in Los Angeles, and we took it for granted that the world was rushing
in a body to buy this disk. We worked a week in Spokane, grabbing four hundred dollars for the week, but somebody sneaked
into our dressing room and stole our money while we were on
stage, a heinous thing to do to a fellow in his home town.

We lost everything we earned, but we didn't brood over it.
We had such a wonderful time cutting up touches with our families and friends, showing our clippings and taking bows, we
figured we broke even. Then we went to Chicago and made our
debut with Whiteman in the Tivoli Theater there. We went into
the Tivoli with misgivings, but, as I've said earlier, we came out
of it thinking we had the world by the tail.

When we weren't putting on our singing-and-piano specialty
act, we sat with the other members of the band, pretending that
we could play instruments, so the audience wouldn't wonder
why we were doing nothing.

Whiteman had me sitting with the orchestra but I contributed

83

nothing instrumental. To make it seem that I was tootling help-fully away I was given a Peck horn to hold—a Peck horn is a small French horn or an alto horn, sometimes called a rain catcher. Mine had a real, working mouthpiece at first but Whiteman took it away from me because I was unable to resist the impulse to fill in orchestral open spaces with exciting glissandos. He had a dummy mouthpiece substituted. "Rhapsody in Blue" has never sounded the same.

Al Rinker was allowed to hold a guitar with real strings, but he too got over-enthusiastic and strummed along with the band when he thought it was playing so loudly no one could hear him. Then the band would come to a pianissimo passage and the clinkers Al produced could be heard. Pops Whiteman finally gave us both prop instruments with rubber strings. Mine was a violin, and I got so I could bow with it right along with the rest of the boys—soundlessly, of course.

Heading east by way of Cleveland, we wound up in New York, where the team of Rinker and Crosby ran into a giant road block. We went on at the Paramount and did exactly what we'd been doing in all the cities, in which—to be immodest—we'd killed the citizens, but in New York, with the same songs, sung the same way, we died. I couldn't explain it then. I can't now. We sang the same stuff we'd put on our records, which had sold well. Whatever it was, the big city didn't want any part of us.

We were prepared to go back to Los Angeles or even to Spo-kane. If we'd never got anywhere or done anything, the blow wouldn't have been so lethal. But to come into New York, the pinnacle of show business, full of hope and confidence, and end up with egg on our faces, just standing there in our high-button shoes with our teeth in our mouths, was heartbreak.

Pops Whiteman stuck with us for a show or two, but after that he was driven to various dodges to keep us active. Among other things, we did a turn in the lobby at the Paramount to entertain the overflow. There was usually a crowd milling around there waiting for the next show, and Al and I went out with a little piano and sang for them, but we got even less response than we had on the stage. The people in the lobby were concerned only with how soon they were going to be seated, and they paid little or no attention to us, although some kindly disposed wait-ees gave us half a bag of popcorn or a swatch of peanut brittle.

Pops also found other things for us to do. When his band opened in his own night club on Broadway, the proceedings began with two big curtains rolling back. Al and I operated those curtains. We were feeling very humble, and were happy to be working at all, even if we were little better than stagehands.

As a part of its repertoire, the Whiteman band played the "1812 Overture." The colorful Tschaikowsky *tour de force* involves a mixture of the Russian national anthem and the "Marseillaise," with a background of bells ringing and cannons going off. For a while we were those bells in the wings. Pops had a big set of chimes, six or eight feet tall, and two hammers to play them with, and toward the end of the "1812 Overture," when the troops are at the gates of Moscow and the city is on fire and the cathedral bells are ringing, we got carried away and belabored those chimes with great spirit. Whiteman had rented them from a music-equipment house, and every second or third day we had to have a new set. Finally the manager of the band went to Pops and said, "How far do you want me to go buying new bells?"

"I don't know what you're talking about," Whiteman told him.

"Those kids are belting those bells so enthusiastically they're ruining them," the manager said, "and we're paying for them." During the balance of our two-week engagement, we were given padded hammers. We always thought the rendition of the "1812 Overture" suffered considerably as a result.

Whiteman was doing a lot of recording, and he worked Al and me into the vocal ensembles. We cut a number of sides which afterward appeared in the "Bix Beiderbecke Memorial Album." We were in on a lot of recordings with the full orchestra, among them some musical-comedy scores. Then Whiteman and his band went to Philadelphia, where we played the Stanley Theater. Pops gave Al and me another chance there. We seemed to be going good, so he put us in the show again. We also made some recordings in Camden for Victor. We were over there two or three times a week, and I was given a couple of solos to do, "Ol' Man River" and "Make Believe," in Whiteman's recording of the Jerome Kern–Oscar Hammerstein II *Show Boat* score.

Those solos stirred up some interest and Pops gave me more of them. Some of the boys in the band, fellows like Roy Bargy, Ferde Grofé and Lennie Hayton, pals of mine, would write me into their arrangements and build me up with the old man. But I still didn't have a solo with the band on stage. Back in New York again, Al and I worked with the band's other singers, the great "Skin" Young, Charlie Gaylord, and Jack Fulton. Together we did harmonic backgrounds for instrumental solos. Whiteman had progressive arrangers—a fellow named Bill Challis and the aforementioned, talented Ferde Grofé, who arranged vocal licks for us for records and for stage. In that way Al and I kept going, but our identity as a specialty act was gone. We were just members of a singing group. Pops tried us as a double a few other times in cafés, but we were still nowhere. New York had us licked. Al and I had lost our confidence, and audiences were quick to sense this fact. Since our routine was based on bounce and gaiety, the audience lost interest if we came out feeling whipped.

Most of the Whiteman band put up at the Belvedere Hotel in New York and I ran up a bill there. When I was a little light with the loot to meet my obligation, I brought an old show-business tradition into play. I told the manager I'd leave my trunk with him and he could hold it for security until I got back from a trip we were about to make with Paul. When I came back, I still didn't have enough money to pick up that Belvedere tab and, having acquired a new if somewhat scanty wardrobe in the meanwhile, I left the trunk there in payment. It may still be there. Full of newspapers, probably.

For a while the jazz immortal, Bix Beiderbecke, was part of Whiteman's band and I roomed with him at the Belvedere. He was tremendously talented musically. The cornet was his instrument, but I sometimes think he played piano better than he did the cornet. He had a superb ear, an inimitable style, and was a serious student of *avant garde* classical music. In that respect, as a jazz artist he was years ahead of his time.

Bix was a disciple of "King" Oliver, and the Dixieland cult, but he took great pleasure and inspiration from the works of Eastwood Lane, Cyril Scott, and Edward MacDowell. Much of the piano he played was based on composition styles created by these composers and similar ones of the period. I recall him playing "Woodland Sketches," "To a Water Lily," "From an Indian Lodge," and others whose titles elude me, and the treatment he gave them was beautiful to hear. It's an everlasting shame he didn't record them.

He had many other favorites, of course, and I often listened to his version of Stravinsky's "Firebird" and "Petrouchka," but the composers I've mentioned above were his favorites.

He also liked to play Debussy's "Afternoon of a Faun" and "Clair de Lune." I am sure he learned them by main strength because at that time he read music very little. Bix was certainly the first popular musician I ever heard play anything like these things on the piano. When you listened to them you got an impression that they were vague and beautiful and that he was almost improvising—the style of harmonization popularly called "cloudlike" now.

Jazz pundits will excuse me if I'm chronologically inaccurate, but I believe that his first recordings were with the Wolverines' Orchestra. He played New York in the middle twenties at the Roseland Ballroom and was a tremendous hit. He must have been quite young then because I am sure he was younger than I, and in 1925 I would have been twenty-one. It was while he was at the Roseland that he made six or eight sides with the Wolverines. One was a record called "Big Boy," recorded by Gennet. I've never heard of any collectors who possess this record or the records by the Wolverines. It seems to me that two of the records with the Wolverines were "The Washboard Blues" and "The Davenport Blues." Davenport was Bix' home town, and he wrote the tune. It was purely an instrumental then, although it may have words to it now. "Washboard Blues" was the immortal lament written by Hoagy Carmichael.

Bix never liked to go to bed, so he always felt terrible physically. He had a bristly mustache straight out of one of the Bruce Bairnsfather "Better Ole" and the "Old Bill" cartoons, so popular in the First World War. It looked like a bad windrow; however, it didn't interfere with his trumpet-playing. It seemed to make his lip stronger, or at least that's what Bix claimed. His lip was always sore, but he said that if he shaved it, it would make it weaker.

He always carried his cornet with him, day and night, sometimes *sans* case, sometimes in a paper bag, and he'd sit in with orchestras any time anyone wanted him to. He rushed around to all the night clubs to play cornet with the boys, getting no rest and having more than a few beers. As a result, he generally felt pretty rough, so much so that if anybody asked him, "How do you feel?" he answered, "I don't ask you how you feel. Why do you ask me how I feel? You know I feel bad. Just leave me alone."

He wasn't bellicose about it, it was just that it annoyed him when anyone asked him how he felt. Anyone who's ever had a "black-dog-riding-on-the-shoulder" type of hang-over will understand his mood. He slept fitfully, and he liked a room equipped with twin beds, so that he could move back and forth from one to the other if he became restless. Every once in a while he'd wake me up in the middle of the night and make me change beds with him. He never exercised. He didn't believe in it. I don't think it fair to call him an alcoholic because he'd go for days without touching the stuff, and he was seldom so under the weather that he couldn't navigate or play the piano or the cornet. In the end, it was his lack of sleep and his physical exhaustion which broke his health and killed him.

Bix was very intellectual, very well read, and as good an authority on new American symphonic music or classical music as anyone I've ever known. When he met others with similar tastes, fellows like Fred Livingston, Chummy MacGregor, Jimmy Dorsey, Howdy Quicksell, they'd sit and fan for hours, discussing this music, playing snatches of it, listening to recordings.

I confess I was playing infield for most of these seminars; it was a little deep for me but there's no question that I derived some profit. Through example, I learned to like good music, and, if not quite to understand it, at least to appreciate and evaluate what I heard for my personal pleasure.

Because of his recordings, he had admirers all over the East. He had a very short memory. When he visited a town and took in a night club and his fans came rushing up to him, he could never remember whether he'd met them before or not. When they said, "Hi, Bix! Remember me, Bix?" he had a series of stock answers which could mean anything. He'd ask, "Are you still down there?" or "Are you still working?" If the one who greeted him was young, he'd ask, "Still going to school?" The guy would say, "Yeah, yeah, I'm still down there," or "No, I left there some time ago," and would go away impressed with how thoughtful Bix was to be so interested in his welfare.

There was a cult for his music while he was alive, but it wasn't so large, so active, or so dedicated as it is now.

Another Whiteman band member was Eddie Lang. Eddie was a South Philadelphia Italian. His real name was Salvatore Mazarro. In the opinion of all the guitar players of his day and many since, he was the greatest one of the craft who ever lived. Eddie could read little music. But he played with all the big radio and recording orchestras. Once he'd heard an arrangement rehearsed, he was not only able to play the guitar part of that arrangement but decorate it a bit. The next time they ran through the number he was solid as a rock.

He was the first fellow to do much single-string guitar solo work on recordings and dance jobs. Single-string means picking the melody out on one string and hitting a chord once in a while to maintain a rhythm.

Eddie had had only the sketchiest kind of education. When I asked him how long he'd gone to school, he'd say, "What's school?" He was quiet and retiring but the things he did he did superlatively well.

When we were on tour Eddie was my accompanist. He came on stage with me and sat beside me, cradling his guitar as if it were a loved bambino. We did most of our songs with just that guitar. Occasionally we let the pit orchestra violins sneak in at the finish or maybe we'd use them in the middle of the song for support. But basically my accompaniment was Eddie's guitar.

When we'd done the first show in every new town we checked into, Eddie remarked, "I'll be busy between now and the second show."

Then he'd visit the local pool hall, case the players there, watch them play a little. Presently he'd get in a game or two and manage to be beaten and to look as if he just fell off a load of pumpkins.

The pool-hall habitués would figure him a musician on tour and loose with his money. For the rest of the week between shows Eddie'd haunt that pool hall. He played it cool, building up a spot for the melon-cutting. He let the locals win a little but when the heavy loot was riding, he turned on his A game and knocked 'em in.

It's my guess that he made more at pool than he did accompanying me. The natural ego of pool players (or any other kind of gambler) is good for a week's exploitation if nursed along carefully. Eddie's rivals always felt when he was knocking those balls in that he was having a run of good luck.

When Eddie played his best at billiards or pool there weren't many amateurs who could handle him. I've watched him in New York play with, and hold his own with, Ponzi and Mosconi and other greats of the pro circuit. The same applied to his card game. He had a phenomenal memory. When he took up contract bridge few he met were his masters or even his equals.

He never played golf but once in a while he'd go with me to a course, pick up a putter, and lick the pants off of me on the putting green.

He was what you'd call a real handy fellow.

Ben Hogan makes me think of him. Anything Ben tries to do he does well.

I've had Ben up to my ranch at Elko. He can shoot better than anybody I ever knew, with either a scatter gun or rifle. He can ride, brand, fix fence. He can run the equipment and repair tractors. And although Ben had a lot more education than Eddie had, Eddie was the same kind of fellow. Eddie never read the newspapers but he always seemed to know what was going on in the way of current or sporting events.

If he'd studied the guitar I don't know whether he'd have been a better or worse player. Maybe if he'd gotten involved with the technique of playing and following musical manuscripts he might not have played with the dexterity and the freedom and the good taste which come instinctively to the natural musician who plays by ear.

Before he died, Eddie Lang used to have great times with the violinist Joe Venuti. They started out together in South Philadelphia, and were partners in a lot of duet recordings. The two made a number of recordings which are still collectors' items. Eddie's passing hit me hard.

He had a chronically inflamed sore throat and felt bad for a year or eighteen months before his death. He mistrusted doctors and medicine. Like many people who came from backgrounds similar to his and who had had no experience with doctors or hospitals, he had an aversion to them. But his throat was so bad and it affected his health to such a point that I finally talked him into seeing a doctor.

Many times afterward I wished I hadn't.

The doctor advised a tonsillectomy. And Eddie never came out from under the general anesthetic they gave him. I don't think they use a general anesthetic now for adults. As I understand it, for an operation of that kind, the patient is anesthetized locally so his respiration isn't affected. Anyhow Eddie developed an embolism and died without regaining consciousness.

It was a great blow. I not only lost a valuable associate in the entertainment business, I lost a valued personal friend, a friend I had fun with and who was loyal to me throughout all of the years we were associated. I've often thought if I hadn't recommended that treatment he'd still be around. On the other hand, if he hadn't had it, the infection might have gone into his blood stream and the same thing would have happened that did happen.

Looking back, life then contained mixed colors, some light, some dark. On the dark side was Eddie Lang's death. On the brighter side was Mattie Malneck's vocal arrangement of "Wistful and Blue" for Rinker and me. With this arrangement we created a new singing style. Nothing for the ages, but a style. The best way to describe it is to say that it was a vocal without words. We sang voh-do-de-oh licks while Mattie, who arranged the vocal and wrote it for us, played the viola as a third voice. It produced something of an unusual effect, and as there had been nothing like it, it was very popular.

As it happened, a fellow named Harry Barris was playing in New York at George Olsen's Club, doing a single and singing riffs. He played hot piano, slamming the top down from time to time to emphasize his licks. Pops Whiteman heard him and liked his delivery and his enthusiasm, and although Barris was doing all right with Olsen, Pops offered him a job with the Whiteman organization. Presently Barris, Rinker, and I were teamed together under the label of Paul Whiteman's Rhythm Boys.

Barris had written a song called "Mississippi Mud." Al and I learned it and the three of us made a platter of it. "Mississippi Mud" was something of a riot in both of its versions. I say "both" because it was first copyrighted by Barris, then a second version was copyrighted by Barris and a man named Jimmy Cavanaugh. Barris worked on three or four other songs, among them "So the Bluebirds" and "The Blackbirds Got Together," and we put together a repertoire of numbers nobody else was singing. And Pops put us on the floor in the Whiteman Club, a night spot which bore his name. The Rhythm Boys left the customers in sections—we fractured them. As far as Crosby and Rinker were concerned, it was a return to our happy days at the Tivoli Theater in Chicago all over again.

About this time Mattie Malneck made an arrangement of "From Monday On" for us. This is significant because, in recording it, we were backed by one of the most remarkable trios ever assembled: Bix Beiderbecke, Jimmy and Tommy Dorsey.

We began to play late parties around town, after the Club Whiteman closed. We played a couple such soirees for Jimmy Walker and we worked a few whingdings for Buddy DeSylva, and for other celebrities, among them Bea Lillie. I've never reminded Bea of this, although we worked together later in pictures, for we didn't do too well at her party. We couldn't seem to get the attention of her guests. There was a lot of elbow-bending and conversation going on in a big drawing room, and if you can't get a crowd like that to listen to you at the start, you're a blown-up tomato. We had two miniature white pianos, one for Rinker and one for Barris, and I stood between them, slapping away at a cymbal in my hand, and we set up quite a din ourselves. But the party had gone too far. Our noise wasn't enough to stop 'em. However, even though we were cool at Bea Lillie's, we were well paid.

We were so flushed with success that inertia set in and we

didn't bother to learn any new songs. When we weren't working, we spent time in Harlem at the Cotton Club listening to Duke Ellington and Cab Calloway, Ethel Waters, and other Negro entertainers, and we didn't do too much rehearsing. Moreover, we got a little tired of each other—as youngsters will. We couldn't decide which of us was boss. Every three or four weeks we decided to break up, then the next day we'd get back together again.

That on-again-off-again routine wasn't conducive to hard work. The success of an act like ours depends upon developing new material all the time, for a piece of material which might be good when it's fresh can be useless in ten or twelve weeks. Naturally, Whiteman was disgusted with us. We were supposed to go on his next concert tour with him, but the stuff we were doing wasn't suitable for a concert-type program and, as I've said, we hadn't bothered to learn anything new. So Whiteman booked us for a vaudeville tour over the Keith-Orpheum circuit. He equipped us with a big cardboard figure of himself, and he made a recording of an announcement in which he said, "Ladies and gentlemen, I take great pleasure in presenting to you my Rhythm Boys. I hope you are entertained by them and that you will give them a warm reception."

When the curtain went up, it disclosed the cardboard figure of Whiteman on a dimly lit stage, and his announcement blared at the audience through a loud-speaker. Then the lights went up and we were seen in the center of the stage, with Barris slamming the piano top down, me frim-framming a cymbal with a wire fly-swatter, and all three of us locked in a "righteous" beat. We were supposed to play thirty-nine or forty solid weeks. But we didn't play them very solid. There were times when we didn't show up at all. Being young, we were irresponsible. Life was our oyster or, to use a phrase popular then, our "bowl of cherries." We took a little time out to savor it.

There were trains we missed, and times when our baggage didn't arrive. We didn't let such mishaps interfere with our golf.

We got in a game every morning if we could find a course. Once, when we were supposed to go to Columbus from Cincinnati, I got mixed up handling the transportation and we went to Nashville, Tennessee, a couple of hundred miles out of our way. As a result, we missed the first three days of our Columbus engagement.

Because of such misadventures, the Keith office in New York with which Whiteman had booked us began to take a dim view of us and our future value, and after our week in St. Louis, Keith very nearly canceled us. We were supposed to do our regular singing act, but we'd been exposed to so many comedy teams on tour and had stolen so much material from them that our act had changed. We were doing an opening song, ten minutes of comedy, and a closing song. We had put on a gag mind-reading act, with Barris in the aisle working the audience while I was on stage wearing a turban. Cued by some remarkably corny and obvious hints from him, I'd guess what was in people's wallets. Rinker played an incidental piano and helped Barris with the audience. We'd made this change in spite of the fact that a large part of our audience-appeal lay in the fact that people who'd bought our recordings came to hear us sing. We ignored that in favor of our new conviction that we were side-splittingly funny. I recall one of our sparkling interchanges.

Barris asked, "How can you cure a horse of frothing at the mouth?"

"Teach him to spit," I replied.

The local manager must have beefed about us to Keith's New York headquarters, for after a few days of such hanky-panky he hold us that he had news for us; either we went back to the original act Keith had bought or we'd be canceled. We promised to reform, but three shows later we weakened and returned to our "witty" stuff again. The curtain closed in front of us before our act was over. We ran offstage to put the blast on the stagehand who'd rung it down, and encountered the manager.

"That's all in this house for you, boys," he said.

He asked us where we were due next. When we said Rockford, Illinois, he told us, "You'd better change your act or you'll be thrown out of there, too." Chastened, we went back to singing and the populace of Rockford had to do without learning how to cure a horse of frothing at the mouth.

Barris was and is remarkably talented. He writes songs as easily as other folk write a letter. In addition, he can sing and he's a good comedian. But while he could do all of these things, he knew he could do them. And because he gave the impression of knowing all there was to know, Al and I called him "Little Joe Show Business." He'd started ahead of us. He'd worked a tour or two with Gus Edwards. This gave him more experience than Al and I had, and he dominated the thinking of our act—the planning of it and putting it together.

In the years that have elapsed since our Whiteman days, Barris has had a lot of good jobs. Not long ago he put together an act with three other song writers: Shelton Brooks, who wrote "Some of These Days"; Archie Gottler, who wrote "America, I Love You"; and Gus Arnheim, who's authored a number of hit songs. They called their routine: "Then I Wrote." They sat at four pianos pushed out onto café floors. Their act was a tremendous hit. Acts like that are bound to be hits, since their tunes and melodies stir up such tidal waves of nostalgia that they're home free.

Barris has always fascinated me as a physical specimen. Twenty years ago, when I worked with him, he suffered from a racking cough. He slept little, and he didn't weigh much. I made up my mind that he wasn't long for this world. When I see him nowadays, although he still weighs less than a wet dishrag and he still coughs, he is just as enthusiastic as ever. He has a sheaf of music in his hip pocket he's just written the night before—or that day. I wish I knew what keeps him going. It would be worth millions. He operates on something I know nothing about—a new kind of fuel for the human motor.

Al Rinker was dark, curly-haired, soft-spoken. When he did

96

speak, he didn't say much. His kind always goes over well with the girls. The fellow who does all the talking gets nowhere; the fellow who waits for the gabby ones to run out of gas, then moves in, does better. Al has always been very serious about music. He likes good music and knows it when he hears it. He plays a good piano, although by ear. When the Rhythm Boys broke up he continued to be successful. For several years after that he did radio work and produced shows on national networks.

With the conclusion of our Keith-Orpheum circuit tour, we returned to Whiteman's band to discover that Hollywood was standing at the threshold of a new trend, one which was to affect my life powerfully—musical pictures. Urged by Carl Laemmle, Jr., Carl Laemmle, Sr., head of Universal Pictures, decided to film a mammoth musical built around Whiteman and his band. Since Whiteman was by far the most important and best-known figure in popular music, Laemmle thought if he could persuade him to do a picture, Universal would steal a march on all the other studios. In 1930, after lengthy negotiations, a deal was set for us all to come to California—the band, the singers, Whiteman, his valet, his business manager—and make *The King of Jazz*. Since we were broadcasting for Old Gold, Old Gold supplied a special train for us as an advertising stunt. Banners draped over the train plugged the cigarettes.

While we didn't know it, we were to make two such trips. When we arrived the first time, we were given a big bungalow on the Universal lot as a recreation room. We all bought autos— or at least we made the down payment with money which Pops advanced to us, then deducted from our salaries. We loafed for a month while the big brains worked up a story which proved unsuitable for Whiteman. They made the mistake of trying to build him as a romantic lead. He was impressive looking, but what with his thinning thatch and his ample poundage, it was finally decided that he didn't fit the script, so we bundled back into the train, returned to New York and stayed there for a couple of months.

It was in this period that my irresponsible ways and over-friendliness with strangers got me into big trouble. Hoping to find a few congenial souls, I dropped into a speak-easy. Before I knew it, I had become pals with a couple of quiet strangers leaning against the bar. That is, their voices were quiet and their eyes were quiet. Their clothes weren't. I started to drink brandy with them, although I'd never tried that potent tipple before—nor have I ever tried it since—and I remember starting pub-crawling with my new companions. After that a haze set in and a couple of days disappeared.

When I came to, I was parked on a sofa in a strange room. Across the room a group of men with padded shoulders, snap-brim black hats and sallow faces were holding a conference at a table. The group noticed me stirring, and one of them came over to me.

"Have a nice sleep?" he asked.

I shook my head. I felt terrible. My head was one big ache.

"Somebody must have slipped you a Mickey Finn," he said. "We didn't think you'd be safe with the money in your wallet, so we brought you here to sleep it off."

"Thanks for the use of the room," I said. "I'll be going now."

"You'll have to put up with us for a while longer," the man said. "While you were out on your feet, there was a shooting. Somebody got hurt and we holed up here. The boys think you'd better stay with us until we give you the word."

I sat there trying to think about it. My head wasn't functioning and my mouth felt as if it were full of hot cotton. I went into the bathroom and filled a glass with water. I didn't get it to my mouth. As I raised it there was a sound like six autos back-firing, the noise of plaster falling, and choking screams from the next room.

I stayed in that bathroom for what seemed hours, until I heard new voices. Then large, flat footsteps came toward the bathroom door. I turned on a faucet and filled the glass once more. When a policeman opened the door, I was drinking thirstily.

"Who are you?" he asked.

"My name's Crosby," I told him. "I'm with Whiteman's band. I've just come from a recording date. I heard the shooting and popped in to see what was going on."

He looked at me doubtfully.

Many years later I was to win an Oscar for acting, but the acting I did to win that Academy Award was as nothing compared with the acting I did then. Wandering nonchalantly out of the bathroom, I mixed with the gawkers and lookers, the detectives and newspaper reporters with notebooks and pencils in their hands who were questioning a couple of my companions with the padded shoulders and the sallow faces. They had been nicked here and there by machine-gun slugs and their faces were even sallower. The door of the room had been shot open. Bullet holes around the lock had done that. Someone had sprayed the room with lead slugs. One of the reporters who knew I was with Whiteman vouched for the fact that I was no gang member, and I was herded outside by the law with the spectators who had come to stare. There was no trouble herding me out. I let them do it one-hand easy.

The next day I discovered that I had been holed up with a prominent gang leader and his mob. This citizen was said to have been involved in one of the most celebrated mass killings of the alky-cooking-and-running days, the St. Valentine's Day Massacre in a Chicago garage. When I read that, I wanted nothing more than to get out of New York, and I was glad when we got word that Universal had finally cooked up a story suitable for Whiteman and we all trooped to the train and went back to Hollywood.

We worked on *The King of Jazz* for an age. Picture techniques weren't developed then the way they are now, and musical numbers took as much as a week to shoot. Pops had promised me a song, "Song of the Dawn," in the picture. I was to sing a verse and two choruses. It was a big production number and was a tremendous break for me. I rehearsed and rehearsed, then I took time out to see Southern California play California at Los Angeles. There was quite a shindig after the game in our recreation bungalow at Universal. The party involved some tippling, but not to excess. We got gay and exhilarated, but not stoned. Some young ladies were present and I volunteered to take one of them home in my flivver with its top modishly down.

She lived at the Roosevelt Hotel. When I tried to make a left turn into her hostelry—at seven or eight miles an hour—another motorist slammed into my rear and threw us out of the car. My passenger was cut up and I took her into the hotel lobby, found some towels and tried to stanch the flow of blood. While I was thus engaged, a gendarme tapped my shoulder and asked if I had driven the car which had dumped us upon the sidewalk. I said I had. He also had in his clutches the fellow who had run into me, and he took us both to the calaboose for austere overnight lodgings. In the morning Pops Whiteman came down and bailed me out. The charge against me was "reckless driving and suspicion of drinking." My trial was set for a week later. The driver of the second car had to go back to college—his examinations were taking place—and his trial was set for a week after mine.

The day of my trial I'd been playing golf, and I appeared in plus fours, highly colored hose and a sweater to match. The judge, a visiting jurist from Santa Ana, was a militant prohibitionist, but no one had told me that. He asked me about the accident and I told him what happened. Then he said, "It says on the complaint 'H.B.D.' That means 'Had Been Drinking.' Is that true?"

"I had a couple," I said.

"Don't you know there's a Prohibition Law in this country?" he asked.

"Yes," I said, "but nobody pays much attention to it."

He snapped his mouth together like the lid of a roll-top desk closing, and said, "You'll have sixty days in which to pay attention to it."

"What's the fine?" I asked.

"There'll be no fine. Just sixty days." So I was flung into durance vile. After a couple of days my brother Everett came to see me. He told me that Pops Whiteman had tried to hold my song for me, but when I couldn't be sprung, they had given it to another singer, John Boles.

At first I was kept in the downtown jail but finally Everett and Pops between them got me transferred to the Hollywood jail, where my friends could come to see me.

Toward the end of the picture a number with the Rhythm Boys had been arranged. We were to render it with the Three Brox Sisters; it was to be called "A Bench in the Park." They couldn't find a suitable substitute for me, so the law let me out once a day in custody of an officer to work in the film. The cop had the time of his life. To him, being on a movie set was really living. I served about forty days before my sentence was commuted. When the other driver—the college lad—heard that the judge had thrown the book at me, he'd hired a lawyer and had pleaded not guilty. By that time another judge was on the bench, who gave him a suspended sentence.

Whiteman was sore about the whole thing, but when he cooled off he admitted that I'd been a victim of circumstances. I certainly wasn't speeding. I'd had a drink or two, but I was sober.

It seems to me in reading back over what I've written here that there's been a great deal of talk about a character named John Barleycorn. If that's the way it was, that's the way it should be told. However, I'd like to insert a note to the effect that although I was guilty of a few youthful indiscretions in the late 1920's and early '30's, once I got those injudicious moments out of my system I have never let liquor interfere with my work or my capacities.

When we finished *The King of Jazz,* we played theater dates with Whiteman in Los Angeles, San Diego, Seattle, and Portland. It was in Portland that I got into an argument with Pops over a bootlegging bill. A bootlegger who followed the band selling day-old pop-skull claimed that I owed him for a bottle of his sauce. I owed him nothing, and I said so, but Pops Whiteman paid him anyhow and took it out of my salary. I disputed this so vigorously that Pops said, "You don't seem to be too serious. You're just having a good time touring and living off the fat of the land and getting arrested and costing me money. When we get to Seattle, we'll part friends and that'll be the end of it."

I don't want to say good-bye to Whiteman in this tale without paying him a tribute for being so patient and long-suffering with me. I'm impressed by how kind he was. When I was younger and more hot-headed, I used to think he should line my pockets with more gold. But I confess he owes me nothing. It's the other way around.

I have often wondered what might have happened to me if I had sung "The Song of Dawn" in place of John Boles. It certainly helped him. On the strength of it, he got a lot of pictures after that. I must say, he had a bigger voice and a better delivery for that kind of song than I had. My crooning style wouldn't have been very good for such a number, which was supposed to be delivered à la breve like the "Vagabond Song." I might have flopped with the song. I might have been cut out of the picture. I might never have been given another crack at a song in any picture.

AT SEATTLE, Al Rinker, Harry Barris and I left Whiteman, and I wrote Bill Perlberg a letter asking him to see if he could find work for us in California. It was in 1930 and Perlberg was then one of a long procession of booking agents in my life. Bill scurried around putting the talk on people and got us a job at Eddie Brandstatter's Montmartre Café in Los Angeles. The Hollywood whirligig of chance takes some eccentric turns. Perlberg is a big producer now. By an unpredictable turn of the wheel, he produced my latest picture, *Little Boy Lost*.

The Montmartre was a favorite hangout of the film colony, and Barris, Rinker and I were fairly big there. For one thing, after Whiteman let us go, we learned a new song or two and our material improved. As sometimes happens when some fresh instrumentalists or vocalists come to town, we became an overnight fad. Those who "discovered" us asked others, "Have you caught the Rhythm Boys at the Montmartre?" It happened later to a lad named Vallee and to a good-looking youngster named Russ Columbo. Much later it happened to Frank Sinatra. I'm glad it happened to me then because it brought Dixie Lee to the Montmartre.

Soon after, an agent named Leonard Goldstein was booking us. Goldstein has also gone onward and upward with the motion picture arts and is now a big producer. Under his aegis we moved from the Montmartre to the Coconut Grove. Gus Arnheim had decided to form a band and go back into the Coconut Grove, where he'd once been Abe Lyman's pianist. He signed Barris, Rinker, and me, a girl singer named Loyce Whiteman, a tenor named Donald Novis, and got together a band which could do comedy group-singing. When we'd rehearsed for a while, we were a pretty useful unit. The Coconut Grove had a radio outlet two hours each night. We thought this a fine thing, but we had no conception of how wonderful it actually was. Through this new medium we built popularity all over California and as far north as Seattle, Portland, and Tacoma. I found out later that even some of the people in the Midwest used to sit up until three A.M. to catch us.

I've been very lucky. I started with no particular aim—other than the vague general one of wanting to sing and be in show business. I was seeking no great achievement. I just did what I liked to do. It seemed to me that the best way to get into singing and into show business was to go to Los Angeles, so I went there. Through a series of circumstances, I got jobs there and progressed from one phase of show business to another, with the accent always on music.

When we were at the Coconut Grove, Barris wrote his great song, "I Surrender, Dear." "I Surrender" had an exceptional arrangement made by Arnheim's arranger, Jimmie Greer, and the record we cut of it was unusual for those days. Dance bands usually played a number in straight tempo, but our recording had changes of tempo and modulations and vocal touches in several spots. This had much to do with the popularity of the song. Week after week, people demanded that we sing it; we couldn't get off without singing it several times a night. "I Surrender" lit a fire under Barris, and he came through with hit after hit: "At Your Command," "Wrap Your Troubles in Dreams," and "It Must Be True," also with a fine arrangement by Jimmie Greer.

Barris was writing now with a fellow named Gordon Clifford, who did lyrics. I put in a word or two myself, but my contributions weren't important. I helped write the verses, which nobody played. They were written because they had to be in the copy; I sang them for recordings, but I didn't sing them at the Grove.

One of my Boswells has since made the statement that I "wooed my listeners with a husky whisper at the Coconut Grove." That could be true. Some nights, after singing four or five hours, including two on the radio, a husky whisper was all I had left.

With the coming of fame, we became regular callers at Agua Caliente. Since we had Sunday and Monday off, we'd go there occasionally for a week end. What with driving about one hundred and fifty miles each way and playing roulette, golf, and the races and belting a little tequila around, come Tuesday, when I stood or swayed in front of the microphone, my pipes were shot.

Toward the end of our engagement at the Grove we didn't take our responsibilities seriously enough to suit Abe Frank. Frank was running the Coconut Grove and The Ambassador Hotel. But the Grove was his pet. He was an elderly, serious sort who disliked anything that disrupted the even tenor of the nightly routine at the Grove. When people were supposed to appear, he expected them to be on deck. So, when I failed to get back for the Tuesday-night show once too often, he docked my wages. Of course Abe was within his rights legalistically speaking, but I thought he was pretty small about it, so I quit.

I was encouraged in this defiance by an offer from Mack Sennett to make a series of movie shorts for him. I had made one for him already, and working in pictures looked like easy money to me. I made a couple more shorts at Sennett's, then Abe Frank plastered a union ban on me, "for failure to fulfill the standard musician's contract." After that, union musicians weren't allowed to work with me. To get around the boycott, Sennett used a pipe organ or ukuleles or an *a-cappella* choir in the background. Or we worked to canned music, which meant that I sang to a phonograph-record accompaniment.

The way we made those Sennett shorts reads like a quaint

piece of Americana. For two days we'd have a story conference. I was in on it. In fact, everybody was in on it—actors, cameramen, gagmen, and Sennett. We sat upstairs in Sennett's office, a large room equipped with plenty of cuspidors because Sennett was a muncher of the weed. For our title we used the name of the basic song in the picture, like "I Surrender, Dear," "At Your Command," or "Just One More Chance." For our plot we'd start with a very social mother and daughter. I'd be a band crooner with a bad reputation, and mother didn't think me quite right for her daughter. Instead she wanted her apple dumpling to marry some respectable pup; some fuddy-duddy; some very disagreeable character; a young businessman or a rising young lawyer.

Once we had this nugget of plot, Sennett would start "writing." I use "writing" for want of a better word. He put nothing down on paper. His story was really a series of gags. We always would end up with somebody falling in a fish pond or some other device with "punch" possibilities. Sennett would tell me, "This is the scene where you call on the girl, and you know her mother doesn't like you, and you're talking to the girl and her mother comes in and discovers you and tells you to leave the house, you louse, she doesn't want to ever see you again. So you go out, and on the way out, you step into this laundry basket, and you get up with the laundry hanging all over you, and you make an ignominious exit."

"When do I exist?" I'd ask.

"When I drop my handkerchief," he'd say. He'd call, "Camera!" and we were off.

From the corner of my eye, I saw his handkerchief drop. I said, "I gotta go now," stepped into the laundry basket, took my fall and made my ignominious exit. The songs we used were usually shot against a night-club background or in a radio station or at a microphone. We weren't clever or adroit about working the songs subtly into the action. Sennett just said, "Now we'll have a song," and we had one.

He had an endless treasury of physical gags left over from his old Keystone Cop, Mabel Normand, Ford Sterling, Wally Beery days. I'd be dunked in a tank and fish would get down my shirt front or quick-rising dough would envelop me in a gooey bubble-bath. Sennett was a genius at devising things like that. He knew how to photograph them and how to stage them.

Those shorts had a running time of about twenty minutes. Sennett didn't shoot scenes over and over again. Once was enough. With a two-day shooting schedule, he couldn't waste time. At the end we wound up with a chase. I'd get into a car with the girl and we'd start out over the Hollywood hills with the cops or the irate parent in pursuit, while Sennett had his cameraman crank slowly to make it look fast. The finale was me singing the theme song, with the mother won over to my side and beaming happily.

My run-in with Abe Frank was the end of The Rhythm Boys. We lay idle a month or so afterward. I went to see Abe Frank a couple of times to see if he'd let us off the hook, but he said, "You'll either accept the fine and come back to work or you're tacit."

Only a couple of hundred dollars were involved, but his attitude brought out the mule in me. I had my neck bowed like a balky jackass; nevertheless, I had to have work. I was married now, and I didn't want my good-provider routine to lay an egg. I got six hundred dollars for each Sennett short, and while that didn't make me a millionaire, it had made me feel that I could support Dixie Lee if she'd have me. I proposed to her over a plate of chicken in the Coconut Grove, and she said, "I think it would be a good idea."

Neither one of us brooded over-long about the seriousness of the step we were taking. We were very much in love. This was it.

About that time my brother, Everett, entered the picture. He began to handle bits and pieces of my business, and he stirred up interest in me on the part of the Columbia Broadcasting System's president, William Paley. Paley was looking for a singer with an unusual style, and Everett sent him the recordings of "I Surrender, Dear," and "Just One More Chance" I'd made with Arnheim's band. Paley listened to them, got in touch with Everett and asked him to bring me to New York.

This seems a good time to tell about the part Everett has played in my career. It would be dramatic to say that if it hadn't been for Everett I'd be lying somewhere with my head on a curb. It would also be an exaggeration. Everett didn't save me from Skid Row. But he fired me with a spirit of git-up-and-git at a time when things were static for me. He came into my picture when I was disgusted and had little faith in my future. He supplied the ambition I seemed to lack. I'm glad I went along with him for the ride.

Everett's a good mixer. He's a hustler. He knows how to deal with people. He was able to reach Paley and equally important people in the broadcasting business and sell them on my possibilities as a radio singer. Later, he was able to do the same thing in Hollywood and convince the keepers of the keys in the film-flam capital that I'd be a success in motion pictures. He's tireless at negotiating with motion-picture companies, motion-picture producers, radio sponsors, advertising agencies—anyone who feels that he needs my services and with whom it is necessary to strike a contract or revise one already made.

He seems fond of bickering with these people, and he'll drag the discussions out happily for days, weeks, months, even years, if he thinks he can get me a better shuffle. He loves to go to their offices or have them come to his, where he pounds the table and hollers and shouts and walks up and down. He's a trifle hammy about it, but there's nothing hammy about what he's accomplished on my behalf. If I had to deal with those people, my patience would soon be exhausted and I'd accept the deal they were trying to get me to accept or maybe go for a compromise which wouldn't be good for me. But Everett yells and screams and argues until he gets a reasonable facsimile of the arrangements he's trying to secure.

Perhaps it's because he's such a good bargainer that he's not always popular with those for whom I work. They don't like to deal with a fighter who goes the limit in trying to get what he thinks I ought to have. As a result, he is sometimes called "The Wrong Crosby."

I've never had any contractual problems with Paramount since I went to work for them in the early 1930's. Each time a new deal was contemplated between us there was always some basis for understanding. With the exception of occasionally having to ask Brother Everett to go to see whatever studio boss was in charge at that particular time and do a little yelling and pounding on his table and stalking up and down in that boss's office, I've never encountered much difficulty in such negotiating.

When Everett has broken down resistance and when an understanding has been reached, my lawyer, John O'Melveny, picks up the details, sorts them out, and puts them into contractual form.

In addition to being my attorney, Jack O'Melveny is also general attorney for Paramount, but this apparently conflicting situation has never presented any insurmountable situations. Paramount's legal department, headed by Jack Carps, assisted by Sidney Justin and a number of other attorneys, takes care of the studio's run-of-the-mill business and represents the studio in its dealings with me. Jack O'Melveny represents Paramount in dealings with other companies and in business arrangements with releasing organizations or in other affairs peculiarly the concern of picture-production organizations. But when it comes to a matter between Paramount and me, Jack steps into the picture as my attorney and is no longer one of Paramount's legal employees.

I realize that the foregoing may sound confusing but actually everything goes along quite smoothly, or as smoothly as things ever go in show business. I must say that after twenty years, I feel pretty much at home at Paramount, and they've treated me well.

I think I've been smart to have it written into my contract from the start that I am not to be starred alone. I figure anybody in motion pictures needs plenty of help, cast-wise; and to be associated with good actors and big names with marquee strength. If I let them put "Bing Crosby" over whatever the name of the picture is, and the rest of the cast in small type on the billboards or on the main title of a picture or in the newspaper advertising, people would say, "Well, he certainly thinks he's a big shot." They'd expect greater things from a "big shot" than I'm able to deliver. If you share your billing with your fellow-players, it keeps them happy. To a lot of people, billing is mighty important. They like to say "I was co-starred with so-and-so in such-and-such a picture," instead of "I was featured in such-and-such a picture." "Featured" is the billing given to smaller fries. It doesn't have the impact of "co-starred."

Then, too, I feel if the picture's good, everybody in it should share the credit for it and if it's bad, we should all go down swinging together.

And lastly—and selfishly—I don't want to be the only star in the picture, because if it's a cruller, I want some accessories to the crime, some fellow-sufferers. I am averse to having one of my pictures referred to as "Crosby's last omelet." Let somebody else take some of the beaten egg.

When Everett and I went to New York early in 1931 to meet Paley, he worked out a deal for me to go on the radio on a sustaining basis when, as, and if I could get the ban against me lifted which had been slapped on me at the instigation of Abe Frank and which meant that no union musician could work with me. I had had a lawyer trying to straighten out the situation for me in California, but because of my stubbornness, he hadn't been successful. We got hold of that lawyer, had him go to Abe

Frank and make a settlement. Then I was free to go to work for Paley.

There have been many versions of the snafu which interfered with my first broadcast. One version had me not showing up for it because I was suffering from a hang-over. A second had me taking a powder because of stage fright. A third said I failed to put in an appearance because of laryngitis.

This is the way it was: while waiting for the negotiations to be completed between my lawyer and Abe Frank, I'd fallen into the habit of dropping in at four or five night clubs a night. Like a zany, I'd been singing in each of them for the kicks, instead of saving my voice for my radio debut, and my pipes had taken a terrible lacing. To put a complete K.O. on my throat, just before the show I rehearsed in an air-conditioned room. It was one of the first air-conditioned rooms I'd ever been in, and singing in cold air I tightened up so that when I was ready to go on I couldn't push any noise out. It wasn't that I was nervous or had any other kind of shakes, including alcoholic ones.

How could I have had stage fright when I'd been singing for hours each night at the Coconut Grove? I don't think I have ever had stage fright or what we in the trade call "flop sweat" in my life. The pipes just gave out because I hadn't had enough sleep and I'd been singing too much, and the unfamiliar air-conditioning put on the clincher. I might have been able to go on and sing badly, but I would have sounded terrible, so I said, "Let's not do it until I'm ready."

When I finally did appear, I was a new voice with a different style and I stirred up interest. But there would have been no interest if I'd sung my first CBS numbers with a throat ceiling zero. I did my first commercial for Cremo Cigars. For a while I was on a CBS sustaining program, but sustaining or singing for Cremo, no one ever had a hotter orchestra accompanying him than I had. Freddie Rich was the conductor, and he was backed by such musicians as Joe Venuti, Artie Shaw, Eddie Lang, and Manny Klein, to name a few.

In addition to my stint for Cremo, Everett booked me into the Paramount, the scene of my biggest soufflé when I made my first New York appearance with Whiteman. By this time I had managed to build a little radio popularity and was no longer a sleeping pill at the box office, and the Paramount management kept me for twenty-nine weeks. It was during that period that I discovered that there are such things as nodes. It seemed that I had a sprinkling of them on my vocal cords.

I was doing five or six shows a day, plus a couple of broadcasts in the evening, plus benefit performances and recording. And as I say, I was hitting the night clubs, singing in them for the fun of it and not getting too much rest. It is no over-statement to say that most of the time I was singing daily over a sixteen-hour stretch. What with all that wear and tear, I began to sound like Andy Devine with lobar pneumonia singing "Chloe." So I went to a New York specialist, a Dr. Simon L. Ruskin, a very fine throat man and a disciple of the great Philadelphia laryngologist, Dr. Chevalier Jackson, who developed the bronchoscope.

Dr. Ruskin peered into my throat and described what went on there to me. He said that my vocal cords were like two harp strings—mine are probably off of Harpo Marx's instrument—and when I talked or sang, the noise I emitted was produced by the vibration of those two strings. My trouble was that I had over-used them. As a result, my vocal cords had sprouted calluses which resembled warts. A chronic case of such calluses is called nodes.

Dr. Ruskin said I could visit Chevalier Jackson in Philadelphia and have my nodes removed, but that it would be a delicate operation. Maybe the technique has developed now to a point where it isn't so delicate, but the way things were then, Ruskin said he couldn't guarantee what kind of a voice I'd wind up with when they'd trimmed off my nodes. "It might make you a boy soprano or you might sing as low as Chaliapin," he said, "and of course you might not sing at all."

I thought of a few cracks such as "I've always wanted a job in a harem" and "not wanting to cut off my nodes to spite my voice," but those cracks died in the making. Somehow I didn't feel funny. Dr. Ruskin had still another suggestion. He thought that if I cut down my talking to a minimum, the rest would be good for my warts, and the irritation which had inflamed them would subside. For about two weeks I did as he suggested, and my voice started to come back. Only it came back a tone or two lower than it was before. I've never had a recurrence except after singing too long in an air-cooled room or after hollering at a football game.

The Paramount used me as a master of ceremonies. I sang a song or two, worked in with some of the specialty acts, or did straight for visiting comics. Being an emcee turned out to be rather a merry assignment. I found I could be quite the gabby fellow. Often, I came up with *le bon mot* or *le mot juste*, as the case required. Probably something I'd lifted, but it may have been due to the fact that in college and high school I'd been fascinated with words and their meanings. I'd discovered that there was a book called a Thesaurus, and I'd carried it around with me. I'd not only looked up word meanings, but their antonyms and synonyms.

I still get a kick out of words. I may use them badly, but I enjoy trying them for size. As a writer, I'm an amateur who, left to his own whims, leans toward alliteration and other fancy devices to make what I write sound unusual and give it zing. As a part of this semantics kick of mine, I've read everything I could get my hands on, some of it good, some bad, but now and then I revert to normal and toss in a slang or jive word. I can go only so far with the big words; then I have to return to the vernacular to finish what I have to say.

Since my 1932 engagement at the Paramount lasted twenty-nine weeks, they strove to devise something spectacular every week in the way of a production number. One week they had me perched on a giant crane. The machinery for the crane was in the pit, and when the mechanism reached for me on the stage, I climbed into the seat. The crane swung me out over the heads of the audience with a spot focused on me, dangling in space, and I sang my song which was probably something suitable like "Penthouse Serenade."

I did this crane number on New Year's Eve when the place was full of drunks and sailors. As the crane swooped low, the sailors reached up, held it and took off my shoes and socks. They were working on my pants when the crane operator switched on enough power to bring me back to the stage, where I finished my song in my bare feet, clutching my belt. It was a big smash, but the rest of the week I imposed a fifty-foot ceiling on the boys backstage.

Another humbling experience grew out of an argument I had with two friends, Les Reis and Artie Dunne. Reis and Dunne were a piano-voice duet who were appearing at a Baltimore theater. Happening to be in Baltimore, I visited them backstage and we got to kidding about all of the imitators of Columbo and Vallee and me who'd popped up. The popping up still happens. A Perry Como comes along and somebody imitates *him*. I ventured the opinion, "It's not difficult to imitate me, because most people who've ever sung in a kitchen quartet or in a shower bath sing like me."

As a part of their appearance, Les and Artie were running an amateur-talent contest, and they said, "Oh, no. If you went out on the stage and sang tonight under another name, you'd be a big hit. On the contrary, if some guy came on who wasn't Bing Crosby and sang the same song, he'd lay there."

"Why don't we try it right now?" I suggested.

"Are you game?" they asked.

"Certainly," I said.

So I went out and they introduced me as Charlie Senevsky, an unknown who'd entered the contest. I belted a song or two around, but aroused only apathy in the audience. Les and

Artie had two other entrants whose stunt was "imitating Bing Crosby." One of them won the contest. I ran out of the money.

My next tussle with the movies was even more abortive than my original caper with the medium when I was one of the Rhythm Boys. Paramount brought me West to sing a song in a picture called *Confessions of a Co-ed.* But when the picture was edited, I wasn't even on the screen. I was only an off-stage voice, nor can I remember now the name of the song I sang.

It's probably incorrect to say this was my next tussle with the movies. While in the Coconut Grove, one night I was pressed into service by Doug Fairbanks, Sr., to do a song in his picture, *Reaching for the Moon.* The name of this song also escapes me, but I was well paid, which is probably the reason the song eluded the cutter's shears, because someone told me they saw the picture on TV not long ago and I was still in—not good, but in.

But some of the studio's brains must have heard me on the radio, for when Paramount conceived the notion of a picture featuring radio performers who'd attained prominence, they signed Burns and Allen, the Mills Brothers, Kate Smith, a treacle-voiced performer known as The Street Singer—and me. Someone fluffed up a story, called *The Big Broadcast*, which would permit the use of our various talents. Paramount did four or five of those *Big Broadcast* films before they turned to something else. I was in two or three of them.

When I came back to New York from Hollywood, I took an engagement at the Capitol Theater. It was there that I met Bob Hope, who was on the same bill. At that juncture, Hope and I hadn't begun to bully each other. That was to come later.

A T THE END OF my hitch at the Capitol I went back to Hollywood again, this time to stay. My next movie, *College Humor*, was a throw-back in spirit to the late, gay 1920's. It was a mélange of coonskin coats, Stutz Bearcats, hip flasks, and cutie-pies in rolled hose. The picture was, as the title implies, roughly based—very roughly—on the John Held, Jr., version of college life which was even then becoming *passé*. The title was borrowed from a humorous publication of the time. Its hit song was "The Old Ox Road," a bit of symbolism. The Old Ox Road was a petting pit or a smooching station on any campus. There are several places at big universities known for their lolly-gogical traditions—places the students go when they want to pitch a little woo. The soft implication was that The Ox Road was like Flirtation Walk at West Point, for example.

That song still means something special to many a balding ex-Joe College and former Betty Co-ed of the Scott Fitzgerald era who's having girdle trouble now. To many such, it means their first inkling that life could be gay, mad, and bad; it means tumbled, shingled hair and wrinkled plus-fours. But to me the song means a couple of other things. One of them was a noisy, pink bundle, Gary Evan Crosby, who arrived in 1933. Gary is named for Gary Cooper. Coop is one of my best friends; he has been since 1930. Several years later when my youngest son came along, we named him for Lindsay Howard, an associate and another close friend of mine.

College Humor reminds me of the first home Dixie and I built. It was on Toluca Lake, where the San Fernando Valley begins on the other side of the mountains from Hollywood. As the children kept coming, that first home at Toluca grew too small for us, so we built a bigger one near the Lakeside Golf Course, on Camarillo Road.

My next movie was *Too Much Harmony*. It had Toby Wing in it and two rememberable songs, "The Day You Came Along" and "Thanks." Not "Thanks for the Memory"; just "Thanks." *Too Much Harmony* was up to its ears in comedians. There were Jack Oakie, Skeets Gallagher, Harry Green, Ned Sparks, and I don't know how many others. I ran in the middle. I'll never forget the first day of shooting. About all I managed to get in was a few nods, and Oakie dubbed me "Old Hinge Neck." There was very little opportunity to get a word in edgewise, competing with such experienced comedians and ad-libbers.

Oakie was my idea of terrific, and is my nomination for one of the all-time motion-picture greats. He must have studied the silent comedians like Ford Sterling, Chaplin, and Harold Lloyd, because his timing was marvelous. And he could mug with anybody I ever saw. When he was younger he was good looking, had a nice figure, a wonderful smile and an ingratiating manner. He looked the part of "the lad who gets the girl," or at least a serious rival for the girl, so lots of parts were available for him, plus important pay checks.

But he let himself get so pudgy that by comparison he made Oliver Hardy look sleek as a cat. He grew eight or nine chins, and the number of roles he couldn't be cast in because he wouldn't be believable increased.

Since he knew all the tricks, he was tough to work with in a scene. He was a master at upstaging and twisting you around so that his face was in the camera while you talked to the backdrop. After he'd had his way with me, all the audience could see of me on film was my ears, which would surely enough be hard to miss. Jack needed watching closely. But I didn't care. If he got the laughs, that was all right with me. Sooner or later there'd be a spot in the picture in which I'd sing a song and Jack would be in the trunk. So, if I had anything to deliver, I did it without worrying about whether Jack was upstaging me. If I'm doing a comedy scene with a great comedian I like to throw the scene to him and play it straight myself. That way we'll get a good scene, and if we get enough good scenes, we've got a good picture. All any actor whose head is not a blob of bubble gum should care about is to be associated with a good picture. If he ends up with most of the footage and the picture's a turkey, what's he accomplished?

Next along my way was one of Marion Davies' last flings at movie-making. The picture was called *Going Hollywood*, and it had a musical score by Arthur Freed and Nacio Herb Brown. This picture was a pet project of William Randolph Hearst. He wanted his protégée, Marion, to make a musical, and since I'd had some success as a singer and a leading man, he borrowed me from Paramount.

Brother Everett made the deal with Hearst. It was a clash of two great dealers, but while their haggling ended as a photo finish, it turned out to be much better than that for the *frères* Crosby. Our arrangement with Hearst was made on a weekly-payment basis, at two thousand dollars a week, which proved to be a stroke of genius on Everett's part. For it was the most leisurely motion picture I ever had anything to do with. It took six months to complete.

Marion's dressing room was a large bungalow on the lot, complete with kitchen, dining room, dressing room, and office for her secretary. The picture was directed by Raoul Walsh. We called him Rollicking Rockaway Raoul because his natal town was Rockaway Beach, New York. I'd been told that Raoul was a man who liked to live thoroughly, without stinting himself. If this was true, he must have undertaken this picture with relish, because it was one which gave him leeway to indulge his natural bent.

Our average day's shooting went like this: I'd show at nine o'clock, made up and ready to shoot. At about eleven Marion would appear, followed by her entourage of hairdressers, make-up ladies, secretary and—a holdover from the silent days— a five-piece orchestra. This band was not on hand to help her achieve a desired mood. It was there because she liked music, and wanted an orchestra around to keep things lively and to entertain her between shots. If a conference was coming up, they'd get a cue from Marion, take five and knock off. Otherwise they played all day.

When the orchestra showed up at eleven with Marion, it broke into her favorite songs by Cole Porter, Rodgers and Hart, and Gershwin. We enjoyed the musicale until eleven-thirty; then we'd discuss the first scene with Raoul, who, up to that time, might have been leading the orchestra, or practicing driving golf balls into a canvas net on the set, or playing blackjack or rummy with a prop man and an assistant director. By that time it was twelve-fifteen or twelve-thirty. Luncheon was announced for the heads of different departments and the leading players, and we repaired to Marion's bungalow for a midday collation.

Those luncheons were something. Bemelmans himself couldn't have demanded more, and to my Spokane palate they seemed Lucullan. Her servants either brought prepared items from her home or cooked something in the bungalow kitchenette. There were Rhine wines and *pâté de foie gras*, or chicken in aspic, or Bombay duck. Hearst might pop in for lunch or maybe he wouldn't; either way there was a plethora of conversation and an interchange of ideas about current events or social activities. But very little talk about the picture.

Lunch dawdled on until two-thirty. Then we went back to the set. Marion's make-up would have to be re-renewed—which would take time—and I'd need a slight retread. About three the orchestra would launch into a few more *divertissements*. At five we'd be ready to shoot the scene when Marion would suggest something refreshing. Nobody was ever loath, so, thus restored, we'd get the scene shot and start thinking about the next scene.

It was now six o'clock and, flushed with the success of our

first scene, ideas for a second were abundant. But Mr. Hearst could, on occasion, be pretty snug with a buck, and the prospect of the crew going on overtime, double time and "golden hours" —quadruple time—was not one he fancied. So all the creative minds were rousted out of the gate and sent homeward.

It's my guess that in an average day of such toil we wrapped up as much as a hundred and fifty feet of usable film. Maybe not that much. However, there were days when Mr. Hearst laid down the law to us. After such a chastening, we chugged along at a pretty good clip and accomplished a lot. There were a number of musical numbers in the thing, among them a wonderful song called "Temptation." A lot of singers have got effective mileage out of "Temptation" since it was first sung in *Going Hollywood.*

"Temptation" was my first attempt at presenting a song dramatically. In the picture I played an entertainer "with faults." Marion had given me the air for my misdeeds and I'd gone to Tijuana to get away from it all. There I'd gone on a tequila diet, knocked around in a succession of bordellos—in the picture they were called "Tijuana hot spots"—grown a beard and become a derelict. As a derelict I sang "Temptation" to a glass of tequila, while tears dripped into my beard from the circles under my eyes. Through trick photography, a dame's face appeared in the glass of tequila; then, at the end of the song, I flung the glass at the wall and staggered out into the night. It was all very Russian Art Theater.

Going Hollywood put me in the first ten of the Box Office Poll, along with such people as Will Rogers and Wallace Beery. It was the first time I'd come within smoke-signaling distance of that hallowed circle. For, in spite of all the monkey-shines in the making of *Going Hollywood,* it turned into a rather good picture. While Raoul Walsh had fun on a set and had kidded around, his record over the years shows that he can be counted upon to make pictures with entertainment value—lusty epics, pictures which draw people to the box office. *Going Hollywood* was no blot on his directorial escutcheon. Although it took months to make, the result was satisfactory.

Nor do I mean any of this as a blast at Marion Davies. I've told it merely as an example of the way the big movie queens of a by-gone era—stars like Barbara La Marr and Clara Bow and Pola Negri—sailed into action. In its day it spelled glamour. I got in on the twilight of this colorful era. It was quite an experience.

Of all the people I've met in show business, Marion Davies is the most generous, with the possible exception of Dorothy Lamour. Marion came from a Brooklyn family and her heart is as big as Santa Monica. She has a host of friends for whom she is constantly doing anything and everything. Her sense of humor is rich and expansive, she has great charm, and I never heard her put the knock on anybody. A nice gal from where I'm sittin'.

It was in the 1934 film, *She Loves Me Not,* that I made my brave stand against having my ears glued back to increase my beauty. This nuisance had its beginning in the time when I was courting Dixie and was having my trouble with Abe Frank. I played a lot of golf then with a Broadway actor, Dick Keene. Dick was working at Fox, and it was his notion that I'd be a good bet for picture work. He took me to see Jim Ryan, the casting director at Fox's Western Avenue studio. Ryan had me sing a couple of songs and read a few lines, and he seemed to like the way I did them. But after looking me over for a while, he said, "I'm afraid there's no future for you in pictures."

"Why not?" I asked.

"They could never photograph you," he said. "The ears are wingy."

I thought he said, "The years are winging," meaning that I was acquiring mileage. I wasn't very old and I flipped.

"I don't mean your age," he said. "Your ears protrude. They stick out too far. A camera pointed straight at you would make you look like a taxi with both doors open. They'd have to photograph you three-quarter-face or profile, and that would put too much of a limit on the cameraman. I'm sorry."

Dick and I went out feeling pretty crestfallen.

Seven or eight years later I became a parishioner of the Church of the Good Shepherd in Beverly Hills. Jim Ryan is a member of the congregation and we sit near each other. I always get up and go out before he does, and I never fail to bat my ears significantly at him as I go by. We both grin.

When I went to work in *The Big Broadcast*, Paramount shared Ryan's view of my ears as a photographic problem and they insisted on gluing them back against my head with spirit gum. I must admit that I was surprised at what the gluing did to my appearance. I looked streamlined, like a whippet dashing after a mechanical bunny. I put up with the spirit gum for a long time. Then they tried adhesive; then they went back to spirit gum. George Raft's ears were batty, too, but he'd had a muscle cut behind his ears which made them fall back against his noggin without having to be pushed by a make-up man. I wouldn't go for such an operation. I liked my ears the way they were—at least for everyday use. However, I was resigned to pinning them back for screen purposes, although both the glue and the adhesive were disagreeable. Then, too, no matter how firmly they were pinned back, they kept popping out all the time, much to the annoyance of Paramount's make-up department.

One of the scenes from *She Loves Me Not* had to be heavily lighted and the heat kept loosening the stickum until my ears popped out eight or ten times. The tenth time I said, "This time they're going to stay out."

"I've got orders not to shoot you that way," the cameraman told me.

"They're out and they're going to stay out," I said. "I'll be at the Lakeside Golf Club. If the studio changes its mind, tell them to call me there."

That first tee at Lakeside is my refuge when the studio is obdurate about what seems to me a reasonable request. If I'm convinced that they are being bull-headed or are pulling rank on me, I retire there to await developments. Finally a man at the studio called. "We'll shoot them sticking out if you feel so strongly about it," he said. So *She Loves Me Not* was shot partly with them out and partly with them in. In the first part I looked like a whippet in full flight. In the second part I looked like Dumbo. They've been out ever since.

But though I won a victory over stickum back of my ears, I capitulated to another nuisance—cake make-up. This nuisance was wished on me by Harry Ray, a make-up man. He was never around when we needed him, so we called him Mile-Away Ray or The Seldom-Seen Kid. He'd make me up in the morning, then disappear, and my face would grow shiny. We spent a lot of time figuring where he vanished to. There was one theory that he hid in a restaurant several blocks away called, with obvious inaccuracy, the Health Center. An alternate theory was that he flitted around the lot visiting other sets, playing Run, Sheep, Run and Prisoner's Base with the scouts and posses we sent to look for him.

When he was on deck, we engaged in a running debate because I refused to wear cake make-up. I'd used the professional kind in my vaudeville days, but my skin was dry, and it had made my face itch. After it had dried and I'd had it on a while it seemed to grow flaky and I'd go around all day screwing my face up like a man with a tic. I'd developed quite a hatred for it. In the end, the Seldom-Seen Kid played on my college loyalty. Gonzaga was coming to town to play Loyola, and Mile-Away Ray lured me into making a bet on the game. The bet was that if Loyola won I'd wear the make-up he wanted me to wear. Loyola won and I wore it.

Robert Hope, of the non-classic profile and the unlissome midsection, is sometimes goaded by a knowledge of his own lack of physical charms into referring to me as "skin head." I don't have to specify what he means. It's generally known that for screen purposes I wear a device the trade calls a "scalp doily," a "mucket" or "a divot." The technical name for it is a hair piece.

I hate to put it on, and I'm always trying to have interior scenes photographed out-of-doors, so I can wear a hat. Before he died, Buddy DeSylva, former head of production at Paramount, promised me that if I would do a favor for him—I forget just what it was now—he'd buy a story for me in which I could play a rabbi and wear a hat all the time.

Each morning when I get a script, I look through it to see if there's any way I can get through the day without donning a mucket. Not that it's such a chore to put on, but the glue in it makes my forehead itch and I can't scratch the itching places without pulling it off. I'm always plotting ways to do a love scene wearing a hat. In one scene I was to meet a girl at a railway station and greet her with a big embrace and a kiss. "You'll have to take your hat off for this one," the director said firmly.

If he thought I'd give up that easily, he'd misjudged me. "Not me," I said. "This fellow's so excited at seeing his girl he doesn't remember to take his hat off. He's deeply in love with her and hasn't seen her for a long time, so he has no time to think about the social amenities when she arrives. He just grabs her, and after that he's too busy to take his hat off."

In the *Road to Morocco,* I tried to wear a hat in bed, but Dave Butler, the director, was obdurate. I finally talked him into a night cap with a tassel.

Speaking of muckets, Wally Westmore of the fabulous Westmore family, identified with the make-up end of the picture business almost since its inception, has kept me in pictures years longer than I would ordinarily have lasted. It was he and his brothers, the "Marryin' Westmores," who developed the "bowser," as it's sometimes called, which has saved many an actor whose thinning thatch would otherwise have doomed him to an early theatrical demise. Who but Wally could have been taken on a trip to Paris for exterior location shots on my last picture, *Little Boy Lost,* on the unlikely possibility that I might be induced to doff my chapeau and need a hair piece? It was Wally's first trip to Paris and some mornings, following expansive evenings, he got it on backwards, sideways, or tipped rakishly.

Another prop for my manly beauty was forced upon me in a 1935 movie called *Mississippi*. It's fairer to say that I forced it upon myself, for I'd let my weight creep up to one hundred ninety pounds. I was eating a lot and getting lots of sleep, and it had been a long time between pictures, so I'd blown up to an unfashionable one-nine-o. *Mississippi* was a period picture— Civil War—and the pants I had to wear in it were so tight that my extra suet was conspicuous. As a result, I had to be strapped up, and I soon found out why women are so anxious to get out of their girdles.

We're Not Dressing was based on an English play, *The Admirable Crichton*, which had been made into a silent picture. The story of *We're Not Dressing* had to do with a shipwreck and a butler whose ability to meet the problems of living on a barren island after a yacht was wrecked was such that he wound up in charge of things. Before long, his employers were waiting on him. It had been decided to have another crack at the story, this time as a musical. Carole Lombard and I were its co-stars. Burns and Allen, a bear, and Ethel Merman—who is quite a bear herself—were the featured players.

Carole could lay tongue to more colorful epithets than any other woman I've ever known, and more than most men. Oddly enough, you never were shocked when she swore. You felt the way you feel when you're with a bunch of men who're fishing or working and one of them bangs his thumb with a hammer or gets a fish hook in his pants. Under such circumstances, if they swear nobody pays much attention because they're entitled to let off steam. That was the reaction I had to Carole's profanity. It was good, clean, and lusty. Her swear-words weren't obscene. They were gusty and eloquent. They resounded, they bounced. They had honest zing!

She had a delicious sense of humor; she was one of the screen's greatest comediennes and, in addition, she was very beautiful. The electricians, carpenters, and prop men all adored her because she was so regular; so devoid of temperament and show-boating. The feeling of non-gender camaraderie Carole gave the men who worked with her was a victory of mental attitude over matter, the matter in her case being curvy, blond, and melting. The fact that she could make us think of her as being a good guy rather than as a sexy mamma is one of those unbelievable manifestations impossible to explain. All I can say is, that was the way it was.

This led to an experience on her part I'm sure no other woman has ever had, for when one of the lads in our entourage decided to play a strictly male locker-room practical joke on her, it seemed the most natural thing in the world.

The shipwreck in *We're Not Dressing* was shot at Catalina near the St. Catherine Hotel, where we stayed for two or three weeks. It was in November, the water was very cold, and we had to jump from a barge out of camera range into water up to our necks and wade beachward toward a camera on another barge while five or six thousand tourists and people from Catalina were standing back of a rope and watching the scene.

Carole dressed in a tent on the beach. The Katzenjammer-joker type told her that if she was afraid of cold water she ought to get a bottle of oil of wintergreen and rub it over her entire body. Just before the camera began to roll, Carole went to her tent and dutifully doused her body with wintergreen. As many a footballer and track man has learned to his bitter sorrow, wintergreen applied indiscriminately to the skin creates an intolerable burning sensation. The victim instinctively dashes for the nearest shower and turns on the cold water, only to discover that cold water increases the burning sensation, while the playful pals who have suggested the oil treatment roll in helpless mirth on the floor.

The doors of Carole's tent burst open, she appeared practically unclothed, flew to the beach on the dead run, squatted down and began to splash water over herself. Anybody else would have been embarrassed by the eyes peering at her from behind the ropes. Not Carole. She had something else on her mind. Besides, people never did bother her, whether she was in dishabille or not. She didn't understand people who leered. Her mind didn't work that way. She was the least prudish person I've ever known.

For a while she made shrill noises like a narrow-gauge locomotive laboring uphill. Then recognizable words emerged from her. The eloquence of her invective surpassed anything she'd ever achieved before, and the rest of us stood in awe-struck admiration. We also began to look around for places in which to hide. But our supposition that she had a man's point of view was right. Once the wintergreen began to wear off, she began to laugh. I can think of no other woman star who would have gone ahead with the scene after such an ordeal. Carole went back to her tent, dressed, emerged once more, and said, "Now, where were we?" When I think of her I find myself saying, "What a woman!" They haven't made many like her.

A lot of old maids and widows living on small pensions or small fixed incomes were staying on Catalina at the St. Catherine Hotel. It was a family-type hostelry, and our movie company was an exciting experience to the guests. I imagine they wrote to their friends and relatives, "We have a number of Bohemians stopping with us." Our movie company ate at two or three huge tables in the dining room. The smaller tables were occupied by the regulars, who strained their ears to drink in the racy things they were sure we were saying. Carole was annoyed with this constant surveillance and eavesdropping. We were eating breakfast one morning when she came slinking in with that feline walk of hers. All eyes swiveled around to watch her, and she decided that this was the time to make up something shocking. She was the girl who could do it. She had an inventive turn of mind.

She called across the dining room, "Bing!"

"What?" I asked.

"Did I leave my nightie in your room last night?"

The spinsters almost dropped their teeth. I've never heard such tch, tch, tching and gasps in my life. After that they gave us a wide berth. Some of them even stopped eating in the dining room.

We're Not Dressing gave me a chance to try acting as well as singing. The script writers had carpentered a good screen play from tried-and-true material. The story had solidity and continuity. It offered more chance for characterization than the usual musical.

In one sequence, Carole and I were supposed to have an argument. During that argument she was to say something that justified my slapping her face. The script writer had written a diatribe for her so violent that the character I played was justified in taking such drastic action. She asked me not to slap her during rehearsals and, of course, I said I wouldn't. We rehearsed the prop and camera movements until we had them all set.

Then she said, "I'm ready. Go ahead and slap."

When we reached the climax, I let her have one. A light came into her eyes the like of which I've never seen in a woman's eyes before or since. She tore into me, threw me down, jumped on me, kicked me, bit and scratched me, all the time screaming imprecations at my prone figure. The director was so flabbergasted that he forgot to say "cut." Finally the crew members, realizing that what was going on wasn't scheduled, pulled her off.

She wept hysterically, then calmed enough to tell me she had prayed that she wouldn't react that way, but that ever since she was a little girl, if anybody touched her face, even if it was just a pat, something inside of her snapped and she went berserk. It probably stemmed back to some episode in her childhood, the kind of thing psychiatrists nod knowingly about. "Thanks for telling me," I said, dabbing my wounds with a handkerchief.

When they ran off the rushes the next day they had to hang

out an S.R.O. sign. Watching it, I realized for the first time that she had torn off my toupee too. I couldn't tell whether she kicked it off or bit it off, for we were a blur of flailing arms and legs, but it went flying. The scene looked like a remake of the famous fight in *The Spoilers* between Tom Santschi and Bill Farnum. For days Carole was apologetic about the whole thing. It was easy to forgive her. But I saw to it that there were no retakes of that scene. My forgiveness didn't go that far.

Carole dearly loved a rib and she cooked up a good one at the end of the picture. The bear, mentioned earlier, worked all through the picture, and the animal chosen for this juicy part had been selected on his trainer's extravagant representation that this "Bruno" could do everything but answer the phone. After he had been established in the picture and it was too late to replace him, the director, Norman Taurog, discovered that Bro' Bear was not only very dumb, but quite stubborn, and vicious enough to lop off a hand if pushed too far. It was only after trying everything that appeals to bears—employing every trick and device known to trainers and zoologists, and after endless delays filled with blood, sweat and tears—that someone discovered he liked flapjacks and blueberry jam. And with the griddle ever hot and flapjacks flying, Taurog extracted a passable performance from ole Bruin.

Of course, when the picture was finally finished, Norman arrived home to find that Carole had bought the bear and had him delivered, on a very long chain, to Taurog's house as a gift.

I T WAS NOT LONG after *We're Not Dressing* that Dixie and I became the parents of twins. We didn't conform to the custom followed by some in the Hollywoods of letting the gossip columnists know about the hoped-for advent eight months in advance. We were old-fashioned enough to announce the arrival of our sons only upon delivery.

But when our twins were in the offing complications set in which we couldn't control. About the sixth month, Dixie had a siege of false labor and the doctor was alarmed for fear she would lose the baby. He thought she ought to have some X-rays, and the X-rays disclosed that there were going to be twins. Somehow or other this news leaked out, as things will leak out in a hospital where there are nurses, telephone operators, and X-ray technicians.

The news-leak didn't annoy me as much as it otherwise might have done for I had something more important to worry about. The X-ray showed that one of the twins had his body arranged in such a position that it was interfering with the functioning of one of Dixie's kidneys. She claimed later that it was Dennis. And when he grew older and she kidded him about being cantankerous, she added, "You started out that way."

Her doctor put her to bed, kept her quiet, and sent her to the hospital at the end of seven and a half months, so he could keep an eye on her well in advance of delivery, because he wanted the babies to grow as much as possible before birth.

I checked in at the hospital every day, but as luck would have it the day I left the hospital and went to Santa Monica to play in a golf tournament, the twins were born. It was no surprise to Dixie that I was on the golf course then. That's where I spend most of my time anyhow. But it gave her a beautiful opening if anybody asked her if I played much golf.

"He wasn't even there when the twins were born. He was out playing golf," she'd say, giving it the full Eleonora Duse–Sarah Bernhardt treatment.

Sometimes, after she was through needling me, I noticed people who didn't know either of us very well looking at me as if I were the jerk of the world.

I've tried to keep my personal life pretty much to myself. I do my best to live my life outside of the fan magazines, night clubs and other public places. But it's tough to do in Hollywood. I make no complaint but sometimes it's onerous.

The studio publicity departments face the task of publicizing a star, and his pictures, and anything that concerns that particular star is grist for their mill. Even trivialities about them are news, if he or she is big enough in the public estimation. The studio publicity department must accommodate the people who publish, edit, and write fan magazines, and who need material on the stars. Sometimes it's difficult to turn a studio down when it wants such material, although I've always tried to avoid publicizing my home life. I don't mind having a camera turned on me at golf tournaments or at public appearances or when I'm at work, but I think that a man's private life should remain private. Ronald Colman made it, but I guess I'm just one of the boys. I don't have his remote dignity, and none of his ability.

About this time I imported the rest of my family to California. Everett was already there, but it seemed a good idea to close the Crosby ranks and have Larry and my father and my mother by my side too. There was no possibility of advancement for Dad at the brewery in Spokane where he'd begun as a book-keeper. He was getting along in years, and since my youngest brother Bob had struck out for himself, and my sisters were married, nobody was home with Dad and Mother. It occurred to me that it would be nice to have my parents taking it easier in a more clement climate. I took a house for them and put Dad in charge of handling my banking and taking care of the securities I'd squirreled away. He came in about ten each morning, had lunch, and worked until two. Then he went to a ball game or to the races.

He took some trips to New York and went to the Kentucky Derby every year. He was able to do all the things he'd wanted to do all his life, but had never been able to do because he'd been too busy feeding seven mouths. The last ten or fifteen years of his life were happy ones for him. Being able to make them that way gave me more satisfaction than anything I've ever done.

Dad was a convivial soul who loved to get around and about, and when he finished his stint at the office—generally around mid-afternoon—he had a regular tour that he made every day. Armed with the most recent news clippings about me or my kid brother, Bob, he'd drop in at Paramount, the Finnish Baths, Oblath's Restaurant or some of his other favorite places, or the haunts of some of the friends he'd made in Hollywood. He drove himself on these tours and Mother never knew who he was likely to bring home for dinner or for a Bourbon poultice. Often as not it was some hitch-hiker whose personality had appealed to him. Our family nickname for Dad was "Hollywood Harry" because of his ability to cover the local scene.

Gary Cooper's dad was one of his friends, and sometimes they covered the beat together. I don't think Gary's dad ever carried his son's clippings with him; in fact I don't think Gary kept any clippings.

Like Mother, Dad went to the races a great deal, but as far as I know he never went up against the mutuels. It was purely a social contact with him; an opportunity to get around, see some of the boys, mix a little.

During his last illness he'd been semi-conscious for some days when one afternoon he rallied and sat on the edge of the bed.

"Where are you going?" the nurse asked. "I'm going home," was his reply, and he did—his last one.

He was a cheery man. He liked everybody and I think everybody liked him, which is a better epitaph than most men have.

It was when my dad came to California to be with me that a building was put up to house the Crosby Enterprises. The business ventures I'd gotten myself into (or into which Everett had launched me) were using office space at the Paramount Studio, but we'd gotten so involved in so many activities we needed more room. There was a building for sale on the Strip, so we grabbed it, put offices on one floor and rented the rest of the building. It isn't an imposing edifice. It's just a four-story California stucco job, but it houses everything we have in the way of enterprises, as well as acting as a repository for our records and files.

Living in California has done a thing to my mother I get a jar out of. She has very high moral principles and is almost puritanical about "the way people ought to live," particularly members of her family. She had some brothers who were a little on the toss-pot side, and for that reason she hates strong drink, although she doesn't mind beer in the house. She is also a cigarette hater. She still doesn't allow my sisters to smoke in her presence, although they're grown women with children of their own. In fact, one of them is a new grandmother. My mother claims that if they want to attract men or hold the ones they already have, they can attract them better by refraining from puffing and inhaling and exhaling.

But since she came to California, she's become a devotee of the race tracks. During the local race meetings she goes every day and plunges a two-buck show bet on the favorites. She and her lady friends take off in the morning, eager and sharp as tacks. They buy all the newspapers, study the selections of each expert in each paper, and buy all the tip sheets available and the *Racing Form* and the *Daily Telegraph*.

After they've done their homework they agree upon a "consensus opinion." This means that they select one horse in each race with the overwhelming majority of selections in his favor. Then they back their choice with a deuce in the third hole. It's not a very desperate procedure, but they squawk as if they'd been defrauded when their favorite runs out of the money. Sunny Jim Fitzsimmons used to say, "There's a hundred and one ways a horse can lose a race." My mother knows them all and she never fails to comment upon them. She knows all of the stock beefs. The jockey pulled the horse. The horse wasn't trying. Its owner wasn't trying.

Her little weakness is most amusing to her sons. Betting on the races is no indication of a lack of moral principles. But it is gambling, and gambling in her book had always been a shady activity. If anyone had told me twenty years ago that she would end up betting on the races, I'd have told him he was off his rocker. Now I think it's wonderful that at her time in life she's able to find and enjoy such an interest.

During my last year of high school and my first two years of college, a boy named Leo Lynn was one of my classmates at Gonzaga. One day in 1931, when I was new at Paramount, I was going into the studio and I saw Leo behind the wheel of a foreign-made limousine. He was wearing a chauffeur's cap but I recognized him right away. I couldn't forget him. He'd been a real shenanigan character in college, putting on impromptu entertainments and mimicking various actors and athletes.

When I'd said hello, I asked, "What are you doing?"

"I'm driving for the English actor, Clive Brook," he said.

"How'd you like to work for me?" I asked him.

"You've hired a man!" he said.

Brook wasn't annoyed at my theft of his chauffeur. Leo found a substitute to take his place, and Clive is so aloof, in the traditional English manner, that I don't think he knew Leo was gone. In addition to chauffeuring for Dixie and acting as a factotum in the Crosby household, Leo was my stand-in. Contrary to the public's understanding of such things, a stand-in doesn't have to resemble the one for whom he stands in. Leo has my skin pigmentation and he's about my height. That's all the cameraman requires.

Leo is grateful to me, too, and perhaps the best way to describe how he feels about me is to report a thing that happened when I was at Pebble Beach playing in the annual invitation tournament. Trying to do any good for yourself in that event is about as tough as doing it in the National Amateur. The Pebble Beach draws almost the same field that the National attracts and it's played over one of the world's toughest courses. I'm lucky if I qualify, let alone beat any of that field.

While I was at Pebble Beach, Leo ran into Johnny Burke in Hollywood.

"Where's Bing?" Johnny asked.

"He's up at Pebble Beach for the tournament," Leo told him.

"How do you think he'll do?" Johnny inquired.

Leo looked at him scornfully and said, "If he's feeling good he'll win it." Leo's loyalty is unreasonable and illogical, and I have been careful never to disillusion him. A man needs all the people like that he can get.

Of late, Leo has so many things to do for me that he has no time to stand in for me any more. But he still has time to take care of his "request list." If you're a star just about to start a picture, you make out a list of people you'd like to have given jobs as extras in the film. If they're registered with the Guild, the assistant director tries to land them a few days' work as the picture goes along. I have such a list myself but Leo also has one—I suppose he calls it the "Lynn-Crosby request list," which is ten times longer than mine. He's very persistent about it and he needles the assistant director until, before one of my pictures is finished, almost all of his protégés are given work as extras.

An extra is paid sixteen-fifty a day, but, if he has a line to say or something special to do, his pay jumps to twenty-five dollars a day. So Leo's pals are after him to ask the assistant director to give them a line, even if only a one-word line.

One of the names on Leo's "request list" is that of an ex-pug. Leo engineered the pug into a De Mille Biblical picture being made at Paramount, along with five or six of his other ex-fighter pals. The sextette played characters in and around Jerusalem. While De Mille was getting ready to shoot a scene the pug asked Leo if he couldn't fix it for him to have a line.

"I'd like to get more money," the pug told Leo.

"You're getting sixteen-fifty now," Leo said.

"I'd like more," the pug told him.

"Look," Leo said. "Christ is only getting twenty-five bucks a day and you're just one of the bums in Jerusalem."

It was true. An extra was being photographed as an off-screen shadow to give a suggestion of Christ passing by. His pay check for the impersonation was twenty-five dollars.

When my folks came to California, Leo drove my mother and father wherever they wanted to go. He drove for Dixie a lot too and ran errands for her when I was out of town.

It's not far off the truth to say that he's become part of the family. He's seen all my kids grow up and spoils them outrageously. He brags about them and tells everybody how good they are. They call him Laughing Leo, because he's got a big, hearty laugh, a real belly job.

All my movies are great to him, whether they're good or not, and he carries my latest clippings around with him to show people, carrying on where Dad had left off. So, in addition to being my valet, chauffeur, stand-in, and conductor of grand tours of the studio for friends who come from out of town, he's my self-appointed publicity man. He knows everybody in Hollywood and everyone at the studio knows him and likes him.

I know this book is supposed to be about myself, but it's difficult for me to write it that way. Not because I'm modest, but because my memory is porous as to the interesting things which have happened to me, except in connection with people I've known, friends of mine. One such is Dr. Arnold Stevens. He has been our friend and family doctor for twenty-five years. Although Steve trained at Washington University, the Mayo Brothers Clinic, and Loma Linda, has a Master of Surgery degree from the University of Minnesota, is a member of the American Board of Surgery, and lectures almost constantly on the Pacific Coast before various medical groups, he insists upon calling himself a country doctor.

He fancies that he's free to make so free and easy with this fact because early in his career he practiced medicine for a few months in the little town of Clifton, Arizona.

He is considered one of the best surgeons on the Pacific Coast. I've watched him operate myself several times, and he's the coolest, most collected artist with the scalpel I've ever seen. Not that I've seen many, but his whole demeanor impresses the watcher with the fact that he has great confidence and ability. However, when he leaves surgery he's in a vacuum. Tales of his haziness and his inexplicable idiosyncrasies rival those of the legendary absent-minded professor. Perhaps the real reason why his mind wanders so (except when he's concentrating on medicine or surgery) is because of his concern for his patient. To Steve each patient becomes a private, personal thing. In other matters, in everyday, commonplace details of life his actions are, to say the least, very vague indeed. Steve remembers only one phone number, the telephone exchange and number of his office. If he's in his office and wants to dial his wife at home he dials his own office and, naturally, receives a busy signal. If somebody's in the office with him he looks up and says complainingly, "The line's busy. How can Jean talk that long? I've been calling her all afternoon." Whoever's in the office with him will say, "Hey, why don't you try dialing your home number?"

Steve smiles sheepishly, looks down at the phone and says,

"Well! What do you know? I've been calling this one, haven't I?"

The good doctor carries with him a little book of phone numbers when he's out of the office. When he wishes to call somebody, he pulls out the book, looks up the person's name and number, puts the book back in his pocket, goes to the phone and dials the same old number, the one for his office. If it's during office hours his nurse answers, and if it's after office hours the exchange operator answers. This startles Steve, and he asks, "Who's this?" The operator or his office assistant says, "Doctor, what number do you want? I'll dial it for you through the switchboard."

Johnny Burke reminded me to insert a classic Doc Stevens item in this. It concerned the time several years ago when Burke ran into the doctor in front of his office. With Steve was his young son, Arnold, who was standing beside his bicycle. When Steve meets a friend or patient he always has something private or confidential to talk over with him, some great secret to impart. This particular time was no exception, so he said to Arnold, "Would you leave us for a few minutes? I'd like to talk to Johnny."

"Sure, Dad," the kid answered. He hopped on his bike and started away.

"Wait a minute," continued the doctor. "Remember what I said about the bike." Arnold took off and Steve began his conversation with Johnny. John interrupted him to ask, "What's about the bike, Steve?"

"Well," answered Steve, "Arnold's been acting up lately. He hasn't been doing his lessons. So I took the bike away from him for two weeks."

"What was that he just rode away on?" smiled Johnny.

"Well, I'll be darned," said Steve, looking after the boy merrily wheeling up the street.

There are a hundred such stories about Steve but I like one which happened just recently. Peggy Lee was giving a small dinner party at her home for Danny Thomas, who had just co-starred with Peggy in the motion picture, *The Jazz Singer*. Steve is so notorious for his bad memory for names that on the way to the party his wife Jean briefed him on the name and pursuits of the guest of honor. Just before they entered the house, Steve once more asked her the name of the fellow for whom the party was being given.

"Danny Thomas," said Jean slowly, hoping it would sink in. Steve said, "Danny Thomas."

She said even more slowly, "Danny Thomas." Then they went up the steps and rang the front doorbell.

Inside Peggy Lee's maison, Steve recognized a face he'd seen on TV and in pictures and, walking right up to Danny Thomas, he slapped him on the back, shook his hand and said, "I'm sure glad to meet you, Mr. Kaye!"

When we gave Steve a ribbing about this, he tried to cover up by saying, "I'll bet he thinks I was kidding him!"

Being in the business myself, I will vouch for the fact that this is definitely not the way to "kid" an actor.

One of the activities my family was able to help me with when they rallied around was handling the financial affairs connected with my recordings. When I started to make records with the Brunswick Record Corporation, Jack Kapp was the recording manager. To my sorrow, Jack is no longer among the living, but when a disk outfit called Decca was born, Jack went over to Decca from Brunswick and wound up as its president. It was Jack who formulated my recording plans. He even selected the numbers I sang. He was wise enough to have me work with a variety of bands and sing duets with different artists, so as to give the listeners a change of pace. This policy helped keep me alive as a recording artist long after the average performer is washed up.

Jack's progressive plans for me were due to the fact that he had a much higher opinion of me than I had of myself. He was always striving to make me the top figure in recording. He selected things for me a cut above ordinary popular songs, although of course I sang those, too. In fact, Jack saw to it that I achieved a musical variety very few other recording artists—with my limitations—were able to. I sang hillbillies and blues, ballads and Victor Herbert, traditional songs and patriotic songs, light opera, and even an opera aria or two.

Jack wouldn't let me get typed. He kept me spread out. In addition to his desire to make money for Decca, he took a personal interest in me. This resulted in my getting the cream of the recording dates and opportunities.

I also worked with a lot of different arrangers. An arranger is the guiding spirit in making a successful record. He is the one who makes the vocal sound good, or he can kill a good vocal or a good song if he's not skillful or not interested in the singer. Jack always had a lot of those fellows available. Whenever a good arranger or a good band was free and without previous contractual obligations, he grabbed them for a few dates with me.

If there was a chance to get the Boswell Sisters, or the Andrews Sisters, or the Mills Brothers or the Dorsey Brothers or Woody Herman or Duke Ellington or Louis Armstrong or Louis Jordan, Jack would give me an opportunity to work with them. That kind of backing contributes a lot toward the success of a record. This is particularly true of Louis Armstrong. On any record we made together, I was really supporting Louis instead of vice versa.

Louis Armstrong is a great friend of mine. He has been one for twenty-five years. I first met Louis in Chicago when he was playing a ballroom there. He'd just left King Oliver's band and had his own band. I met him again in California twenty-two or twenty-three years ago when he was playing Frank Sebastian's Cotton Club in Culver City. Harry Barris and Rinker and I used to go over there and hear him all the time. Louis never had a very good band. I don't know why. He always was great himself but he never seemed to have very many good men playing with him. I think the reason his records are so successful now is because he has good side men and good support from the orchestras he works with when he records. And good arrangements, too.

So far as his style is concerned, he doesn't seem to age a bit. Nobody has been able to imitate it successfully. A few men try to play a cornet the way Louis plays this instrument and a few try to sing the way he sings, but nothing happens. When Louis plays he soars. When he sings he bubbles.

Louis is quite the corresponder. Wherever he goes he sends me post cards. He sent me a card from Sweden which read: "Dear Pop: Everything over here is Skol. But I'm the skolinest cat in Scandinavia."

During the past six or eight years I've used Louis two or three times a year for broadcasts whenever I can catch him in town or, if I happen to be East when he's there, I grab him with Jack Teagarden for a couple of transcriptions. Louis is wonderful to work with. When you're out there in front of a microphone with him, you can throw the script away. You don't have to worry about a thing. He is so amusing and so colorful when he works that everything he does goes over heavily. Even before he comes on he's got his audience in the palm of his hand. They're ready to enjoy his music. He's a great fellow to stand alongside of. When you bounce off somebody like that you don't break.

Jack Kapp had a lot of trouble talking me into recording "Adeste Fideles." Being only a crooner, I felt that I didn't have sufficient stature as a singer to sing a song with religious implications. But Jack insisted that "Adeste Fideles" through the years had virtually become a Christmas carol. So I recorded it. I'm glad I did.

"Silent Night" was different. I didn't feel that it fitted into the carol category. Moreover, I thought it would be wrong for me to take income from the sale of such a record. The way I saw it, it would be like cashing in on the Church or the Bible. But brother Larry came up with a suggestion. He set up a fund for the children then being taken care of by American missions in China. The plan was to take the royalties from "Silent Night" and pour them into this fund. In that way I'd avoid cashing in on a religious song. We helped clothe and support those kids until the Government, looking for fresh tax money, ruled that our scheme was illegal. By that time we'd probably put a quarter of a million dollars into that worthwhile cause.

When the Second World War came along, Larry assembled an entertainment unit composed of a chorus line, a band, four or five acts in all. It played the camps and it was financed with money from the "Silent Night" fund. I went along with the show sometimes myself.

I had something to do with another song, Irving Berlin's "White Christmas," which has become a modern Christmas carol by popular acclaim. Every Christmas it booms out of department store loud-speakers over the heads of shoppers and street-corner Santa Clauses. In the trade, "White Christmas" is known as a standard. Anything heard seasonally is a standard, and "White Christmas" certainly deserves that classification. It's a great song with a simple melody, and nowadays anywhere I go I have to sing it. It's as much a part of me as "When the Blue of the Night," or my floppy ears.

It was no sacrifice on my part to be loyal to Jack when other recording outfits tried to lure me away. The idea of working for anyone else was preposterous to me, and I never gave those offers serious consideration. With Jack I felt that I was in the hands of a friend and that whatever he told me to do was right. Not that we didn't come some recording croppers together, but we had some good ones, too, and the good ones were usually songs Jack picked out.

Those who are now in charge of production at the various recording companies tell me that to awaken popular interest in a record they've got to produce a new "sound"; an unusual combination of instruments or voices which record buyers haven't heard before. If you can do this, they say, you've got a chance to turn out a hit record. It doesn't matter what the material is like or how good the song is or what it's all about, how it's done, or how it's performed. It's just whether it features an unusual sound which hasn't been heard before.

To tell the truth, I don't think I'm capable of producing any new sounds. I've used up all the sounds in my system many years ago.

Right now it seems time to talk about the interesting activities of the song pluggers. Or, as they prefer to be called, "Publishers' Professional Representatives," if you please.

Out of the welter of song material a firm receives each year— and it may run into the thousands—probably five or six songs are selected annually as potential hits, things the publishers have confidence in. These are the ones they work on. They'll take one such song and put on what they call a "drive" for a month or so. The intrepid song plugger, armed with acetate recordings and sheet music of the ditty for demonstration purposes, and loaded with extravagant claims as to its merit, will tour the areas to which he is assigned. He'll visit night clubs, radio and TV stations, theaters, restaurants, any place where music is played, for the period of the drive. He makes a determined effort to get every singer, instrumentalist, group, or band leader to use this song in the period during which the drive is on. Such a program, as can be readily seen, is calculated to develop national enthusiasm for the song and jump it into the hit status.

It is my guess that one of the most colorful and experienced members of the song-plugging craft is an old friend, Tubby Garron, who, in his own words, says, "I may not be the biggest liar in show business, but I'm not worse than second."

Personally I must say if he isn't first, I'd be at a loss to say who is. Tubby's been around ever since I've been barking ballads, and I guess a good many years prior to that as well, because he claims he's the fellow who gave Al Jolson the song, "Waitin' for the Robert E. Lee" back in the early 1900's when Al was a Johnny Come Lately. He claims this is the song that put Al over and he stands ready to do the same feat for anybody who'll use his current plug tune.

In point of fact, it would be difficult to name any singer in the last fifty years who Tubby doesn't claim to have made.

He'll demonstrate a song on a street corner, cocktail saloon, hotel lobby, any place he can get anyone to listen. And he disdains use of a microphone. He says he was a singer before such gadgets were invented and he will be singing long after they go out of date. He has a voice like Fog-Horn Murphy and he also decries the current inability of many of the present-day singers to use their hands effectively. Baseball coaches say, "No hands, no infielders." Tubby says, "No hands, no singer."

When he's on the road I always send him a telegram to Seattle, Portland, or wherever he happens to be. In that wire I discuss in extravagant terms some non-existent oil enterprise in which we are supposed to be engaged together, or an apocryphal picture venture of ours or other fictitious high-finance enterprises. He flashes these wires around radio stations and hotel lobbies where the disk jockeys can see them and immediately establishes himself as a man of some consequence. He adds that, of course, song plugging is just a hobby with him.

He carries a little vial of crude oil with him which he's bought at a service station and exhibits it as a specimen of his latest big strike in Texas, Oklahoma, New Mexico or elsewhere. One night on the San Francisco *Lark* going north, I introduced him to the president of a large oil company. Tubby immediately engaged him in conversation about oil, the oil business, oil prices, likely location of new fields, representing himself as a big operator. About ten o'clock I went to bed and the following morning the steward in the lounge car told me that Tubby had had the oil company president on the hook until two or three o'clock, buying drinks and discussing Tubby's non-existent oil holdings. He carries with him what is known in the trade as a Carolina bankroll. That is, a cucumber with a couple of dollar bills wrapped around it and tied with a rubber band. He flashes this any time there's a question as to his solvency.

His motto is, "Be brave, love each other, and be nice to old people." And I must say he lives up thoroughly to every tenet contained therein.

One time we gave him a surprise dinner party at one of the local restaurants. There were three or four hundred guests on deck. On the dais were such personages as Henry Ginsberg, then president of Paramount, Buddy DeSylva, then in charge of production, and most of the leading singers and bandsmen. In the audience were all of the members of the industry who could fight their way into the function. Tubby, of course, arrived with no knowledge of what was in store and when he came into the vast dining room and saw the signs plastered over the wall, greeting him and paying him tribute, he sensed the significance of what was about to happen. For a minute—but only for a minute—he was all humility. Then he rallied, strode to the front of the stage and, shaking his finger at his fellow song pluggers, he shouted, "You're all for me tonight but in the morning you'll all be jealous as hell again."

In a profession famous for tenacity, he is the most tenacious of all. Once when he was unable to stir up sufficient interest in one of his songs, a song in which he had his usual confidence, he went to a busy intersection in down-town Los Angeles, climbed to the top of a lamp post and burst into three or four choruses of "Rose-colored Glasses" while perched there. Naturally, news-papermen took pictures, there were several front-page stories about it and the song was given quite a boost. In fact, it became a sizable hit.

If there's ever a lull in any theater while he's in there, if a picture breaks down or if an intermission is called for the sale of popcorn, Tubby is eight to five to jump to his feet and launch into his latest plug. Or at least he'll go as far as he can before the ushers escort him to the sidewalk.

Although I don't think he ever has more than eight dollars in his kick, he will aver at the drop of a question that he's one of the richest men in town. "I have a Cadillac, a swimming pool, and I go to the bank every morning and change my money for brand new bills," he proclaims.

Honestly, I hate to think what life around the studios would be without him. He comes in every morning, always with the same hilarious routine. He's a shot in the arm, a tonic, and a great little fellow to have around.

One of the things that always seem to interest writers assigned to me is this question: "You seem to have as many men fans as women fans and your voice and your manner seem to please both sexes. To what do you attribute it?"

I'll give the answer I've always given. It applies particularly to my singing. I think—and I'm confident that my assumption is correct—that every man who sees one of my movies, or who listens to my records, or who hears me on the radio, believes firmly that he sings as well as I do, especially when he's in the bathroom shower. It's no trick for him to believe this because I have none of the mannerisms of a trained singer and I have very little voice. If I've achieved any success as a warbler it's because I've managed to keep the kind of naturalness in my style, my phrasing, and my mannerisms which any Joe Doakes possesses.

They feel no kinship for a singer with a wonderful register and an elaborate range. They realize that he's achieved something they can never hope to achieve. But it's my hunch that most men feel that if they had gotten the opportunities I've had, they could have done just as well. I don't doubt that there's a lot of truth in that. I'm certainly not a handsome figure, being on the short, dumpy side, and with hair that is thinning or has thinned. I have no glamour, no continental suavity, no bedroom eyes. So they figure I'm just one of the guys they run into every day at the pool room, or at the ball game, or at the office, or out hunting, or on the golf course.

Once or twice I've been described as a light comedian. I consider this the most accurate description of my abilities I've ever seen. That's just about all I am, a light comedian. I'm not a very funny fellow and I'm not a very serious fellow either. Neither do I give off a terribly romantic aura.

I don't always get the girl in a picture. Sometimes the ball bounces the other way. I'm quite often the fellow who rides off into the sunset leaving the other fellow with the girl. Most of the big figures in motion pictures, the Tyrone Powers, the Gables, the Coopers and the Charles Boyers—I could name scores of them—have glamour, are handsome and romantic. I have none of those attributes. I'm just like the Mr. Averages in the audience who watch the glamour boys on the screen and listen to the little woman at their side sighing like a furnace.

That was why the title *Mr. Music,* which Paramount gave to a picture I made in 1950 with Nancy Olson, made me uncomfortable. The picture didn't do too well at the box office, and I've always thought it was because its title was unfortunate. Any time you name anybody Mr. So-and-So, you're in trouble. It sounds as if the one named is claiming more than he's entitled to. I fought against that *Mr. Music* title because I thought it would put me in a position of claiming to be a leading figure in the music world. But the studio thought otherwise. In fact, that "leading figure in the music world" angle was the one their ads and their exploitation played up.

I think it soured a lot of people on me. Pin a name on a stage or screen actor like America's Boy Friend or The Orchid Man, or Mr. Music on a singer, and he's behind the eight-ball. People go to see him with a "he's-gotta-show-me" attitude. It's easy to turn such a label into a gibe. It can bounce. That *Mr. Music* title took in too much territory for anybody, especially me, since I know relatively little about music.

I've heard it whispered that my memory for lyrics is full of wide open spaces where nothing comes to rest for long; that through the years I've tucked so many songs in my head I can't remember the words. The truth is I can generally remember the words of the old-timers, the standards; but I forget the words of songs that achieve a fleeting current popularity—the kind I sing only two or three times on the radio before over-use and juke-box exhaustion kill them. I never really learn them. I can remember the words of several hundred standard songs, but I'd be hard put to it to think up even the first eight bars of some of the new stuff.

For lots of people, old songs have a sentimental association with something pleasant that happened to them or with a time when they were doing fine. For example, I'm always being asked to sing songs I sang at the Coconut Grove more than twenty years ago. Probably those who make the requests romanced their wife there before they were married and the songs they heard at the Grove recall these happy occasions.

Oddly enough, back in my Coconut Grove days, writers described my voice as "having a 'cry' in it." I suppose what they meant was "having a sob in it." I don't remember using that phrase myself.

It was Hope who thought up the vulgarization, "groaner," for the word "crooner." I've been asked, more times than I could shake an answer at, when the word crooner was invented. As far as I know Rudy Vallee was the first to be called that, although a case could be made out for the prior claim of the vaudeville-and-night-club headliner, Benny Fields. As for defining the word, it originally meant someone who sang with a band and crooned into a small megaphone or made mooing noises into a microphone. In France they call a crooner a *chanteur de charme*. I suppose this means a singer of charm, although it seems a loose term to describe me.

Crooner connotes a slurring of words until they're mashed together in a hot mush in the mouth. When I'm asked to describe what I do, I say, "I'm not a singer; I'm a phraser." That means that I don't think of a song in terms of notes; I try to think of

148

what it purports to say lyrically. That way it sounds more natural, and anything natural is more listenable.

Time was when I let lyrics roll out of me without thinking how they sounded. Playing some of the records I made in the 1930's, I notice that in many of them I was tired; my voice was bad and had a lot of frogs in it. The notes were generally in key, but sometimes I barely made them and they sounded strained. But I paid no attention to whether they were bad or good when I made them. And they sold. They were popular. When I play back some of the records I've made in the past year or two, they're too vocal. They're over-sung. I'm listening too much to what I sing when I sing it, and it makes me self-conscious. If I have any lasting or durable personality I am unaware of it. Some scribe once wrote that I am as typically American as Will Rogers. I shrink from any comparison of myself with the great Will. He was one of the sharpest wits who ever worked in show business. I saw him when he took Fred Stone's place in *Stepping Stones* after Fred was injured in an airplane accident. Will came on stage with no material; nothing prepared, and did about twenty-five minutes all alone up there discussing current events, and when I say current, I mean just that. Many of the things he talked about and many of the things he lampooned were things that had just happened within the last twenty-four hours. He didn't use a single set routine or a joke. And he got howls.

I've never met anybody else in show business who could have done that.

I met Will a few times and had a speaking acquaintance with him. While I never knew him very intimately, he was a man I admired and loved sincerely. I was in a night club in Saratoga Springs when the news came over the radio that he'd been killed in Alaska. A radio broadcast was going out from the night club and the producer of the show called me over and said, "Will Rogers has just been killed. They're having a memorial program all over the system. Will you sing 'Home on the Range'?"

I'd had a few drinks, but I sobered up and sang "Home on the Range" with a tear in my eye and a catch in my throat. It was one of the hardest things I've ever had to do. There was no preparation, no warning. I set a key with the orchestra leader and a minute and a half later I had started "Home on the Range" as requested. But it was mighty hard to finish.

Comes now a mention of my employment by the Kraft Music Hall, beginning in December, 1935. I had been broadcasting for Woodbury Soap and Chesterfields, but when I went with Kraft I was with them for a long, fat decade.

Once more, as with Jack Kapp, I fell into the hands of a man who took a personal interest in developing me. He was the writer of the show, Carroll Carroll. Its producer was Cal Cuhl.

In addition to doing radio work, Carroll had written for a number of publications. He seemed to have an ear for the way I talked, and he encouraged me to incorporate as many of my own words as possible into the script. He'd send a script around to my home and I'd try to rewrite the speeches he'd written for me so as to make them sound even more like me. And I'd try to put in little jokes if I could think of any. Most of them were clumsy and pointless, but once in a while I hit something mildly amusing and Carroll wouldn't delete it if he thought it had a chance of getting a laugh. The way we worked together resulted in the next thing to ad libbing.

The names of those who appeared with me on the Kraft show are a Blue Book of the loftiest talent in show business, but I had fun with them just the same. Those longhairs go for humanizing in a big way. They love it and the audience loves it, too. I never had any trouble with them about song material, the dialogue we were going to do together, or what we were going to talk about.

We were careful never to make my guests seem tawdry or

cheap, or trick them into buffoonery. They got a kick out of yaketing about baseball or horse racing with me, and I'd sing an aria with them (although it was difficult to find an aria I could handle) and they'd sing a scat song with me.

I imagine over the ten-year span, at one time or another we had every important opera or concert name on the show, some of them many times, like Rose Bampton, Risë Stevens, Lotte Lehmann, Piatigorsky, Grainger, and others. I'll never forget Chaliapin, the giant blond Russian with the steely blue eyes and lusty good humor. I suppose he was the greatest basso who ever lived. When he zeroed in on one of those rich, low notes, the diapason he developed must have jiggled the needle on the Pasadena seismograph. Merely being in the same room with this man was a thrill. I met his daughter a couple of years ago in Paris and she told me when the Germans were closing in on Paris in 1940, Feodor collected some mortar and brick and walled up his great collection of wines, whiskies, brandies and liqueurs. He was determined that none of these priceless vintages should fall prey to the unappreciative Teuton palate. It had never been re-opened, so I offered at once to place my crew of openers and tasters at her disposal. She was agreeable but time never allowed. This may well be my next mission abroad. "Anyone for Chaliapin's cellar?"

So everything was daisy until I launched my battle for a transcribed radio hour. At the time that warfare was practically front-page news. There was great opposition to the notion, not only from Kraft, with whom I'd been for ten years, but from the whole radio industry.

I had confidence that a show on tape would be just as satisfactory entertainment-wise as a live show, better in many ways.

There were two reasons why I wanted to transcribe my radio shows. The first, and most important one, was that it gave me a chance to do a better show. By using tape, I could do a thirty-five or forty-minute show, then edit it down to the twenty-six or twenty-seven minutes the program ran. In that way, we could take out jokes, gags, or situations that didn't play well and finish with only the prime meat of the show; the solid stuff that played big.

We could also take out songs that didn't sound good. It gave us a chance to first try a recording of the songs in the afternoon without an audience, then another one in front of a studio audience. We'd dub the one that came off best into the final transcription.

It gave us a chance to ad lib as much as we wanted, knowing that excess ad libbing could be sliced from the final product. If I made a mistake in singing a song or in the script, I could have some fun with it, then retain any of the fun that sounded amusing.

A second consideration—and a mighty important one to me personally—was that it would give me a chance to get around the country more if I could tape in advance. If I had to go to New York, I could do two or three shows ahead, which eliminated the necessity of transporting a cast and musicians across the continent. If I wanted to go fishing or hunting or play in a golf tournament, that too could be arranged.

Then, too, once when we knew a musicians' strike was coming off, we taped ten or twelve weeks' shows in advance. We knocked them off in about two weeks, working every day and every night. This gave us a chance to stay on the air with good shows while the strike was being settled.

But everybody was against the idea—the networks, the sponsors of other shows, the advertising agencies. They thought it might hurt the network financially. They felt that if entertainers were allowed to tape, they could sell to individual stations instead of having to use the network. Then at the psychological moment when the issue seemed in the balance, Philco said that it would be okay with them if I taped a certain number of shows.

The way it worked out, it didn't seem to hurt the networks. To my mind, the only things which lose impact on tape are sports events, or important news events. There's little question but that ball games re-created from telegraph reports are about as synthetic as you can get.

The tape idea has been a boon to Bob Hope, too. He bounces around the world more than anyone I know; any week he might be in Alaska, in South America, in China or in Europe, and he'd have an awful time doing his shows live. He uses tape almost exclusively. So does Jack Benny. Almost everybody on the air is taping now.

It's wonderful for Groucho Marx because his shows are mostly ad lib in character and he would lose much of his informality and much of his humor if he had to confine himself to his script and stick to a time limit. His show—he also films it for TV simultaneously with his broadcast taping—often runs an hour. He edits this down to twenty-seven or twenty-eight minutes. But out of an hour of ad libbing and feeling free to talk as long as he likes about anything that comes up, he gets a good show. Also, he never knows what his guests are going to say. Maybe it'll be a little racy and might offend if it went out over the air without a chance to censor it first.

I've heard a lot of talk from people about what a break it was for Al Jolson when I gave him two or three radio spots. There was talk that it revitalized the old boy and gave him a second birth in show business.

Al did as much for me as I did for him. Signing him was a lucky stroke for me. Some of the best radio shows I've ever had involved Al. If they helped Al make a comeback—that is, if he needed a comeback—they helped me as much. Al happened to me at a time when I needed good shows, and getting him to go on with me gave me a big boost.

He was indefatigable. If you'd let him, he'd sing all night. Some people had trouble controlling Jolson on the radio because he wanted to do the things that had been successful for him for so many years on the stage, in vaudeville, and in pictures. Al loved to do things for a studio audience which were strictly visual. His gestures and his mugging would make the audience in the radio studio laugh, but the people listening at home were baffled. They figured they weren't in on the gag and that they were being left out of things. It steamed them. Radio producers didn't think those things were good radio fare, and for that reason Al was in Coventry. But Bill Morrow, my writer, had the knack of handling Jolson. He would talk Al out of those things so reasonably that Al would think he was getting his own way.

Strangely enough, in spite of his yen to do visual entertainment, Al hated TV. Every two or three days he'd call Morrow on the phone and say, "Well, I caught so-and-so last night on TV and he was lousy." Or, "I've seen this or that TV show. It's through. It's had it."

He hated to see good performers dissipate material and routines developed over years in show business on one TV shot and then drive themselves into a nervous collapse trying to think of something fresh. I always felt Al had little to fear from this monster. TV should have been his dish, if anyone's.

Mississippi was the first time I'd worked with W. C. Fields, although I'd met Bill on the golf course and in the local bistros and he was one of my idols. His comedy routines appeared spontaneous and improvised, but he spent much time perfecting them. He knew exactly what he was doing every moment, and what each prop was supposed to do. That "my little chickadee" way of talking of his was natural. He talked that way all the time.

Bill was getting along, but he was still hard to shave on a golf course. He couldn't hit a long ball, but he was marvelously clever with his hands. And he was a terrific putter. I guess he got his superb co-ordination from having been a juggler in his vaudeville days. And he was a master at manipulating the betting arrangements on the first tee. Looking at his brightly blossoming nose and his graying locks, more than one optimist figured he could take him, but Bill made a lot of tax-free coin on the golf course.

During the war Los Angeles had a mysterious and never fully explained "Jap air-raid" scare. The anti-aircraft guns around the airplane plants fired for hours and made a terrific racket. Bill was no type who walked briskly home from the office each night in a Chesterfield and bowler, carrying a tightly rolled umbrella and a brief case full of sales reports to analyze. He was more apt to roll home lit with inner alcoholic fires, his progress sounding like the passage of a frigate firing broadsides. Somebody explained the commotion by saying, "Those weren't A.A.

guns. It was just Bill Fields going home late from Dave Chasen's restaurant."

Bill had a house on the shore of Toluca Lake near the Lakeside Golf Club. His lawn went down to the edge of the lake. He had a small arbor there where he sat and drank bourbon and practiced his comedy and juggling routines. Toluca Lake attracted flocks of geese and Bill complained testily that he had to quit practicing because they hissed him.

I'm always fortunate in being associated with a Bill Fields, a Fred Astaire, a Bob Hope, a Barry Fitzgerald, or some other talent-loaded individual; it's like hitting a triple parlay at the races. Which brings me to the day in 1939 when Hope came along. I'd worked with him in 1932 at the Capitol Theater in New York, but not since. He'd come to Paramount originally to make B pictures, but for some inexplicable reason he caught on fast and became a favorite. Then one day someone decided to team us in a picture called *The Road to Singapore*. It was a lucky hunch for everybody involved. The widely publicized Hope-Crosby feud was not a planned vendetta. It was a thing we fell into. It grew out of the fact that when we appeared on each other's radio programs and in the *Road* pictures, it seemed easier for our writers to write abusive dialogue than any other kind.

When our Hatfield-McCoy routine became a byword with the public, we did nothing to derail it. We developed and expanded it and pitched in merrily to think of insults to hurl at each other. When we're doing a radio show, Hope shows up at the studio with libelous comments about me penciled on his script. He writes more during rehearsal. I do the same. We may even think up a few verbal barbs after the show goes on the air.

Hope's very nimble at this sort of thing and I can only remember sticking him once, but I'm proud of that once, for I had him really blubbering. He had made some disparaging remark about my figure, and I said, "I just got a load of your rear when you walked away from the microphone, and you looked like a sack of cats going to the river." He went dead for almost a minute. He thought up a rebuttal later, but in our league, if you don't come up with a reply right away, it's three strikes and sit down.

Our first *Road* picture baffled its director, Victor Schertzinger. Victor was a nice fellow and he'd directed some fine pictures, but he'd had little experience with low comedy. He was an experienced musician and, although he knew nothing about hokum, Paramount signed him to direct the first *Road* picture because of his musical background. He was a quiet fellow, used to directing his pictures in leisurely fashion. His awakening was rude. For a couple of days when Hope and I tore free-wheeling into a scene, ad-libbing and violating all of the accepted rules of movie-making, Schertzinger stole bewildered looks at his script, then leafed rapidly through it, searching for the lines we were saying.

When he couldn't find them he'd be ready to flag us down and to say reprovingly, "Perhaps we'd better do it the way it's written, gentlemen," but then he'd notice that the crew was laughing at our antics. He was smart enough to see that if we evoked that kind of merriment from a hard-boiled gang who'd seen so many pictures they were blasé about them, it might be good to let us do it our way.

So we had more trouble with our writers than with our director. Don Hartman, now production head at Paramount, was one of the writers. The other was Frank Butler, who still writes *Road* pictures and who collaborated on our most recent tour, *The Road to Bali.* Hartman and Butler didn't like the way we kicked their prose around, and it didn't help that when they visited our set we ad-libbed in spades. When Hope called out to Hartman, "If you recognize anything of yours yell 'Bingo!'" Don left the set in a huff to register a beef with the production department.

We were curious as to what the front office thought of our antics, so when the eleven-o'clock rushes were run off, Hope and

I sneaked up to the projection room. All the studio executives were in there; the door was ajar, and we could hear those inside guffawing. They even roared when Hope stopped the action and talked directly to the audience, a most unorthodox procedure. So we knew we were in.

The basic ingredient of any *Road* picture is a Rover Boys-type plot, plus music. The plot takes two fellows, throws them into as many jams as possible, then lets them clown their way out. The jams are plotted in the script, and although they're bogus situations and on the incredible side, they're important because they hold the story together and provide a framework for our monkey-shines. Gags can't be played against gags; they have to be played against something serious, even though the serious stuff is melodramatic. Hope and I invent many of these gag escapes from predicaments as we go along, and to prevent our imagination from flagging, we prevailed upon Paramount to employ a pixie in human form, Barney Dean. Barney looks as if he'd posed for one of the seven dwarfs in Disney's *Snow White* —not Grumpy, but one of the merry ones—and he's just about their size. He showed up on our set one day peddling Christmas cards.

Hope and I remembered him from our vaudeville days. Barney had done a dance act with a party named Tarradasch. Barney's real name was Fradkin, so the team bore the improbable title of Fradkin and Tarradasch. I don't know how Fradkin and Tarradasch ever got bookings. Tarradasch could tap a little, but Fradkin just shuffled. If Tarradasch grew tired or wasn't feeling too well, the audience heard no taps at all. When the booking shortage grew so acute that no food was coming in, Barney gave up dancing and formed another act with another pal, Jim McDonnell. In this new act he played a pesky little stooge, and McDonnell was a big, tall, suave straight man. Every time Barney pulled an inane line on McDonnell, McDonnell hit him and Barney crashed to the floor. They broke their act in at a theater in Chicago, a house where knockabout, baggy-pants, putty-nose comedy went over big because the audience liked their fun gamey and unrefined.

When the Paramount-Publix circuit talent scouts caught the Dean-McDonnell act, the audience was unusually riotous, so they booked them. Unfortunately for Dean and McDonnell, they opened their new booking in Montreal in a neighborhood house before a sedate family audience. When Barney told his first joke and McDonnell and Barney hit the stage floor, the audience made a noise not unlike "tsk-tsk." When Dean and McDonnell kept right on knocking themselves—and each other —enthusiastically out, the tsk-tsking turned into an ominous booing.

That was the last of them as a team. Barney returned to New York, then came to Hollywood as a stand-in for Sid Silvers, who was making a picture at Metro. As it happens, Silvers was at war with the director, the production staff, and the writers on the picture, and Barney was constantly striving to pacify him. He was afraid that Silvers would talk himself out of a job, and if that happened, Barney would be out of a job, too. "Take it easy, Sid," he begged. "You're flirting with my job."

When, despite Barney's frantic flapping of olive branches, the job finally flickered out, Barney took to selling Christmas cards. He'd dropped in to see us, hoping to sell us some. Hope and I were reminiscing with him when he pulled out one of those bits of pasteboard with your fortune printed on it that you get from a penny weighing machine. Barney read: "You are gifted with great business acumen. You are very well fixed financially. There's nothing in your future to indicate that you'll lose your great fortune."

"If I go back to my hotel and find they've locked me out of my room," he told us, "I'm going to sue the weighing machine people."

"Why don't we have Barney sit around on the set and if he thinks of anything amusing, suggest it?" Hope said. "Even if we don't use it, it may serve as a springboard for another gag."

Which was why we used our influence with the brass to have him put on the payroll as a writer. He was given an office with a secretary, but he'd never seen a secretary except on the street, and he was afraid of his. Day after day, his secretary sat alone in his office, until we told him, "You can't let that poor girl stay there all alone. Why not at least write a letter to your mother?"

For a moment Barney looked frightened. Then he said triumphantly, "But I haven't got a mother!"

When we finished shooting that first *Road* picture, he stayed with us, and if Hope's not making a picture, Barney works on one with me.

Barney had quite a time in 1947 when we were on location for *The Emperor's Waltz*, a non-Hope picture—at Canada's Jasper National Park. Jasper Park is like Yellowstone. A lot of animals, including black bears, wander around loose. These bears are fairly tame and tourists feed them sugar, but they can be mean if the sugar is taken away from them too fast or if there's a cub about. I don't think that Barney had ever been off the pavement before and certainly the only wild animals he'd ever seen were well caged. We arrived there after dark, and were walking from our bungalow to the main dining room when a big hulk came lumbering along in the dark, followed by a couple of cubs.

Barney, who still shows traces of the fatherland's accent when he gets excited, asked, "My Gott, vat's that?"

"Those are bears," I told him.

"Who needs them?" he asked querulously.

He's very good at thinking up visual gags, but he does more than that. He keeps us from using things which might be considered in bad taste. Influenced, no doubt, by his Montreal fiasco, he is instinctively sensitive to such material. Sometimes, when Hope and I get going in a scene, we are carried away and, before we know it, we say things we wouldn't say if we had time to think about them calmly. That's when Barney speaks up. He had quite a battle with Hope once over a line in which a booby trap in the way of a possible *double-entendre* was concealed. Hope thought it was harmless, but Barney said he couldn't use it.

Finally Hope gave up and said to me with awe in his voice, "Just think. We raised this little Frankenstein ourselves."

Barney stands about five-foot-two or three inches. He's bald-headed and his habitual expression is intense as if the cares of the world are resting on his shoulders. His feet are so tiny that he has to buy his shoes in the boys' department. His hands are so small that he drops everything he picks up.

When he was going overseas with Hope to entertain the troops in the South Pacific he pulled a memorable crack. But first I'll have to creep up to that crack with a little background. Barney's a great baseball fan. So much so that his idea of Shangri-la is a Sunday afternoon double-header. Being a base-ball magnate myself, I'm not supposed to bet on the game and I don't, but like any other ball fan, I'm aware of the fact that the betting fraternity at ball parks hangs out back of third base. If you're a gambling man and you want to bet on baseball, there are usually kindred souls lurking behind third base who'll bet either way you want to go, or wager on each ball if you like.

Barney always sits behind third base or he did until recently when his doctor told him that the emotional wear and tear of sitting there was giving him an ulcer. He still spends some time back of the hot sack "to get the action" or "get the scam" as he calls it. This means finding out "what's the price" or "what are they doing today and who do they like." Then he comes back, sits down and sweats out the result, chewing his program as a cow chews its cud.

Now back to his overseas trip with Hope. Barney had been briefed and given shots but before he took off, he had to fill out a questionnaire. It asked, "Whom do you want notified in case of an accident?"

"Just tell the boys back of third base," Barney wrote.

One of my proudest possessions—I guess probably the pos-session I prize most after my four boys, if I may be said to possess them—is a five- by six-foot oil painting by Sir Alfred Munnings, probably the finest painter of horses and sporting scenes of this generation and formerly President of the British Royal Academy. The painting depicts a fox-hunting scene with five or six horsemen magnificently mounted, wearing the red coat and black cap and with the pack of hounds in the background. The party is going out on the moor. It is truly quite a picture. One night we had a party which ran into the wee small hours. The last guest to leave was Barney Dean. Mr. Dean was, shall we say, feeling "drowsy," and I led him to the door, thinking to assist him into his car. As we reached the door, he turned for a minute and looked at the painting, then looked up at me and, pointing at the painting, he said to me, "How come we never do that any more?"

Some years ago, when he first came to Hollywood, he was crossing Hollywood Boulevard in the middle of the block. About halfway over a traffic policeman grabbed him and wrote out a ticket for jay-walking. Barney looked up at him quizzically and said, "How fast was I going?"

One of the best things that's happened to me is a one hundred and forty-five-pound Irish leprechaun named Johnny Burke, who's written the lyrics for such songs as "Pennies From Heaven," "I've Got a Pocketful of Dreams," "Moonlight Becomes You," "Sunday, Monday or Always," "Swinging on a Star"—an Academy Award winner for 1944—"Annie Doesn't Live Here Any More," "Scatterbrain," and "An Apple for the Teacher." Johnny had known Dixie when she worked at Fox and he'd written a song for her then called "The Boop-Boop-a-Doop Trot." Later Dixie and I had a lot of laughs over that title, but in the late 1920's it was considered very jazzy.

It is Johnny Burke who says that he has met at least a hundred and twenty taxi drivers who claim to have helped me out of the Coconut Grove when I was singing there and "was wobbly on my pins." He also claims that there's another large club

of those who "saw a slightly tipsy Crosby fall through a drum."
I run into scores of such "eye witnesses" myself. They are
blood cousins to the hundreds and hundreds of people who
went to school with me—or with any other star. When people
tell me that they have a friend who went to school with me I
ask, "What school?" They usually say "North Central" or "Lewis
and Clark," two public schools in Spokane which I never
attended. I just tell them, "Yes, that's true," and let it go at that.
But when they say they have a daughter or a niece who went to
college with me, I have to tell them that Gonzaga isn't co-
educational.

Johnny Burke's appearance is deceptive. He looks guileless,
but he's the most enthusiastic rib artist I've ever known. A good
rib artist never lets sentiment or friendship interfere with his
rib. During the last World War a number of fliers from an air-
field near Monterey were in Hollywood on leave. I'd done a
few shows at Monterey for those fliers, had put in a little golf
with them and had sat in on several jam sessions with them, too.
So, in an effort to return their hospitality, I invited ten or twelve
of them to Hollywood to tour the studios and to attend one of
my broadcasts. To climax their week in town, I threw a party for
them. It was a nice party; I'd lined them up with dates, everything was going great, and they seemed to think I was a good
guy. But the truth is, I was having as much fun as they were.

Burke chose that moment to have an attack of ribitis. He
found two or three of my guests leaning against a bar, and
asked, "Having a good time?"

"Wonderful," they said.

"You know, of course," he told them, "that Bing just does this
for publicity. Actually, he's quite a louse." His rib began to
pick up pace, and he ran me down in every conceivable way.
For a while they tried to laugh it off; then they began to see red.
Finally they swung on him and he yelled for help.

Johnny wouldn't have minded a poke on the kisser. A genuine
rib-steak artist thinks it a mark of distinction to have a black

eye; this means that his rib was highly successful; but two or three hulking fliers coming at Johnny at once were too many for him.

But it was when I was working in *College Humor* that Johnny outdid himself as a ribber. He wrote some of the songs for that film and as a promotion stunt the studio and *College Humor* Magazine held a country-wide beauty contest to select Miss College Humor. The doll who won was given a trip to Hollywood and a bit part in another movie, *Rhythm on the Range*.

The winner was a wholesome, attractive girl of eighteen, Bessie Patterson, from Tucumcari, New Mexico. I don't think she'd ever been out of Tucumcari. When she came to Hollywood to take a bit part in the picture, Johnny Burke dated her. She was a very genuine type, and a great one for kidding herself by saying, "I didn't have shoes on when I came West."

Johnny took her out a lot and they fell in love. But wanting her to have the same tastes and interests he had, he persuaded her to go to the University of Southern California, where she finished a three-year course in a year and a half. As a graduation present he married her.

Not long after that we had a girl singing on my Kraft radio show called Pat Friday. One night the Burkes, Dixie and I, and several other couples were all dancing at Ciro's. Pat Friday was there, too.

When Bessie Burke saw her she asked, "Who's that girl?"

"That's Pat Friday," I said. "The girl who sings with me on the Kraft Music Hall show."

Bessie said, "I know another girl by the name of Pat Friday."

Johnny broke in to ask, "You do?"

She said, "Yes," and he told her, "You win the NBC Pat Friday Contest. If anybody knows another girl by that name, NBC will pay them eighteen dollars and seventy-five cents."

"That's wonderful," Bessie said. "I'll send them a letter as soon as I get home."

A week went by and she said to Johnny, "NBC is the stupidest organization I've ever heard of."

"What's the matter?" Johnny asked.

Bessie told him, "I haven't received a reply to my letter. I posted it myself and I've received no reply whatsoever."

"Did you send any Campbell's Soup labels with it?" Johnny asked.

"No," she said, "are you supposed to?"

"Yes, you've got to send a Campbell's Soup label," he told her. "It's one of the requirements of the contest."

Bessie said, "I'm glad you told me." And she wrote another letter, this time enclosing a Campbell's Soup label. But when another week went by with no flutter out of NBC, she complained again. "I have heard nothing from the National Broadcasting Company," she told Johnny. "If that's the way they run their affairs I don't know how they ever reached the prominence in the industry they're said to have reached."

"What kind of a Campbell's Soup label did you send in?" Johnny asked. "You're supposed to send Chicken Gumbo."

"I didn't know that," she said. "I'll take care of it."

This sort of thing went on for a month. Johnny had her sending in this and that, and she was getting more frustrated and angrier every day.

One night four or five of us, including Bessie, were bowling. She's a powerful girl. Beautiful but strong.

We were talking as we bowled. For some reason we hit upon the subject of ribbing people. Bessie looked at us scornfully and said, "Nobody would go for those ribs you pull. Anybody with sense would know when you're ribbing. I could tell by your faces. I could tell in one minute if any of you were ribbing me."

She had a bowling ball poised, ready to hurl it down the alley and just as she drew her arm back, Johnny asked quietly, "Did you ever hear of Pat Friday?"

Pausing at the top of her swing, she went white. Then she threw the ball down the alley so hard the pin boy was almost decapitated by the whirling pins. Then she got her coat and stalked out of the place.

It took Johnny quite a while to edge out of his quarters in the dog house and back into his own home.

It helps Burke with his ribbing that he has such a wonderful deadpan. He needed that deadpan for one he pulled on Bob Hope. Bob was having headaches over a business he had almost gone into, but thinking better of it had changed his mind. The result was a posse of process servers trying to shove summons papers into Hope's reluctant mitt.

Burke and Hope were playing golf when they saw a couple of fellows out on the course inspecting the water mains. Hope was gun-shy of strangers at that point, and he asked who they were.

"One of those guys is from the District Attorney's office," Johnny whispered. "I know him well." Hope and Johnny were playing a hole near a river. Hope went into that river bottom like a round stone rolling downhill, crawled through a culvert full of mud and ran and walked alternately until he reached his home.

Three or four days later, when he found out who "the process servers" were, he went gunning for Burke. But Burke can be hard to find at such times.

What with this and that, Burke's reputation is synonymous with that of the lad who got his kicks calling "Wolf, wolf," which brings me to the day of January 2, 1943, when my house burned down. The story has been told, but always by others. I've never told it.

The fire broke out one afternoon shortly after Christmas. Dixie always saw to it that we had a beautifully symmetrical Christmas tree, usually done in white, with all the balls of one color. The tree was two stories high and was very imposing. A short circuit in the wire carrying juice to the tree lights started the blaze while Dixie and the boys were home. Nothing burns faster than a dry Christmas tree and this one was very dry and very large. My family stood outside and watched their home burn to the ground.

I had a date to play golf with a friend of mine, Dick Gibson, late in the afternoon. Then, since I wouldn't be home in time for dinner, we planned to move on to the Brown Derby. The house burned down in mid-afternoon and I was paged by telephone around town, but since no one knew where I was golfing, I couldn't be reached. Burke, who was a neighbor of ours then, did most of the phoning. Finally he reached me at the Derby and said, "Bing, this is Johnny. There's nothing to be concerned about, everybody's fine. Dixie and the kids are all right, but your house just burned down."

I thought it a very light rib for him and a bald approach for a guy who was supposed to be so clever at ramming home the needle. "All right, Johnny," I said. "Good luck to you, too. I thought you were more adroit than that!" Then I hung up. No sooner had I sat down than the phone rang again. It was Burke once more. This time he repeated his tale with such passionate sincerity that I believed him. He reported that the fire was out and that he was with my family at Bill Goodwin's house, two doors down the street from us.

I drove out to view the ruins. The house was a shell; the staircases were still there, but the roof was gone. It was during the racing season. I'd won a little on the races and I had two thousand dollars in cash stuck in the toe of a sports shoe in my dressing room. The ways of the human mind are peculiar. There I was with my home gutted, but as I got out of my car and walked through the ruins, I was thinking only of that loot in my boot. The firemen and the fire chief met me upstairs and followed me down the hall through what was left of my house. I went into my dressing room, picked up a shoe, reached in and took out the choker I'd stashed in it. I'd had a cabinet made for my shoes so that their toes would fit into slots. The fire had scorched the heels of some of my footgear, but the toes were intact.

I said good-by to the firemen, who'd watched me, bug-eyed at my treasure hunt, and joined my family at Bill Goodwin's. We were feeling pretty blue trying to figure where we'd live when Dave Shelley, a friend, sauntered in. He'd passed the ruins of my house on the way.

"Hi, Bing," he said brightly, "what's new?"

As a crack it made Bob Hope's "What really started the fire was that somebody rubbed two of Bing's sports coats together" sound like a quip off a very old block indeed.

Dave's remark relieved the tension. Somebody got out a bottle of beer, we had a meal, and assumed a "so what, it was only a house" attitude. The next day we checked in at the Beverly Hills Hotel. Then we moved into one of Marion Davies' houses—one she didn't happen to be using at the time.

I had no answer for Dave Shelley's "What's new?" question at the moment, but about a year later the same Mr. Shelley failed to negotiate a turn in the road out of Palm Springs. He not only banged up his roadster, but himself.

The first call he got at the hospital came from a man named Crosby. When Shelley got the phone up to his ear, the voice at the other end said, "Hello, Davie. What's new?"

Johnny Burke's only trouble as a lyric writer is that, if anything, he's too literate; he hates to write anything obvious. But I remember once when his erudition paid off. A 1941 Hope-Crosby picture, *The Road to Zanzibar,* had been laid in an unidentified country and for political good-will reasons the studio wanted Johnny to write a song in a language at which no nation could take umbrage. This might have stumped a lesser man, but to Johnny it was a breeze. He brushed up on his knowledge of Esperanto and wrote the song in that universal language. He even made it rhyme.

It's impossible to think of Johnny without thinking of Jimmy Van Heusen, too. For several years now, Jimmy and Johnny have teamed together to produce outstanding hits. Jimmy's real name is Chester Babcock, but he thought it so unglamorous that he jettisoned it. When Jimmy went into the song-writing business his first song was called "Shake Down the Stars." I like to spoof him about that song. "It's the most violently wasteful song I've ever heard," I tell him. "A guy rips down the whole firmament because some flutter-brained dame doesn't love him. He sounds like an H-bomb scientist gone nuts."

Jimmy takes all of his exercise, violent or mild, out in song writing. He abhors physical exertion. One day I asked him to go for a walk.

"Not me," he said.

"Why not?" I asked.

"Walking's corny," he replied scornfully.

Outside of writing music, his only hobby is flying. He's a fine pilot. During the war he was a test pilot for Lockheed. He still flies his own plane. He's got a lot of ratings, commercial, instrument ratings, he's passed them all. He's a thorough flier, a safe flier, and a good one.

He's determined to remain a bachelor. Lots of girls have set their caps for Jimmy but they could never interest him. He takes them dancing, but that's as far as he goes. He's elusive.

Which brings me to a little anecdote about Dr. Shurr. The scene was Boston's Ritz Carlton Hotel. I was there with Johnny Burke and Jimmy Van Heusen, striving to render them a little assistance in connection with the opening of a musical play, *Nellie Bly,* for which Johnny and Jimmy had written the words and music. It was in some difficulties and they were under the impression that if I would proffer a suggestion or two it would help them whip it into shape. Regrettably, my assistance was of no benefit and the show closed shortly after it reached New York.

But to get to Dr. Shurr. He's a famous character on Broadway and around Hollywood. He was the agent for Bert Lahr and many other important musical-comedy personalities, as well as for musical-comedy producers, writers, dancers, and singers. For all I know, he handles dramatic people, too. He is one of the biggest and best agents in the business. At casting Broadway musicals he's the best.

He's very popular, very well liked, very colorful, and quite a dandy. He has his suits made by a tailor with the high-sounding title of "the ultimate in tailoring for gentlemen in the theatrical business in New York."

Dr. Shurr is the Grover Whalen and the Lucius Beebe of show business. He is the essence of all that is fashionable in men's clothing. He changes his suits two or three times a day. When he shaves in the morning he goes over and over each square inch until he's down to the veins. He owns a piece of a toilet-water company in which Gaxton is also interested, and he inundates himself lavishly with this ineffable aroma every day. Nor does he spare the other unguents, oils, and talcs. When he emerges from his quarters in the morning to go to his office, he's a redolent representative indeed.

The Doctor hates to be alone, even for as much as five or ten minutes. Particularly is this true if he's out of town, or on the road traveling. He was also in Boston sitting in on the bedside conferences for *Nellie Bly*. He was an agent for Victor Moore, who was in the show, or for Billy Gaxton, I can't remember which—maybe both.

We were to go back to New York the next day on the noon train but before we parted company after the night performance, he extracted a solemn promise from Burke, Van Heusen, and myself that we would be sure to call him in the morning when we were ready to take the train. He wanted to breakfast with us and go to the station with us in a cab. He didn't relish the idea of being alone for even that short period of time. We promised we would, and went to bed. At least the Doctor did. The rest of us hit a few night clubs and arrived home about three or four in the morning. We had some scrambled eggs and when we'd tucked them away it was six-thirty or seven o'clock. One of us—I can't recall which one—suggested that we call the Doctor and tell him to get dressed right away, since an emergency had come up in New York and we were taking the eight o'clock train.

"My God, wait for me," the Doctor said when we reached him on the phone. "Don't go without me. I'll be right down."

"You've got only forty minutes," we said, "but do the best you can and we'll wait for you. Send your bags downstairs and come here to our room."

Thirty minutes later the Doctor burst into our room. He was carrying his coat and a bag of toilet articles. His tie was stuffed into his pocket. His face was criss-crossed with crimson streaks where he'd nicked himself shaving. His hair was uncombed.

After calling him, we'd gone to bed and were half asleep. It was quite a little time before we could cool the Doctor off and send him back to his room, where he paced nervously until we left.

He told me later that the thing which had upset him most about our rib was the fact that a number of people had seen him in the elevator with shaving soap in his ears.

O NE OF MY FAVORITE movies was *The Birth of the Blues*. It
was made in 1941, with Mary Martin as my leading lady.
The story paraphrased the career of the Original Dixieland Band
and was set against a New Orleans background. In it, a song
written especially for the film, "The Waiter, the Porter and the
Upstairs Maid," was buttressed by such classics as "Melancholy
Baby," "Wait Till the Sun Shines, Nelly," and the "St. Louis
Blues"; an array which was, as they say in France, *formidable*.
But my principal recollection of that picture is the great jazz
trombonist, Jack Teagarden.

Jack was one half of the famous "Big Little Gate" who played
with Paul Whiteman when I sang with that band. Jack was the
"Big Gate," the guy who swung the band. His brother was "Little Gate."

Jack was cast as one of the members of a band and sat with his
legs over the tailgate of a wagon—the way the New Orleans
bands once played—while he made with his sliphorn. Those
wagons toured the streets of the Crescent City, the blaring
music advertising various bordellos. These tailgate musicians
even played on their way to and from funerals. They didn't play
dirges or laments at such times. They figured the one who was
gone would like something with an upbeat.

Another member of the jazz cult whose talents we utilized in
pictures was Wingy Manone, the cornetist and scat singer from
New Orleans, who supplements his billing over the cafés where
he works with the legend, "Come in and hear the truth." I always had a great admiration for Wingy. He worked for us in

another Mary Martin picture called *Rhythm on the River,* made in 1940. As followers of jazz well know, Wingy has only one arm, and every Christmas Joe Venuti sends him one cuff link.

Like many of the good ones before and during his time, Wingy never learned to read music. But he always wanted to play with the big orchestras, particularly with Benny Goodman. And Benny promised him if he ever learned to read the notes, he'd give him a flier in the brass section.

Once, when Benny was playing New York, he got a wire from Wingy, who'd been working Chicago, averring that he'd learned to read perfectly and adding that if Benny would send along the fare, he'd join him immediately. Benny got up the fare for transportation on the *Twentieth Century Limited,* and two or three days later Wingy showed up and took his place in the brass section of Benny's band at the afternoon's rehearsal. They put the third cornet part in front of Wingy and Benny gave the downbeat. Of course the spots meant nothing to Wingy and he was lost after the opening bar or two.

When they finished Benny came over to him and said, "I thought you told me in the wire you'd learned to read."

Wingy said, "I did. But man, it's amazing how rusty you can get on those long train trips."

I remember *Holiday Inn* because in it Fred Astaire danced himself so thin that I could almost spit through him. In *Holiday Inn* he did one number thirty-eight times before he was satisfied with it. He started the picture weighing one hundred forty pounds. When he finished it he weighed one hundred twenty-six. In *Holiday Inn* I danced a little, too. At least, I did a modified buck-and-wing shuffle, with off-to-Buffalo overtones. But when you're in a picture with Astaire, you've got rocks in your head if you do much dancing. He's so quick-footed and so light that it's impossible not to look like a hay-digger compared with him.

One of Hollywood's pet descriptions of a studio head is "a little Napoleon." Nunnally Johnson once said, "A little Napoleon is an executive who can walk under a bridge table." One-time Paramount executive Manny Cohen came close to filling this qualification. He was about four-feet-eleven or ten; well under five feet. Manny arranged a deal for me to be in a picture to be called *Doctor Rhythm*. Bea Lillie, Mary Carlisle, Andy Devine and a few others were to be in it too. In one of its sequences Andy Devine, who played a zoo keeper in New York, became tipsy and, filled with pity for the animals, began to liberate them.

Scurrying around, the assistant director signed up three hundred and fifty monkeys belonging to a circus man who was laying off in town. Some of the monkeys were pretty valuable; some were just ordinary monkeys. With them, the studio leased a big cage a hundred feet high and fifty feet wide, equipped with a door through which the keeper could go in and out.

There was some discussion as to how things should be handled so that when Devine opened the door, we wouldn't lose the monkeys. "Listen," the assistant director said, "I've worked with monkeys before. We'll put a big net over the set out of camera range and when Andy lets them out and they come out of the door and run off scene, they won't be able to get any farther than the net."

The circus man who owned them didn't think that would work. "You ought to build glass walls around the set," he said.

The assistant manager said that was unnecessary and Andy played the scene, opened the gate and let the monkeys out. The first monkey ran up the net, took it in his hands, ripped a big hole in it and three hundred and fifty monkeys romped through the hole.

Most of them didn't stop there. They scampered through the studio and out into the streets, the highways and byways. A few of them stayed on the lot and set up housekeeping in the lofts of sound stages. But most of them left there recently.

For days people were calling up to report that they'd found monkeys in the rumble seats of their cars or under their beds. The studio took an ad in the paper announcing an offer of five dollars to anyone who brought a monkey back to the studio. We were getting monkeys from as far away as Compton and Long Beach. These had jumped into the backs of parked automobiles; when the car pulled into its owner's garage, and he switched off the ignition and stepped out, there would be a monkey staring at him.

All this monkey business inspired a writer and co-producer buddy of mine, Herb Polesie, who was working on the picture, to make a disrespectful crack. Herb came to work one morning and said, "There's a fellow out at the front gate who's leading Manny Cohen by the hand and wants us to give him five dollars. What'll we do?"

I remember something else about *Rhythm on the River* because of Jimmy Cottrell, a prop-man pal. As I've said, I'd gone to school with Jimmy in Spokane, but when he left school he became a fighter and I'd lost track of him. I ran into him again in Hollywood when he quit fighting and was looking for something to do, and I helped him land a job at Paramount as a property man. He's been there ever since.

When *Rhythm on the River* came along, Oscar Levant's name had become one with which to conjure in the entertainment world. Oscar was on "Information Please," he'd done concert tours, he'd appeared as a soloist with some of the country's biggest orchestras. He'd written a humorous book and it had had a respectable sale. His quips and cracks were grist for the Broadway and Hollywood column mills. It so happened that in *Rhythm on the River* there was a character who matched Oscar's personality, so he was hired for the role.

The first day of shooting, Cottrell was busy readying his props when Levant shambled onto the set looking like a treeful of owls. He's a chain smoker and his hands were stained with nicotine. His blue serge suit was so thickly covered with tobacco ash that it almost covered the spots where he'd spilled coffee. He drinks fifty or sixty cups of coffee a day, and what with caffeine and nicotine plucking his nerves like a harpist, he sleeps only in fits and starts. He's also a thorough-going hypochondriac, and his pockets are stuffed with pills and tonics. His collar is usually half open, he wears a black string necktie, and his cuffs are frayed. He won't mind my describing him this way because if he were describing himself, he'd do an even more corrosive job.

Lowering himself into a chair, he yelled for coffee, and Cottrell brought it to him. A few minutes later he yelled for more coffee. This went on for some time, while Cottrell eyed him critically. He hadn't quite dug Oscar. He was still casing him.

Finally he asked, "Who are you?"

"I'm in this picture," Oscar told him.

"What part do you play?" Cottrell wanted to know.

"I play the part of Starbuck," Oscar told him.

Cottrell shook his head as if wondering what stupidities the studio would commit next. "You're playing Starbuck, eh?"

"Yeah!" Levant said.

"I can't see you in that part," Cottrell said, and walked away, leaving Levant smoldering at having a prop man lay him out like that. Usually it's Oscar who pushes people into the grease.

Cottrell came over to me and asked, "Who's that joker over there with cigarette ash all over him who's ordering coffee like he owned the joint?"

I said, "Levant," but it meant nothing to Jimmy. It rang no bell.

"Who's Levant?" he asked.

I tried to tell him, but Jimmy is a great one for original impressions. He said, "He's not going to get much of a ripple out of me."

Several days of armed neutrality and glaring went by; then Oscar discovered that Cottrell had been a boxer. Levant's an avid boxing fan and this knowledge began to temper his ire at Jimmy's treatment. Next he found that Cottrell had been a baseball player, and next to boxing and music, Levant loves baseball. This gave them another common bond, and at the picture's end they were very buddy-buddy. It has always seemed hilariously incongruous to me that Levant, the dilettante, the sophisticate, the musician, the saturnine pundit, should establish a Damon-and-Pythias relation with an ex-pug. But to them it doesn't seem peculiar. They still correspond voluminously. It's my bet that their letters would make absorbing reading. I'd rather have their collected correspondence on my bed-side table than the exchange between George Bernard Shaw and Ellen Terry.

Cottrell identifies himself to those he meets with, "I'm the fellow who taught Bergman how to box in *The Bells of St. Mary's.*" Under his tutelage, Ingrid became real handy.

I remember working in a picture at Universal with Mischa Auer and Joan Blondell. Jimmy Cottrell was prop man on that job, too. Dave Butler directed it, but I can't recall its name. When a bathrobe was called for for the Russian actor, I got Jimmy to put "Golden Gloves, Moscow, 1917," on its back. Dave Butler thought it a neat touch and left it in the picture. But the funniest stuff in that picture concerned a drummer named Jack Powell and never got on the screen at all.

The film included a song number done in a café. A trio of girls dressed as waitresses sang a little of that song. I was a waiter and I sang a little of it, too. In fact, everybody in the café grabbed a little of it.

Dave Butler came up with a notion for a culmination of the scene with the chef beating out a chorus and a half on the pots and pans, the stove, and the icebox with drumsticks. With the chef all over the joint with those sticks the way Dave saw it, it would be a real syncopated thing. The only one we could think of to do it was a drummer named Jack Powell, and he was in London. But by this time the number had progressed to such a point that we just had to have such a drummer.

So Powell was flown from London to Los Angeles at great expense. And he practiced with the music department for a couple of days while we were shooting something else.

Finally we were ready to do the number.

We started at nine o'clock in the morning. Usually a number of that type, running about two and a half minutes on the screen, can be shot in a day—including all angles. The rest of us got our part done by the middle of the afternoon. Now we came to Jack Powell. While the first part of me singing and the girls singing was being shot, the kitchen formed the background. It was one of those kitchens opening into the front of the house, so anybody working around the stove and the sink is visible. Dave Butler told Jack, "You're not doing anything in this first part, so you stand back there and make like a chef. Make a move now and then from one stove to another. You'll just be a blur, but we'll at least establish that you're around."

After a while Cottrell had come to Dave and had said, "How far do you want this Powell guy to go?"

"How do you mean?" Dave asked. "What's he done?"

"He's cooked about six dozen eggs and he's used up three sacks of flour," Jimmy said. "He's throwing eggs up in the air and catching them and breaking them and he has flapjacks going and he's flipping them around and it's costing the studio a fortune in props."

Dave quieted Powell down and finally we got to the drum artiste's part of the number.

Somehow he just couldn't seem to get it to come in right. Powell had his own patented vaudeville act in which he did blackface. He'd start with drums on stage, jump down into the orchestra pit and drum there; then he'd drum up and down the proscenium arch and on the stage floor. He was pretty good with his own act that he'd been doing for years, but when we gave him a tune he didn't know, he was in the men's room. He didn't know where he was. He was lost.

He'd get right down to the end, then get so excited he'd break a stick, hit something too loud for the sound track, or some other thing. The extras were still there—with their overtime pay running up—and everybody else was hanging around. Nine-thirty came, then ten o'clock. Shortly after that there was one take in which we thought he was going to make it sure, but once more, just before the end, he broke a stick.

"Get another stick," Dave told him. "We'll do it again."

"I haven't got any more," Powell said.

"What did you do with them all?" Dave asked.

"I autographed them and gave them away this morning to visitors on the set," Powell told him.

Jimmy Cottrell wired some sticks together and Powell finally got it right. At the end, when it was all over, everybody gave him a big hand and he made a little speech. "This," he said, "has been the most touching tribute ever paid to me. I want you to know that I'm glad you appreciate my art."

Then he collapsed. His eyes fluttered shut like a tragedian who has played *Hamlet* so many consecutive times that flesh and blood refuse to stand the emotional and physical wear and tear another second.

When we revived him with cold water and fanning, we persuaded him to autograph one of the wired sticks and give it to Dave.

Dave is ordinarily an articulate guy. This time, our gift struck him dumb.

What with flying Powell all the way from London, the whole business cost about thirty thousand dollars.

An ex-actor himself, Dave Butler is also an ex-stunt man, and he believes that all actors should do their own stunts. He did and he can't see why everybody else can't. Dave was shooting a scene in *The Road to Morocco* focused upon Hope and me walking down a narrow street in a Moroccan village. As we walked, a tribe of Bedouins came down from the hills to sack the town and to find us. We were supposed to see them coming a half-mile away and start walking fast. As they got closer, we were supposed to break into a trot, then into a run. Just before the raiders' horses passed over the spot where we'd been standing, Dave promised to holler to us over the loudspeaker so we could jump. I started walking, then running. I still didn't hear the horses' hooves but Hope couldn't stand the suspense and dived into a doorway.

I didn't see him go and kept on running, but now I could hear those horses and feel their hot breath on my neck. Dave never did holler to jump. Finally I jumped through a window, and the horses missed me by a whisker. I pulled myself together, cut and bleeding, and Dave said, "Let's do it again. You jumped too soon. It ruined the scene."

Dave's big and jovial looking, but there must be a mite of sadist in him somewhere. Because of the things he did to us, Hope called him The Murderer.

He is one of the loudest men at an athletic contest I have ever known. It's easy to tell who he's rooting for five minutes after the game starts. And the invective he hurls at the members of the opposing team is pretty difficult for that team's adherents to stomach. A couple of years ago, when the Cleveland Browns played the Los Angeles Rams for the professional football championship, Dave was in the stands rooting in his usual raucous, fog-horn fashion for the Rams. Seated in front of him was a delegation of thirty or forty people from Cleveland who, of course, were seething over Dave's cracks and his fealty to the Rams. Finally one of them shouted, "Shut up, will ya? We're getting sick of you and the Rams." Dave rose to his feet, threw his chest out proudly and cried, "Sir, I went to Rams!"

Once Al Rogell was directing Madeleine Carroll and Sterling Hayden in a love scene set on a desert island in the Bahamas. It was just a sand pit with a lone palm tree in the background. They were shooting the scene on an island a little off Catalina. After rehearsing the scene several times, the lack of action in the background worried Al a little. He didn't care for just the leaden blue sky. Seeking to remedy this defect, he asked Cottrell, who was the property man on the film, if he couldn't have some birds or something flying around in the background to give the scene an impression of reality. The way it was, it looked as if it were being shot on a sound stage somewhere, and he was trying to rectify this impression.

Cottrell said he'd see what he could do, and after lunch he gathered up all the left-over garbage and took it down to where the shooting was going on. When Rogell had rehearsed the scene a couple of times Jimmy said, "Let me know when you want the birds," and Rogell said, "All right, any time now."

Cottrell took the garbage down by the beach and threw it in the water; Rogell called "Action!" and his players went into the love scene. They'd barely finished the first few sentences when a million sea gulls appeared from nowhere. Screaming and diving, they created so much pandemonium it was hard to tell actors from crew or crew from sea gulls. Rogell jumped to his feet, mounted a near-by platform and screamed, "For God's sake, send them through one at a time!"

I thought *Here Comes the Groom,* made in 1951, was a funny picture. Frank Capra, who directed it, starts with a good script, but if he feels like it, he varies it as he goes along. If an inventive mood strikes him, he's quite likely to think up something better, as he did in *It Happened One Night.*

He has an unusual feeling about the music in his films. He won't allow any of it in one unless it comes in naturally. He says that in real life people don't carry orchestras around with them. To his audiences it appears that a character in a Capra picture actually makes any music they hear on the sound track. If Frank wanted me to sing a song while I was riding a horse, he'd have me playing a guitar or banjo or an accordion and accompanying myself, or he'd have somebody ride beside me playing. For this reason, he's had many fights with music departments and with song writers who like to hear their songs supported by a big string orchestra. Me, I take a neutral position. But it seems to me that if it's O.K. to score a picture for music, it should also be permissible to use an unseen orchestra when somebody's singing. On the other hand, the way Capra staged the song, "In the Cool, Cool, Cool of the Evening," written by Hoagy Carmichael and Johnny Mercer for the film *Here Comes the Groom*, helped it win the Academy Award as the best song sung in a motion picture in 1951.

When we were shooting *Little Boy Lost* in Paris in the fall of 1952, we had trouble blocking off streets long enough to make the shots we needed. Parisians are traditionally jealous of any invasion of their personal liberties, and Bill Perlberg and George Seaton, who were making the film, had to use a lot of diplomacy and tact.

One day, after spending hours trying to shoo spectators away from the camera, we succeeded in dislodging everybody except one fellow. He stood his ground like Horatius at the bridge. Apparently he saw in us a threat to *liberté, égalité,* and *fraternité.* "I was in the last war!" he declared proudly. "I shall not move!" Nor did he. We had to pick another location.

The traffic in Paris is a highly confused operation, a sort of automotive poker game in which each driver tries to bluff the other. We were waiting for the traffic to stop so we could get a shot near the Place de la Concorde, when a two-car accident occurred. The driver who was in the right went up to a traffic policeman and I heard him ask for the arrest of the fellow who'd caused the accident.

"Please!" the traffic policeman said with dignity. "I direct traffic. I do not witness accidents."

That night I got into a traffic jam myself about seven o'clock and I asked my French driver where all the traffic policemen had gone. "At this time of the evening they go home in disgust," he said. "It becomes just too confusing."

But, with the exception of my own, it's my favorite country. For a variety of reasons, of course, not the least of which is the food. But principally for its people. I admire their individualism, their unyielding opposition to any invasion of their personal rights or liberties. They don't have many, but they certainly cling to what they have.

In France, it seems to me everybody minds his own business,
and as long as what he's doing in no way interferes with his
neighbor, he's not bothered. I grow very annoyed with the type
of American who goes to Paris for a couple of weeks, lives in a
swanky tourist hotel, haunts the night clubs on the Champs
Élysées, and the chi-chi restaurants; then seeks to qualify as an
authority on France and the French way of life. This is comparable to a Frenchman spending a similar time on Broadway, and
judging our people on the basis of that experience. You have to
go into the homes, the small towns, to know the good, solid people and learn something of their language, their ideas and point
of view.

I'm no pacifist, but I believe I can understand something of
the Frenchman's reluctance to suit up and jump into another
war. They've been invaded three times since 1870. Go to a small
French town, of say eight hundred population, visit the church
and see there the plaque in the vestibule listing the young men
who lost their lives in the First and Second World Wars. There
are two, and sometimes three hundred-odd names. Gives one
to think, *n'est-ce pas?*

But back to show business. Most of us are bedazzled by the
luster which surrounds the name "Barrymore." There was the
brilliant and incorrigible John; there's Lionel, the reliable and
steady; and last, but not least, there is the regal and imperious
Ethel. I've known John and Lionel casually and have worked
with them on occasional radio programs. I've also worked with
Ethel on the radio; but it wasn't until I made *Just For You* with
her that I had the opportunity to know this great lady, close-up.
Shortly before the picture went into production, an incident at
Romanoff's restaurant gave me an inkling of what she's like.
Across the restaurant, Miss Barrymore was dining with friends
while the princely Mike and his *maître d'hôtel* were engaged in
a whispered colloquy back of my booth.

"She has to be told!" I overheard.

"I'm not going to be the one to tell her!" the *maître de* said.

"It isn't right for us to keep it from her until she's finished dinner," said Michael.

"You tell her," the *maître de* said.

"Not I," said Mike.

So it went; then they separated and went their ways. Just what was it they didn't want to tell her about, I wondered. Perhaps it was a death in the family or some serious illness of an old friend. Later, when Mike stopped by my booth, I asked him the meaning of the muttered conference.

"Haven't you heard?" he asked.

"No," said I.

"Brooklyn was licked today in the play-off," he said.

It was my first indication that the Queen of the Barrymore clan is a deadly serious sports fan. Later, when we began to shoot *Just For You,* we had had a radio installed on the set and were listening to the Los Angeles Rams play the Forty-Niners. Ethel approached just in time to hear the announcer say, "Oops —there's a fumble down there."

She said, in deep disgust, "Sounds like we're back in the Ivy League." And this in spite of the fact that the dreams she gave the bushy-haired Eastern All-Americans of the early 1900's must have interfered with their pre-game sleep.

I had her passionate concern with sports confirmed later when the picture we were making got under way. After Joe Louis' fight with Rocky Marciano, in which Joe was badly beaten by a fellow he could have knocked out in a single round five or six years before, I was talking about the fight with Ethel.

"Poor Joe," she said, "he couldn't counterpunch any more. He's lost his timing. All he had was his old left jab. What a pitiful way for a great fighter to go out."

On the basis of an incident which occurred when she was a young girl, it's difficult to figure her fondness for sports. As she herself told me, her father was an Englishman who came to this country to live after he had married her mother. He hadn't been here long before he became a rabid baseball fan, and went every day to the old Polo Grounds. He took Ethel with him although she was still a moppet. When the Giants lost he remained until the last fan had left the stands, bombarding all within earshot with caustic comments on the umpire, the players, the managers, and the outcome of the game. This embarrassed Ethel so much that she usually ran away and left him there. The result was that she got lost several times. So thoroughly lost was she, that, as she told me, "My nanny would have to come and reclaim me at a police precinct station."

I noticed that when Ethel was rehearsing her scenes for our picture, apparently she was not concerned with her lines, the business, or the props. But when the director finally said, "Let's take it," her first take was perfect. Past experience with other actresses hadn't prepared the director for such perfection, and he asked for another take as a matter of course. The more the scene was shot the worse Ethel became. Like any true champion, she'd built herself for one major effort, and that was it. She was amazed that the director insisted on taking the scene over and over.

"Is he making a collection of these things?" she asked me with some puzzlement.

From where I croon, she is truly a wonderful lady. It's my notion that the true test of a person is the number of friends he has—especially old friends, whom he's known for years and who, though they may have diminished in importance or professional stature, or in the amount of worldly goods they've hung onto, are still cherished.

Ethel Barrymore passes this test *summa cum laude.* The people around her, and the people she spoke of, were people she had known for years. It was obvious her only interest in maintaining their friendship was because she liked them and was loyal to them and fond of them.

I often find in my business people who go through phases. As they increase in importance they lose old friends and acquire new ones. These cycles continue until they reach the top. They for-

get the friends who were close to them when they had nothing—
people who liked them for themselves. My memory may be at
fault on this, but I think it was Walter Winchell who made the
observation, "In show business you meet the same people coming down you met going up."

Miss Barrymore has never forgotten that maxim.

Earlier in this story I talked about making *Going My Way*,
but I haven't mentioned the public's reaction to my playing
Father O'Malley in it. There were unexpected repercussions to
that role. Not everyone approved of the fashion in which the
young priest was humanized. I'd gone to a Jesuit school and
I'd always found priests very human and not unlike the boys
they taught, but in some South American and Latin countries
movie-goers objected to the priest I portrayed wearing a sweat
shirt and playing baseball. I got a sizable amount of critical
mail from those countries, reproving me for my "undignified
conception of the role of a priest."

However, His Holiness, Pope Pius XII, saw the picture several times and wrote a letter in which he described his enjoyment of the film, and said he thought it good to have the priesthood so humanized.

I'd heard of the public identifying actors and actresses with
roles, but this was the first time I'd got the full treatment myself.
Not long after *Going My Way* was released, I attended a dinner
party at the home of my friend, Jack Morse. Before dinner, cocktail canapés and hors d'oeuvres were served, among them toasted
frankfurters on toothpicks. They were served by a gray-haired,
motherly-looking maid from the Ould Sod. It happened to be
Friday, and when I absent-mindedly took one of the frankfurters,
I thought she'd have a stroke. "Holy Mother! Father Crosby!"
she burst out, snatching it from my hot little hand, "you're not
going to eat one of those!" Obviously she was subconsciously
thinking of me as the priest I'd played, and the fact that "Father
O'Malley" would eat a meat canapé on Friday upset her.

The other guests collapsed with laughter, and she retreated in confusion to the kitchen. I was a little confused myself.

It wasn't long after that when an aunt of Dixie's came to visit us. She hailed from a small town set deep in the hills of the South, where the citizenry seldom get to see a movie, and when they do, they take it to heart. She'd been with us for a week when she heard me say I was planning to play golf with Humphrey Bogart.

"Good heavens," she protested, "you wouldn't play golf with such a man!"

"Why not?" I asked.

"I saw his last picture and he's the worst man you've ever seen! The idea of a priest and a gangster getting together on a golf course!" she snorted.

The maid and Dixie's aunt weren't unique in confusing me with Father O'Malley. From Africa and from China and Japan came letters addressed to me as Father Crosby or the Reverend Crosby. All kinds of communities and towns wanted me to drop whatever I was doing, visit them for a while, and form little singing groups for children to keep them out of trouble, the way I'd done in *Going My Way*.

Some joker at Paramount made the suggestion that it would be a great gag if I bobbed up for a moment in Bob Hope's next movie garbed as a priest. Now and then we make a fleeting appearance in each other's pictures for a laugh, and laughs being hard to cull, we're always ready to use any suggestion that might pull even a light rumble out of an audience. But I was unhappy about this particular touch of genius. I was sure it would prove offensive to a lot of Catholics, as well as non-Catholics who didn't feel that the character I portrayed in *Going My Way* should go for clowning around in other people's movies for laughs.

Shortly after I'd turned this idea down with a resounding thump I happened to be visiting in Spokane and I discussed my decision with Father Corkery, the president of Gonzaga University and a classmate of mine. He was glad that I had felt the way I did about it, for in his opinion—as in mine—the stunt would have been in very bad taste.

When the picture was released and became one of the greatest box-office money-makers in all movie history, thousands of people asked where Leo got his conception of Barry Fitzgerald as Father Fitzgibbons.

My own answer to this question is that Father Fitzgibbons was a blend of several priests. I should know because I was there when he was being born in Leo's head. My own idea is that one of the priests who inspired the conception of the priest role in *Going My Way* might have been a priest whose parish for years was Palm Springs. He's retired now, having called it a day when he was eighty-two. He was delightful and excessively human. Thirty-five to forty per cent of his congregation were—like myself—fugitives from the motion-picture colony who dwelled in Palm Springs from time to time.

If I came in late with a pal, he would very likely stop in the middle of a Mass, turn and say, "So, you just made it. Mr. O'Brien and Mr. Crosby are here, folks. It's very nice of them to show up. We ought to give them a hand, but I don't think this is the place for it."

There's one story about him I like. It was getting chilly in Palm Springs, and one Sunday quite a few of his flock had colds. They were honking their heads off, which was quite upsetting to the good priest. Finally, digressing from his topic, he said, "There's a good deal of hackin', coughin', sneezin' and snifflin' goin' on in here which is very distrachtin' to your pastor, so distrachtin' that it is difficult for me to keep my mind on what I'm tryin' to say.

"If ye have colds," he went on, "ye can't help coughin' and hackin' and sneezin' and snifflin', but I should think you would take some stheps to avoid contractin' these colds and comin' here and annoyin' me as you're doin'. Ye come here to Palm Springs, and the gentlemen among ye, ye wear the shorts and the tropic shirts and when the sun goes down behind the mountain, it gets a little cool.

"And the lhadies amongst ye with your bare midriffs, your sun suits and your Bikini bathin' suits, you're not dacently dressed. You should follow the example of your pastor. I've lived here forty-some years and I wear long underwear from Novimber 'til May. And I've never had a cold in me life. If ye'd folly my example and clothe yourself properly ye wouldn't be havin' these colds and you wouldn't be comin' to church and distrachtin' your pastor."

Having given this advice, he resumed his topic and finished his sermon. He'd gone back to the Altar to the Offertory of the Mass when a horrid thought struck him. Wheeling, he cried to the congregation, "Mind ye, now, I change once a week." Then he finished the Mass.

I wouldn't be leveling if I said that when this picture was being made I was conscious of doing a better or different job than I'd ever done before. All I knew was that Leo McCarey let me do what I wanted to do and read my lines the way I wanted to read them. Not that he let anything slipshod slide by, but he strove to achieve a natural delivery of our dialogue through under-directing rather than over-directing, as some do. He must have felt that if this picture was to have a chance, and if the characters in it were to be acceptable, they would have to be portrayed as natural, normal, and homey, rather than as pious and sanctimonious.

Leo has a genius for getting the kind of performances out of people that do not look like performances, but rather people being themselves up there on the screen. Even knowing this, I never felt that we were producing any masterpiece or anything akin to greatness. I don't think Leo did either. We had a lot of fun making the picture. Working with fellows like Frank McHugh, Barry Fitzgerald, and a woman like Risë Stevens, was an enjoyable chore. In fact, chore is much too strong a word for it.

I've been told that I'm relaxed and casual. If I am, I owe a lot of it to golf. Golf has provided relaxation which has kept my batteries recharged when I put too heavy a load on them. It doesn't matter what my professional or personal problems are, when I step onto that first tee I get a sense of release and escape. When I concentrate for three to three and a half hours on trying to play a good game, the studio, my radio hour, and the fact that the latest oil well in which I've invested is spouting water are unimportant.

The medics concede that a three- or four-hour respite from tension and knotty problems is of tremendous value to anyone who's stretching and straining to wrest a living from life as it's lived today, which is certainly no soft touch. When you get back to your work after such surcease, you feel more like wrestling with it.

In my opinion, competition on the links has removed more carbon knocks and emotional burrs from human minds than all of the psychiatrists' couches. I'm a fanatic on the subject, but golf is a game which not only brings out the best in individuals but those who play it are ready and willing to channel it into paths which contribute to the public weal.

For the past seven years I've sponsored a golf tournament at Pebble Beach, California. Before that we were five years at Del Mar. Play is held on the three golf courses in the area. The proceeds are donated to local charities. The event kicks off at the Cypress Point Club; then, the second day, the field plays the Monterey Peninsula Country Club. On the third and last day of the competition it tangles with the exacting championship course at Pebble Beach.

I personally pick up the tab for all expenses incurred in connection with the tournament, including prize money. The entire proceeds—gallery receipts plus program and advertising sales —go toward building recreation centers for youth in the area and for clinical needs of the community. In six years we've raised one hundred fifty thousand dollars, and have built or have helped build recreation centers in Carmel, Monterey, Seaside, and Pacific Grove.

Although there are cash awards for each professional on his own ball, the tournament is a pro-amateur event. I select and invite the amateurs, and they play at their regular club handicap. The competing amateurs are given watches or other trophies, but I see to it that they are not cup-hunter types. Most of them come to Pebble Beach for a good time and to get in some good golf along with the nation's best professionals.

Once in a while a sleeper gets in, some amateur who's been laying in the grass all year turning in high scores to give himself a high handicap and thus pull off the *coup de main* at Pebble. Such a prize was won one year by Ed Oliver and partner. Ed, through no fault of his own, found himself teamed with an amateur who represented himself as an eighteen-handicap player. Cursory investigation failed to disclose anything wrong with this representation, so the amateur was allowed to play with eighteen shots. This meant that he had a stroke on every hole on the golf course and any he parred would give him a birdie on that hole. To the stupefaction of everyone else, he shot seventy-four on his own ball, in a round which included eight pars and three natural birdies, an impossible performance for a high-handicap player.

After this links blitz was over, the voluble Jimmy Demaret was moved to expostulate, "And he had two other birdies which he was ashamed to turn in."

The dates we play are not particularly advantageous weather-wise, but in seven years we've only been forced to cancel one day's play because of Mother Nature's unfriendliness. The first day's play at Cypress Point in 1951 was played in a howling gale and intermittent rain squalls, and, as a result, the scoring was high.

Having placed in the morning when the weather wasn't too bad, Jimmy Demaret was the early leader and he was all set to do a show with us that afternoon and evening at Fort Ord when we began to receive calls from Cypress Point saying that many of the professionals wanted to come in off the course, wash out the day's play, and come back for a fresh start on the morrow. Demaret, a debonair Texan, famous for his flamboyant wardrobe as well as his bang-up golf and his sense of humor, was indignant at the suggestion. "Little breezy," he said, "but in Texas we'd consider this a wonderful day for a picnic." He was happy with his seventy-four.

Some of the professionals came back to the club house from the course, complaining that they couldn't play because the high winds made it impossible to keep a ball on a tee. Peter Hay, the likable Scotch professional who rules the area, was aghast at the suggestion that play be discontinued. He made the point, "There's no rule in the book which says you *have* to put the ball on the tee."

Play continued and Demaret was the eventual winner, although the second day's play had to be canceled out because the water was standing inches deep in places on the course and the wind was continuing high. Paired with Bob Hope, Jimmy finished second in the amateur-pro division. It would have been wonderful if Hope and Demaret could have won it. I had an eloquently disparaging speech all prepared to deliver to Hope when I handed him his trophy, and when another fellow turned up the winner, I had to think up new material.

This other fellow was Bill Hoelle, an employee of mine in a rather juicy enterprise on the Pacific Coast, an affair called Minute Maid Orange Juice Distribution. Hoelle sank a full three iron off the beach on the eighteenth hole to tie for first place with his partner, Art Bell. This beat me out of a first-place wager I'd made in the Calcutta Pool on another team. As a result of Hoelle's devastating stroke, for a time I thought of shipping him to Paso Robles to sell french-fried pecans, but I relented and decided to keep him on the payroll.

The professionals who show up at Pebble Beach are naturally interested in the financial awards, but the tournament also has attractive social aspects. It's a merry week. The field is an unwieldy one to get around a golf course in a day. This makes it necessary to set starting times as early as six forty-five A.M. Six forty-five in the morning can be a little cold and dewy at Pebble Beach in January. It's a sobering sight to see some of the athletes stagger from their beds at that unearthly hour—some of them hung over from the preceding night's wassail—and move on to the first tee ready to sweep the dew.

There are many house parties in the locality during the week end and guests come from all over California and the Northwest and even from points east for fun and golf. Not only is Pebble Beach one of the toughest golf tests in the world, but it takes a stern competitor and a rugged team to survive the extra-curricular activities which go with the tournament. The players are entertained lavishly with cocktail parties, dinners, and late-evening shenanigans.

Because of this factor, a serious training regimen is almost impossible but everyone has a good time and the gallery sees spectacular golf.

One year a damsel who was rather on the adventurous side took in the tournament. She was a spectacularly lacy-looking beauty, dressed to the teeth. The younger, unattached players in the field hung around her like jackasses around a thistle patch. But the only fellow who seemed to be making time with her was a quiet young professional—diffident and shy—whose attentions, we supposed, went only as far as buying her a sandwich now and then.

Now this chick wore a hat calculated to make Hedda Hopper flip in frustration. It was one of those wide-brimmed straw affairs popular with tourists returning from Mexico. It was decked with straw ornaments and bangles dangled from its brim and from its peak. Naturally, she became known to all the cognoscenti as "Madam Hat."

Going into the third day's play, the shy young professional was one of the leaders in the field. But the night before the final rounds he took the lady, hat and all, to a movie. Next morning he announced that he'd gone directly home after the flick because he wanted to get lots of rest and prepare himself for his final championship effort.

He was paired with another leader in the tournament and the two of them were followed by a tremendous gallery. On one of the holes he hit a diving hook off the tee. The ball disappeared into an almost impenetrable jungle. He worked his way into it, followed by those members of the gallery hardy enough to battle the brambles. They wound up in a glade deep in the wildwood. There, under spreading cypress branches, was the hat. Not the lady—just the hat. The galleryites eyed him inquiringly and the silence was thunderous. Such was his embarrassment that it took him three strokes to get out. He couldn't have played worse if he'd played the hat. After that he took four or five bogeys in a row.

Lawson Little lives at nearby Monterey, and his home is the scene of nightly festivity for his fellow professionals who visit Pebble Beach. Lawson is so widely known for his skillful mixing of palatable Martinis that his abode is called "Gibson Gulch." For weeks before the tournament he prepares for visitors by filling his basement with gallon jugs of a six-to-one proportion. Once a day he goes down and gives the jugs a half turn so their contents won't settle too much.

Lawson also keeps a steaming cauldron of chile bubbling in the kitchen, surrounded by all the trimmings, such as tamales and French garlic bread. There's little doubt that he gets his associates in such physical condition that he could win the tournament himself if only he refrained from partaking of his own hospitality. Not only is he a fine golfer but he knows the three golf courses on which the tournament is played and the conditions which prevail on them better than any of the visiting players.

He and his partner, the convivial Francis Brown, always sell very high in the Calcutta Pool which precedes the tournament, but because of his expansiveness as a host and because Brown is not exactly anti-social, they have never made an impressive showing.

Then there's Biff Hoffman, the ex-Stanford fullback and a four-handicap golfer who's a regular participant in the tournament. Biff fancies himself as a whistler although his entire repertoire consists of a whistled imitation of Henry Busse playing "Hot Lips." Everyone is fond of Biff, but all hands have heard his performance so many times that it's turning brown around the edges. To say that its appeal has withered and died is to put it mildly. There was quite a party at Lawson Little's one night which Biff attended with me and another couple, but about midnight we had to go on to another place and we said, "Come on, Biff, we've got to go."

"I can't go now," he said.

"Why not?" I asked.

"I haven't whistled yet," he replied.

We persuaded him to go along to the other party anyhow. It turned out to be a nice affair, complete with a pianist who had been imported from San Francisco to play incidental music during the soiree. More than once I saw Biff talking with the piano player and apparently coaching him for an anticipated command performance of "Hot Lips à la Hoffman."

Presently Biff drifted over to me and said in disgust, "I guess I can't whistle tonight."

"Why not?" I asked.

"That piano player is a 'hacker.' He can't play 'Hot Lips,'" he replied. To a golfer, a "hacker" is a player who's always in a trap flailing away at his ball as if killing snakes.

One year Biff was paired with Clayton Heafner, a top professional from one of the Carolinas. Heafner is imbued with a serious approach to the game. On the night before the first day's play, Biff over-estimated his capacity a little and showed up on the tee suffering from a rousing case of whips and jingles. More specifically, the "Biffer" was a trifle shaky. He should have been at home resting, instead of teeing off into the teeth of the gale which was blowing.

Clayton played good golf all day. He did his best on every shot. Biff did his very best, too, but he spent most of his time in the trackless timber and mountainous sand from which the course is carved. He hadn't helped Clayton on a single hole.

Eventually they reached the sixteenth tee. The sixteenth is a par-three hole with a carry of two hundred and twenty yards over ocean to green, and it is a world-famous hole to golfing *aficionados.* Usually if the team playing that hole is in a contending position, one of the two goes for the green with a booming wood shot. Then his teammate plays it safe to the left and is content with a chance for a possible three or a sure four if the first player flies his tee shot out to sea. Biff looked the situation over critically, tested the wind with a wet forefinger, and said to Heafner, "Clayton, shall I go for it or play safe?"

"Mistah Hoffman," drawled Clayton in his Southern drawl, "why don't you put that lil' piece of rubbah in your pocket and go for a walk in the country?"

I don't mean any of this to indicate that the tournament is a big ball with everybody getting baked while they're there. Quite a lot of serious golf is played—some beautiful golf—by the world's greatest players, and I take considerable pride in the assistance the event gives to deserving projects in the Monterey-

Pebble Beach area. In the 1953 tournament alone almost forty-five thousand dollars was raised for charity.

As the Scotch say, "Goff's a humblin' game." One day you play over your head, the next you're just a hacker, and you don't know why. Anyone who lets himself grow egotistical about his game is building for a fall. There are bound to be days when you simply can't move that rubber at all. The game provides a constant challenge which you can meet in pleasant surroundings and in good company.

This is just as true of the exhibitions I play with Bob Hope and with various professionals as it is of my nine-hole tussles with my son Linny. Over a period stretching from 1941 through 1945 Hope and I played for the Red Cross, for other war-time charities and for bond drives. When we played for bond drives we held a bond sale on the eighteenth green at the conclusion of our match. Our articles of golf apparel, the balls we'd played with, our clubs, anything we had in our baggage, were auctioned off and the money went for bonds.

We played in so many cities and on so many courses that I lost count of them. Sometimes we'd tour with a couple of pros—say Byron Nelson and Ed Dudley; Jimmy Demaret and Lawson Little; or Jug McSpaden and Toney Penna. Sometimes Hope and I took a couple of the local pros or a brace of leading local amateurs.

It must have been good for our game. It gave us a chance to play before lots of people, and under divers conditions, and on all kinds of golf courses. And it gave us an opportunity to play with good players. Being something of a mimic, I was able to ape some of their good shots, their swings and their style, and this didn't hurt my game. However, I wondered sometimes if watching our game didn't set the stars we played with back a few years.

In New Orleans, when we were staging a bond auction sale at the conclusion of a match, the winning bid always seemed to be offered by a Miss Gustafson. When our things were auctioned off, a Miss Pearl Gustafson bought something. Then a Miss Ginny Gustafson came up with the high dollar, Miss Angie Gustafson topped the rest, and so on. When the sixth Miss Gustafson came forward, Hope asked if all of the Gustafson girls were sisters. She said "Yes."

"Good grief!" Hope asked. "Didn't your father ever hear about Ovaltine?"

This crack broke up the bond sale for a few moments, I promise you.

On one occasion during the last war, Hope and I were entered in the Texas Open. We were in company considerably over our heads. Ordinarily the tournament committee would have given us the cold shoulder, but since the proceeds were to go to the AWVS, we were allowed to play. The idea was that our antics and our attempts to play top-flight golf would attract more paying patrons than those who usually attended open events in Texas.

On the first day, Hope and I were paired with Byron Nelson and Ben Hogan. Our gallery was a sizable one. The caddie I'd drawn for the afternoon was a tall, lean, colored boy. He stood about six-feet-four; his feet resembled a couple of Gladstone bags. An irrepressible twinkle of good humor gleamed in his eye.

To the surprise of the gallery, Hope and I managed to get off the first tee fairly well. It was a short, par-four hole, and we had second shots of about a hundred and forty yards. What was even more surprising, Nelson put his ball out of bounds and Hogan drove into the rough and found himself an almost unplayable lie. For his second, Hope hit a good shot, but it caught the top of the trap and kicked down into the sand. Hogan came out short of the green. Nelson put his on the back green, but he lay three. I happened to catch a second shot with the right quiver of my legs and arms, and it finished about six feet below the hole—an easy putt for a birdie.

As I fought my way through the gallery to the green, I could see the headlines on the morning sports pages: CROSBY OPENS TEXAS OPEN WITH A BIRDIE. I reached the green and stood there nonchalantly leaning on my putter, while the other members of the foursome holed out. Bob lagged his up for a five, as did Nelson. Hogan pitched on about twelve feet above the hole, missed it and took five. My great moment had come. I had to wait until my caddie got through the gallery, but he finally ambled through an aperture, walked onto the green, and sized up the situation.

We went into an intimate colloquy. "You know this shapes up as a birdie," I said, "and I'd sure like to make it. But I want to get the right dope on the break and the speed of the green. You've been caddying around here for quite a while. You ought to be able to give it to me."

"Well, now, let's see," he said, putting my bag down on the edge of the green; "you want me to give this the full study?"

"If you will," I replied.

He walked up to the hole and surveyed the terrain above and below it. Then he got down on his knees and studied it from both sides, while the crowd of seven or eight thousand waited. I took my place back of my ball and waited for his report. Finally he shuffled over to me.

I whispered, "Which way shall I putt it?"

"Maybe we'd better go out this way a little the first time," he said, waving his hand to the right. That "first time" unnerved me; and there *was* a second time, too. My first putt carried past the hole and I had to make a four-footer for a par coming back.

On the fifth hole I had a chance to get on the green with my second shot, but the distance puzzled me. I called him over again and asked, "What do I need to get home?"

"Mr. Crosby," he said, "I don't even know where you live."

I eyed him sharply. I wondered if he was getting his material from Hope, but he was such a dead-pan character I couldn't tell.

I played pretty well for me, and was fairly happy with the

round until the sixteenth, where I drove two into the water, dumped my fifth shot into a trap guarding the green, blasted the next one over the green, and got down in twelve strokes. On the way to the next tee I asked my caddie if he had put down my score for that hole.

"Couldn't do that," he said.

"Why not?" I asked.

"I can't spell 'chaos,' " he said. No one has ever been able to convince me that Hope hadn't rehearsed that one with him.

Another one of my golfing recollections involves one of the most popular and better-known song duos of the late 1920's, Pepper and Salt. Pepper's real name was Edward Culpepper, and his professional name was Jack Pepper. This pair, while probably not so well known or so well paid as Van and Schenck, commanded a good salary in vaudeville. They played only the top circuits, and had been seen and heard in a couple of first-chop Broadway productions.

I crossed paths with Pepper and Salt several times in vaudeville. I became pals with one of the members of the team, Jack Pepper. Jack hailed from Dallas, Texas. He had been married for about ten minutes to Ginger Rogers, who was then a dancer. In the early 1930's the Pepper and Salt team split up. Salt wound up in charge of a radio station, a job which also included singing as well as running programs.

Pepper clung to vaudeville. He did a single and played night clubs. But as his girth increased and his thatch thinned, demands for his talents dwindled despite the fact that he could sing like a bird. Jack had an expansive conviviality. Jolly times meant more to him than split weeks. I have known him to turn down cushy vaudeville routes so he could be present for the racing inaugural at Saratoga in August. Jack's favorite expression was "Have fun now; get the bread later." Many a time when I met him around New York and I asked him how things were going, he replied, "Lots of laughs; lots of bread in the house." He sang an occasional song in Jack White's Club 18 and did straight for Frankie Hyers or Pat Harrington. Or sometimes he stooged in vaudeville for Jay C. Flippen, Ben Blue or others of similar stamp.

The year, as I recall it, was 1943. Bob Hope, Jerry Colonna, and I were on board a train from El Paso to Dallas, with a sprinkling of musicians and a soubrette or two. We were en route to play a golf match and do some shows at the local air bases, after similar stints in El Paso.

One mid-afternoon our gin-rummy game was broken up by the delivery of a telegram addressed to Hope and me. When the porter handed it to us Bob opened it. It read:

DEAR CHAPS: I AM OWNER AND OPERATOR OF A NIGHT CLUB, AN EXCLUSIVE DINE-AND-DANCE SPOT ON THE OUTSKIRTS OF DALLAS. WOULD YOU TWO FELLOWS AND COLONNA MAKE AN APPEARANCE FOR ME THERE TOMORROW NIGHT AND HELP ME GET A LITTLE BREAD IN THE HOUSE.

YOUR OLD BUDDY-BUDDY, JACK PEPPER

We studied the schedule of events laid out for us the following day in Dallas. We had a luncheon date with the mayor and other civic officials; a Red Cross golf match in the afternoon; an appearance at an air base in the evening. But that appearance should be over about nine o'clock. This seemed to allow us ample time for an appearance at Jack Pepper's Club, so we went back to our gin game and gave the matter no further thought.

Next morning Pepper greeted us at the depot in Dallas. His figure had grown aldermanic. His face was red and perspiring, and he was obviously laboring under a burden of anxiety.

"Why didn't you answer my wire?" he demanded.

"It wasn't necessary," I told him. "We're all set. We'll go out tonight and do a show for you."

"That doesn't do me any good now," he complained. "I've had no opportunity to publicize it. If you'd wired me yesterday, I could have had it in the newspapers this morning, and on the radio stations last evening."

"Well," I said, "let them bang away at it on the stations this afternoon. Here's another idea: print about ten thousand circulars announcing our appearance, and give them away at our golf match. What with the circulars and intensive by-word-of-mouth steaming up, you ought to be able to entice loose members of Dallas café society into your deadfall."

Except for a few glimpses of Jack and his shills racing around the course handing out bills and making announcements over the public-speaking system that the Hollywood stars, Colonna, Hope, and Crosby, would appear that night at his club, we didn't see him again until nine o'clock that evening, when we'd finished our show at the air base. Jack met us there, bundled us into a car, and we started for his bistro.

He should have described the location of his night spot as on the outskirts of Fort Worth, because it was almost a sleeper jump from Dallas, but once we'd glimpsed it, I could see why Fort Worth might have objected to that. We arrived before a rustic lean-to which looked, I imagine, something like Daniel Boone's first outpost. It was flanked by a postage-stamp parking lot, where we were greeted by a gangling Western type, introduced to us as "Waxahachie." Jack described "Wax" to us as not only the master of ceremonies of the floor show but as electrician and spotlight man on the side. When not thus occupied, he parked cars.

There were no cars in the parking area, and no patrons had arrived when we entered the club. The orchestra, composed of a girl drummer and an organ, was wailing away at "Don't Sit Under the Apple Tree with Anyone Else but Me." The dance floor was a hole in the ground about twenty feet square and ten feet deep. Stairs led down to it. It reminded me of snake pits I'd seen at carnivals. The patrons—once they arrived—would sit around the rim of this hole in the ground, on rustic furniture, before rustic, lamplit tables.

"How about a little belt before the people arrive?" Jack queried us nervously. When we said we were agreeable, he darted into the kitchen and returned with a bottle of something which he jovially described as "Old Whipping Post," or some such buck-and-a-quarter potion. We sat around for a while, hacking gingerly at this leopard sweat until ten-thirty or a quarter to eleven, but the place was still empty. Pepper noticed our looks of concern, and said reassuringly, "Dallas is a very late town. People never come out until eleven or twelve o'clock, but once they come out, they throw their loot around and stay up until the last dog is hung and the pup shot."

The telephone rang and Pepper answered it. We heard him engage in conversational exchange with the party at the other end of the line. Jack's voice said, "Yes, they're here—all three of them—Hope, Colonna, and Crosby. . . . You don't believe it? Wait a minute; I'll put one of them on."

Taking his cue, I went to the phone and identified myself. A feminine voice laced with a jigger of rich Texas accent asked, "Haow do I know you're Bing Crosby? Sing me a little song."

I gave her a few bars of "Blue of the Night."

"Oh," she cried, "I can't tell whether it's you by just those few little bitty old notes! Sing me a whole song!"

"What song do you want to hear?" I asked.

" 'I Surrender, Deah,' " she said.

So I sang it to her—the whole song—even throwing in the high finish. Not good, but high. At the conclusion I could hear a pattering of applause from the other end of the line.

Then she asked, "How do I know Bob Hope is there? Put him on."

I called Hope to the phone, which was no trick. He'd been fighting for it ever since I'd picked it up, and he went through the same routine, only he substituted a five-minute monologue for a song. Next Colonna went on the Bell Network. He sang "On the Road to Mandalay" and did a few cross-fire gags with Hope and me.

Pepper, who was sweatingly impatient for us to finish, snatched the phone and asked. "How soon will you be over, and how many are in your party?" He heard her reply, and his face fell. He put the receiver back on the hook and came back to our table, his brow heavy with care.

"What did she say?" I asked.

"What did she say?" he repeated bitterly. "She said now that she'd heard the show she wouldn't have to come over."

We went back to belting away morosely at the Old Whipping Post once more. It wasn't long before the phone rang again. This time we were smarter. We merely identified ourselves without giving ample performances. As a result, we lured a party of twelve out to Pepper's place. They arrived about midnight. When they showed, we put on an hour's show in the snake pit and they bought eight dollars' worth of drinks and hamburgers. Pepper did some bits with us, and Waxahachie was featured heavily, too. It was a small audience, but enthusiastic, and we scored nicely, even if Pepper's take was a little light. However, what with Old Whipping Post soothing and sustaining him, he didn't brood long, and at one o'clock when we closed up and started for the depot, where our train was waiting to take us to San Antonio, Pepper had appointed himself a member of our troupe.

Three days later he was still with us. When I asked him what would happen to his club in his absence, he said casually that near the end of our evening there he had bequeathed the place to Wax, mortgage and all.

I don't think Jack's ever been back deep in the heart of Taixus. After that he went with Hope to Europe and to the South Pacific on entertainment tours, and landed quite a bit of work in vaudeville and night clubs. As far as I know, he's still up to his eardrums in fun and laughs and plenty of bread in the house.

My favorite story of golf as a character-rearranger is one I not only witnessed but participated in. It goes back quite a way but it's still vivid as a neon sign in my mind. When Al Rinker and I first hit California, we served a stretch with the motion picture-stage presentation outfit Paramount-Publix. For a few months we alternated between Los Angeles' Metropolitan Theater (now the Paramount) and San Francisco's Granada.

A frequent visitor backstage at the Metropolitan—he was there nearly every evening—was a young Scottish golf professional, named Jock McLean. After a few weeks Al and I became quite friendly with him. Jock was an amateur song writer and was incurably stage struck, but he paid for his coffee and cakes by being a pro at an exclusive golf club in the Los Angeles area.

Rinker and I were already badly bitten by the golf bug. In fact we were as golf struck as Jock was stage struck. Any time we could wangle free from our Paramount-Publix chores, we struggled around the Griffith Park Golf Course. Angelino golfers of the late 1920's will recall that Griffith Park was not the well-manicured layout it is today. Not to put too pretty a face upon it, it was rugged and it had sand greens, a feature which is anathema to a dedicated golfer. It's impossible to pitch to such greens. We played short and tried to roll our ball up on them and the inability to pitch direct to the pin took a lot of the pleasure out of the game. Brooms were parked by the greens to smooth the sand before and after putting.

Our new friend, Jock, was employed at a club where the lay-out was grass and where the greens were the finest in the West— the equal of those anywhere in the country. We importuned Jock for a chance to play his course, but since it wasn't within his province to give us his permission, we were unsuccessful. To overcome this impediment, Al and I held a pow-wow and came up with a Machiavellian gimmick. We manifested sudden interest in Jock's amateur song compositions and he grudgingly gave us permission to play the course if we promised to reach it early in the morning (around six o'clock) and depart before nine when the first members teed off.

In other words we could play the course but we were to keep out of sight. This meant that we got up at five in the morning to drive to the course but it was worth it, because it seemed the only chance for the Crosby-Rinker entries to appear on such a good track.

Jock claimed that it would cost him his job if it were known that he'd given us permission to play. He particularly warned us to avoid a multi-millionaire member, whom I'll call Kimberly. It seemed that Kimberly was irascible and a difficult man to get along with in every respect. He was especially truculent about any use of the course by outsiders. Not only that, but he was also the club's Scrooge. Penurious, mean, bitter, he was a chronic complainer about the food and service. He was constantly embroiled in quarrels with the House and the Greens Committees as to their shortcomings in performing their jobs. He was so niggardly hardly anyone would caddy for him. He never contributed to the Employees' Christmas Fund, and was forever thumping the table in favor of economies in the club's administration and facilities. In other words, he was quite a heavy. Rinker and I made up our minds we'd steer clear of him.

We played this course almost daily, and followed Jock's admonitions religiously. We wet our feet with the early morning dew and never ran into any of the members. One morning, however, we started later than usual and by eight-thirty were only on the tenth green. The tenth was a par-three hole of about a hundred and fifty yards. I was getting set to putt when I looked back at the tenth tee and saw an old gaffer bending over to tee up. It was too late for us to hide in the trees, so we stepped off the green and stood to one side near a sand trap. Our idea was to let the elderly chap play onto the green and then continue on through us.

He smacked a good one with his number five wood, but it had a hook on it. It landed short of the green to the left, took a bounce and rolled right toward me. Impulsively, and without knowing why, I kicked it toward the green. The ball carried a low-lying sand trap, bounced twice, and plunked smack into the hole, coming to rest wedged between the stick and the inside of the cup. While Rinker and I stood there fascinated at the result of my drop-kick, the old gaffer picked up the little canvas bag in which he carried his two or three clubs and approached the green.

"What'll we do now?" I asked Rinker.

"Let him look for it," he said.

On the green the old party looked around, then into the sand trap, interrupting his search from time to time to throw suspicious looks in our direction. We remained speechless, concentrating on a flock of blackbirds passing overhead, and a man who was mowing three fairways away.

Finally the searcher asked, "Did you see a ball come this way?"

"Yes," I said, "it went on the green."

"It's not there now," he said.

"Maybe it went into the cup?" I said.

"What?" he screamed. He dropped his clubs, ran to the green, pulled out the pin, saw the ball in the hole, jumped up and down and waved his arms. He topped off this performance by rushing up to Rinker and me and embracing us.

"Seventeen years," he bellowed, "and this is my first hole-in-one. And I've got witnesses. You saw it, didn't you?" We nodded.

"This calls for a celebration," he declared. "Come into the clubhouse."

We pleaded that we had work to do but he was insistent. "You've got to testify for me," he said. "I must prove I made a hole-in-one. None of the members will believe it. Why they won't believe I even hit the green."

So we went along to the clubhouse. En route I threw out a few conversational feelers to see if it was safe to let him in on the truth about his "hole-in-one," but I could see what repercussions such a revelation would have. The very least would have been to cost Jock his job, so I gave up.

Inside the clubhouse he banged on doors, had the bar and the kitchen opened, dashed into the office, got his secretary on the telephone and told her to invite a lot of the members for a celebration luncheon that noon. Then he had the bar man open champagne. We told him once more that we had to work but he wasn't going to let us get away until the other members arrived and we'd testified about his ace.

"I've never given a party before," he chortled, "but the one I'm going to give will be a pip. You're my honor guests."

After Rinker and I had taken a few belts at the bubbly, our eagerness to get to the theater in time for the matinee diminished. By lunch we'd forgotten there was a matinee, or a theater, or show business, for that matter. We'd progressed to a point where we could describe that hole-in-one graphically from the moment the ball left the tee, describing a course like a white string stretched in the sky until it entered the cup. We eliminated, of course, any mention of the nudge I'd given it. Each member had to hear our story as he arrived. At one point there was an embarrassing moment when Rinker and I couldn't agree as to whether the ball carried in on the fly or had bounced three or four times before plopping into the jug.

The luncheon, tippling, toasting and celebrating continued until past mid-afternoon. It was only then that we realized we'd missed the matinee. But we were considerate enough to phone the theater and tell them that we'd make the supper show at a quarter to seven.

We made it all right. In this case, the audience, generally small and undemonstrative at that time of the evening, was largely composed of country-club members, led by the enthusiastic Kimberly. After the second show everybody adjourned to Coffee Dan's for dinner and later we went on to the Coconut Grove. When we left Kimberly about two A.M. and went home to bed, he was still being sustained and cheered by a few of the more hardy members of the club.

Next morning, the papers carried stories of Kimberly's feat. There were pictures of him standing with us in front of the locker room, and there were details of his background.

A day or two later Jock McLean dropped in to see us. We

were afraid we'd have to tell him the truth and reveal our deception. But Jock was all smiles. He had with him an embossed envelope with our names on it. We tore it open and pulled out the enclosed card. It was a two-months' guest-privilege card at the country club. We'd been proposed and seconded by Kimberly, who was the club's vice president.

"We'll just have to go out there some afternoon and wait for a mellow moment to reveal what happened," I told Rinker. "We can't go on letting this old boy spend all this dough on us and making nice gestures when the reason for his gratitude never really happened at all."

"Yeah," Rinker agreed feebly, "that's what we'll have to do."

"It's not so much what we did," I said, "it's the fact that we let him go on believing he had an ace that's so reprehensible."

So we went out to the club on several different occasions for lunch, and we played around in afternoons when there were no matinees, but certain things had begun to happen at the club which made us think twice about springing our revelation. Kimberly, who had always been snug with a buck, was becoming practically profligate. He put up trophies for a caddies' tournament. He established a fund for caddies who fell into financial difficulties because of sickness or lack of work. He gave two or three big parties for the members, bought I don't know how many sets of clubs and other equipment from Jock, and was working on a plan to retire the mortgage a local bank held on the club property.

His entire personality and approach to life had changed. And as the weeks went by, the change became even more evident. Rinker and I went to San Francisco for a month's engagement, then to Oakland and San Jose. Two or three months later when we came back, we were at the club again playing golf with Kimberly.

By this time he'd been elected to an important post in the Southern California Golf Association and was interesting himself in solving the problems faced by that group. He had become an important figure in local charities and was devoting himself to civic improvement.

Which should do as proof that golf is quite a thing when it comes to popping its practitioners out of their ruts. This is true not only spiritually but geographically too. After you've slogged your way around the same golf course so many times that every divot drying in the sun is an old friend, you're apt to be seized with an uncontrollable desire to try your skill on somebody else's golfing backyard.

This urge to see whether the grass is not only greener elsewhere but easier to sail a ball over can lead far afield. Some day I'm going to add the Duchy of Luxemburg to the list of places over which I've dragged my clubs.

I'd been up at St. Andrews playing in the British Amateur. I'd had a rather big night in London and gotten home just in time to shower, shave, dress, and drive down to Dover to catch a small Belgian boat of the packet class for Ostend. I had a few Dubonnets and some luncheon and it felt very confining and stuffy inside.

Walking around the deck to get a little air after lunch, I encountered a very distinguished looking gentleman and asked him where he was from. He said he was from Luxemburg. I've always been intrigued with this light opera, Graustarkian-type little country. I don't know too much about it. I guess no Yankee does. In fact, I hadn't heard much about it until Perle Mesta went over there as our Ambassadress. But I'd always been fascinated by it. So I asked this fellow, "What do they have there, a king or queen?" It was, he told me, a duchy.

I said, "Oh, a duchy, eh? Do they have a duchess?"

He said, "Yes, a Grand Duchess."

"Have you ever seen her?" I asked.

He said, "Yes."

"Do you know her?" I wanted to know.

"Oh, yes," he said, "she's my wife."

I was talking to the Prince of Luxemburg. I was a little embarrassed. I could have done a backjack into a *pousse-café*. You could have knocked me over with a napoleon slice.

This fellow was the Prince of Luxemburg all right, but a very nice chap. Very nice, indeed. When we got to talking, he spoke better English than I did. He told me he had been a great friend of General Patton's. In fact, he'd been attached to General Patton's staff as a liaison officer between the Third Army and the French. I told him that I, too, had spent some time with the dashing Patton. We swapped some yarns about him and recalled some of his exploits.

But apparently my nosiness hadn't offended him, for he invited me to visit him in Luxemburg and catch a little golf. "You'd like the Grand Duchess," he said.

I regret that I couldn't make it. I'm sure I would have had a wonderful time, getting to know the Grand Duchess and playing golf. It's not every day you get a chance to drive a long tee shot into another country if you catch one good.

Phil Harris is fun to play with. He never stops wise-cracking on the course. One day we were playing with Milt Hicks, a fellow club member. Milt is built like Herman Hickman, the ex-Yale football coach. Hicks plays pretty good golf, mostly in the low seventy's, but his stance is peculiar as he crouches over the ball. Phil Harris calls him The Land Crab. He takes terrific lunges at the pellet and when he hits one the ground shakes for yards around. He doesn't get much altitude, but lots of yardage off the tee. He hits them what is called quail high; sizzlers about two feet off the ground. Phil says he's a menace to the field mice.

Milt loves to use a nine iron when everybody else is using a four or five to reach a given green. In other words, he likes to show how strong he is by using a club which is constructed to hit a ball only one hundred and ten or one hundred and fifteen yards, but by closing the face of his club a little and using all his muscles, he is able to knock it out one hundred and seventy-five yards. When he goes into this strong-boy act he rips up divots as big as footballs, and rocks, grass, little pieces of glass, and fragments of sea shells whiz through the air.

On this particular afternoon we were all playing the first hole on the Thunderbird course. We had all driven pretty much alike. I was away. I played a four iron, Phil played a five iron and Hicks said to his caddie, "Give me a nine iron."

The caddie said, "Now, Mr. Hicks, you're not going to use a nine iron. It's too far."

"Yes he is, he's going to use a nine iron," Phil said. "We're going to bury a dog out here this afternoon."

When the unseemly laughter had subsided, Hicks stepped up to the ball, took a lunge at it and knocked it onto the green, one hundred and seventy-five yards away. It was by all odds the longest nine-shot I've ever seen.

All of which goes to prove the soundness of what I call the Crosby Law: "Never needle an opponent when he seems to be the underdog. Only needle him when he's out in front."

Then there's the story of Lou Thomas, once Lakeside's finest putter, but a man so meticulous on the greens, so insistent on silence that playing with him was sometimes a trial. One day he had a twelve-footer on the fourteenth green. Truman Bradley was just inside of him with a ten-footer. Lou surveyed his putt from the upper and lower angles—from both sides, tested the wind, spent five or ten minutes reading the contours, the grass, even the roots. He picked up some loose blades of grass, some lint, tiny bits of sand, then turned to his caddy and asked, "Was this green cut this morning?"

"Yes," the caddie replied. Whereupon Lou putted and missed.

Truman, who had spent this long interlude leaning on his putter with ill-concealed impatience, stepped up to his ball and stood over it for a moment waggling his club. Suddenly he stopped, straightened and turned to Lou's caddy.

"What time?" he inquired.

Or there's the one about Bissonette, a colorful, if somewhat eccentric player at Lakeside. He was in a foursome playing the sixteenth one day and when they reached the point on the fairway where their drives should be, they found three of the balls, but not Bissonette's. A ten-minute search of the area met with no success. Finally, when they were about to give up and go along, Biss said to his companions, "You know something?"

"What?" they asked.

"I never drove," was his shattering disclosure.

A little anecdote about Ben Hogan and Jimmy Demaret might fit in here. As everyone who follows golf probably already knows, Ben and Jimmy were kids together, caddies together, and have been practically inseparable throughout all the years. They are two very contrasting personalities, but are great friends, nevertheless. Demaret is swashbuckling, ebullient, a gay blade of the fairways; Hogan is dour, taciturn, serious, and intense. Strangely enough, they had never hooked up head and head in a tournament until the finals of one of the PGA championships in the middle 1940's in Portland, Oregon. The PGA is, of course, one of the top tournaments for the professional golfer, one which all of them are eager to win at some time in their career.

Hogan trounced Demaret mercilessly, something like ten and nine as I recall it. Some weeks later, when I ran into Demaret in Los Angeles, I asked him about the match, wondering, in view of their old friendship, whether Hogan had been cordial or companionable during that long and dreary day.

"Did he say much to you?" I asked.

"Only two words," replied Demaret. "'You're away.' You know, Bing," he continued, "all I saw all afternoon was fanny and elbows."

"Fanny and elbows?" I questioned.

"Yes," replied Jimmy. "Every time I looked around he was taking the ball out of the hole."

On the golf course, Demaret constantly needles Hogan. But he seldom gets any kind of a reaction. However he did steam

Ben pretty good once when they were both visiting me at the ranch in Nevada for a couple of weeks. They came up to do some hunting and to lie around fishing a little. They got there about noon and after lunch we got in the jeep and went up on the tops of some of the ridges to have a look around to see where the bucks were, so we'd have an idea of the right places in which to hunt the following day.

We were high up when we saw some deer down in a valley break for cover. Catching sight of them all we jumped out of the jeep and ran to the edge of a cliff to see just where they had gone. On our way back to the jeep a sagehen jumped up. A sagehen is a bird about as big as a cock pheasant. This one got up with a tremendous flurry and when he'd flown seventy-five or a hundred yards, Jimmy, who was carrying a thirty-thirty carbine, raised it to his hip and shot.

To the surprise of everyone, he hit the bird dead center, really distributing him. It was an incredible shot. Jimmy turned to Hogan and said, "When you improve on that I'll shoot my next shot."

They were there two weeks and Jimmy never fired again. He went along hunting with us every day. He deer-dogged for us on horseback, kicking the deer out and stirring them up, but he never fired a gun again. He said to Hogan, "If you get me a deer jumping off a cliff, in the air, or pop one out of a helicopter, I may shoot. But I'm not going to shoot any old deer just running along on the ground or standing still. I've got to have them in the air."

Then Hogan, or "Blueblades," as Demaret calls him because he grinds his teeth in his sleep at night, grinned sardonically.

Along toward the end of their stay we were hunting up around the nine-thousand-foot level. Someone got a deer down and we were dressing it out. Hogan had crossed a gorge about three hundred yards away. Another deer broke out of the brush and started up through the snow. Hogan dropped to one knee and fired. He hit the deer somewhere near one of its shoulders. We heard the thud; and the deer fell in the snow.

Because of the depth of the gorge across which Ben had shot, it was impossible for us to go directly to the place where the deer fell. It was necessary to climb on our horses, go up around the top of the mountain, and come back in from the other side. It took about an hour to do this and when we arrived there, although there were plenty of indications where the deer had fallen and quite a bit of blood in the snow, there was no sign of the buck.

We never did find that deer. He must have been merely pinked by the bullet, then he fell, and slid down into some crevasse and sneaked out of there. I hope the coyotes didn't get him. When you get a deer wounded and don't find him, it always bothers me.

"Well," Jimmy said, "I guess you didn't hit him."

"Of course I hit him," Ben said. Then turning to us for confirmation he asked, "Didn't I?"

"Yes," I said, "I thought I heard the bullet hit and the deer certainly went down."

"I think he just tripped," Jimmy said.

"Tripped!" Ben yelled. "How about the blood all over the snow?"

"The high altitude got him," said Jimmy. "He had a nose bleed."

Jimmy never let up on Hogan about it. He got it all the way home and during the rest of the visit.

In 1948 or '49—I can't remember which year, but I recall that it was the year we made *The Emperor's Waltz* at Jasper Park— I went back there for the Jasper Park Invitation Golf Tournament and was lucky enough to win it. The following year, as my guest I took there with me George Coleman from Miami, Oklahoma. George is also a part-time resident of Pebble Beach. George and I took part in the tournament. Along about the second round, George was matched with a cagey old player from the Midwest, a player he should have been able to handle pretty easily. They were playing a match three or four holes ahead of mine. When they were on the seventh or eighth hole I sent my caddy up to find out how they were coming along. He brought back the news that George was five up.

Toward the end of the afternoon, when I was finishing my round, I saw George and his opponent out playing extra holes. This indicated that the Midwesterner had overcome George's lead and that they were even.

George beat him on the twenty-third and I got the story later. Between the eighth green and the ninth tee, after inspecting George's physique, his opponent asked George if he'd ever done any boxing when he was in college.

"No," George said, "why?"

The gaffer said, "Well, you have such wonderful biceps, such powerful sloping shoulders and flat muscles, you would have been a terrific hitter."

George knew he was getting the old eefus, but he couldn't resist putting a little extra muscle into the next five or six tee shots. He quick-hooked them; they were real coat-hanger types, and they disappeared into the woods which lined the fairways. He needed quite a few holes before he got back on the beam. The worst part of the situation was that he knew he was being needled, but that made it all the worse.

George and I wound up playing each other in the finals. The day before this thirty-six-hole event was to take place I was scheduled to attend a party given by the members of the staff and do a little entertainment for them. There would be considerable banqueting and drinks and George said, "Do you mind if I have an early dinner, take a massage and go to bed?"

I told him that I certainly did mind, that he was coming along with me and eat everything I ate and drink everything I drank so we'd arrive at the first tee in the morning in approximately the same physical condition, making due allowances, of course, for the disparity in our ages and physical equipment.

We both played some pretty sour golf but George beat me about three and two. I think he must have spiked his drinks with water.

One of my closest friends is Harvey Shaeffer. Harvey is a vintage Yale graduate and was a flier in the First World War. Originally he was in the Lafayette Escadrille, then in the regular air service. I say this realizing that if all those who claim to have flown in the Lafayette Escadrille actually flew in that group, it was a bigger organization than Hap Arnold's command in the Second World War.

Harvey is related to the Widem family, a wealthy Eastern tong which has mining interests and steel mills, and one thing and another. But although Harvey was a good student in college, when the family tried him out in a few of the brokerage offices they control or own, he couldn't seem to catch the routine. Finally they told him they were going to give him a crack at finding a buyer for a piece of Long Island real estate which belonged to the family. If he could pull it off, they'd give him ten per cent of the proceeds. Harvey fooled around with the idea for a while, but it was such a big block of ground, consisting of two or three hundred acres, that a considerable sum of money was required to swing the deal—upwards of a million dollars. Getting someone interested was no easy chore.

About that time a Mr. Thomason, a New York banker, passed on. When the proper period had elapsed after Mr. Thomason's burial, Harvey called upon Mrs. Thomason and spoke with her as follows: "Mrs. Thomason, your husband was a great citizen, one of the leading bankers of our generation, and a man of great philanthropic interests. I know you'd like to do something to embellish his memory."

"That I would," Mrs. Thomason said.

"Well," Harvey told her, "I have a two- or three-hundred-acre piece of property out in Great Neck, and I think it would be a wonderful thing if you would perpetuate Mr. Thomason's memory by buying this piece of land, developing it into a community and calling it Thomasonville. Such an enterprise certainly seems better to me," he added, "than monuments or marble or stone, or charitable foundations, or anything else you can do, if you really want to make Mr. Thomason's memory live in the hearts of his countrymen."

When Harvey enlarged upon this theme, the widow evinced more than a passing interest. When he was through, she was on the point of agreeing to go ahead with the deal. The price was to be one million and five hundred thousand dollars and Harvey's ten per cent would have amounted to one hundred and fifty thousand—a pretty good start for a young man just starting out in the real-estate business.

He bustled about, calling upon various members of the Widem family who owned parcels of the property he had arranged to sell. He was successful in obtaining clearances from all of them except two old-maid aunts who owned a small five- or six-acre section in the center of this choice piece of ground.

They stubbornly refused to sell. No amount of persuasion or talk of the extraordinary profit they would realize budged them. As a result, Harvey never could get the entire piece to sell to Mrs. Thomason. Since she wouldn't take it on any other terms, he lost the sale.

From that day, Harvey swore off work. So far as I know, he's never done a tap since. He contended that if a deal like that, which he had worked so hard to complete, fell through because of the obstinacy of two old-maid aunts, there was no point in his trying. Thenceforward, he concentrated on polo and golf, principally the latter. Encountering no mysterious brokerage routines or mulish old-maid aunts on his strolls around the links, he became a very good golfer, is rated a one- or two-handicap, and at times even scratch.

He has played a lot of friendly games with the club members at the Meadowbrook, Deepdale, and Wingfoot Clubs, but his hobby is touring with the professionals on the regular pro golf-tournament circuit. One of his relatives is very big in the rug and carpet business, a fact which will become more important as I continue Harvey's saga. On one occasion he happened to be in Texas for a San Antonio tournament. The day the tournament was to start, rainy weather deluged the vicinity. The downfall continued for a couple of days and as a result the tournament was indefinitely postponed. While waiting for the event to start, Harvey practiced pitch shots in his hotel room, lifting the ball into the wastebasket from the rug with a wedge or a nine iron. This did the rug little good. In fact, quite a bit of the nap was ripped off and the strings which held it together were exposed.

When Harvey was ready to check out, the hotel manager told him that his trunk would be held until the rug was paid for. Harvey didn't have enough cash to pick up the tab for a rug, so he wired his relative at the rug-company headquarters to send down a certain sized rug immediately. Even with all possible speed, it was a week before the rug arrived. In the meantime, Harvey was grounded in San Antonio.

But Harvey ordinarily travels light—in fact, lighter than anyone I've ever known, with the exception of Will Rogers. Will often journeyed from Los Angeles to New York with only a toothbrush and comb in his pocket. He'd buy a clean shirt and a pair of shorts in Chicago, and throw the used ones away. Then he'd do the same thing when he reached New York. This took care of Will for the entire journey.

Harvey had a little more impedimenta than that, but not much. He'd come to California for a two months' visit with a dinner jacket, a pair of dress trousers, two white shirts, a black bow tie, a pair of black oxfords, and a pair of gray flannel slacks. He'd play golf in the gray slacks and one of his white shirts, whichever one was dirtier. For evenings there was his dinner jacket and the other white shirt. This wardrobe would last Harvey throughout his entire Pacific Coast stay. And his attire was always correct, even if sometimes a little baggy.

He once nursed an anti-British phase. Why, I don't know. Perhaps he had eaten some bad marmalade, or something. He had many British friends, but he was against Britain as a nation. When his Anglophobia was gnawing away at him most corrosively, he toyed with a number of fantastic schemes to achieve their destruction.

One of his plans was to go all over the United States, collect all the used cars he could find, all the broken-down, discarded junk heaps, and have them delivered in Miami. There he would hire barges, load them with the jalopies, tow the barges into the Gulf Stream, dump the used cars and divert that ocean current from its course, so that all Englishmen would freeze to death.

Again, when the Italians invaded Ethiopia, Harvey was irate but resourceful. He devised a complicated plan for pumping out the Mediterranean and flooding the country. "We'll drown every one of them spaghetti-benders," he vowed, and he sent the blueprints to Haile Selassie. I have no record of a reply. For this, and other ingenious but impractical maritime schemes, Harvey became known as the leading oceanologist of Bayard County, Virginia. In fact the only one.

However, none of Harvey's likes or dislikes were permanent. He learned to love England for the brave stand they made in the 1940 blitz.

I was playing with Harvey in a golf tournament at Lakeside when I noticed that he had developed a case of the shanks. Golfers will recognize this term, but for the uninitiated, it is a disease which infects the short-iron game of a player. The ball, instead of being hit by the face of the club, is hit higher up where the shaft goes into the club's base. This puts a sickening spin on the pellet and sends it at right angles to the line you are trying to follow. It's caused by various things and the afflicted player is helpless unless he seeks succor from some good professional. Its cure differs according to whom you ask for advice.

The "Bandit"

Harvey was shanking all the way around the golf course, but he was putting well, so he was not scoring badly. We came to a short three-par and he hit a cold shank, but it hit a tree off to the right of the fairway, bounced back on the fairway and rolled up on the green, leaving him a three-foot putt for a birdie. "Harvey," I said, "you've certainly got the shanks bad today."

"Yeah," he said off-handedly, "but I'm timing them."

Harvey's golf nemesis was a fellow named Hank Baldwin, sometimes known as "Bandit" Baldwin. His nickname sprang from the fact that he was very adroit at making bets on the first tee and adjusting the handicaps for any match. It's my guess that throughout the years he's beaten Harvey nine-tenths of the time and accumulated a nice little savings account in the process. Harvey labored long and manfully to try to break the jinx the "Bandit" held over him. Actually, Harvey's a little better player than the "Bandit," but when they tee off and the issue is drawn, Harvey just can't seem to get his best game together and beat the "Bandit," and his best game is needed because the "Bandit" is a mighty good player himself.

In addition to his ability, the "Bandit" is very adroit at gamesmanship. For instance along about the fourth hole he would remark, "Harvey, with your physique you ought to get a lot more yardage. Why don't you get your left hand higher at the top of the swing?" or "Don't you slip some with those short spikes?" or later, "I wish you wouldn't wear those glaring white shoes. It bothers my putting." Sometimes he'd ask, "Do you exhale or inhale when you drive?"

These seem innocent observations or questions, but golf is a game of intense concentration and what the "Bandit" was trying to do was to destroy Harvey's. Harvey knew, of course, that he was being needled but that only aggravates the situation.

Once when they were both in Florida playing every day in foursomes, the "Bandit" teamed up with a great amateur-player pal of his. Harvey tried every good amateur in the state, and even imported a couple from Atlanta, for his partner, but every time the "Bandit" stuck him deep, so after taking seventeen or eighteen straight lickings and ruefully considering his dwindling sources of supply, he told the "Bandit" he was through; he was going to find a game with somebody else.

One day he went over to a Miami practice range to hit a few, and as he walked out on the tee he spotted a tall, angular, youthful chap dressed in a pair of blue serge pants, a white shirt and a little linen cap. This boy was about six-feet-two-inches tall and he couldn't have weighed more than one hundred thirty-five pounds with an anvil under each arm. He had a bag of practice balls spread out on the ground before him and he was lacing one-iron shots about two hundred and twenty yards quail-high as if they were hung on a string.

Harvey grew interested and sauntered over to watch the tall boy whistle a few more one-irons out, looking like Walter Hagen in his prime. Engaging him in conversation, Harvey discovered that he was from Boston, that he had a chronic lung condition which made it necessary for him to get away from a rigorous climate in winter and live in a more temperate one. He was holed up in a cheap motel on a very short bankroll.

"Son," said Harvey, "we are about to substantially improve both your living condition and your financial situation. Let's go get your luggage." The lad was agreeable so Harvey drove him to his motel, picked up his bags, took him to the Roney Plaza and installed him in a suite on the top floor, with instructions to the manager that the tall boy was to be incommunicado, no phone calls, no messages, and his meals to be served in his room.

Then he got the "Bandit" on the phone.

The "Bandit" was found at one of the swank beach clubs where, having lost his golf pigeon, he was engaging several elderly ladies in backgammon. Which was the "Bandit's" second-best game. In fact no less an authority than P. Hal Sims once told me Baldwin was one of the five best in the country. Of course the ladies couldn't even warm him up and he was way out in front.

When he came to the phone, Harvey said, "How about a golf game tomorrow?"

"I thought you were through with me?" the "Bandit" reminded him.

"Well," Harvey told him, "I've got to go away in a few days and I thought maybe just one more game."

"Who you got for partner this time?" the "Bandit" jeered. "Snead?"

"No," Harvey said, "just a young boy. A friend of the family's who happens to be down here in Miami. I thought I'd try him."

"I can't afford to leave this game I'm in every afternoon for a golf game unless you're prepared to make a substantial wager," the "Bandit" said.

"I might go for as much as five hundred nassau," Harvey told him. That means five hundred on each nine and five hundred on the match, with an automatic press on the back side. (Translation for non-golfers: automatic press means a doubling of the bet on the second nine holes by the one who lost on the first nine. Clear? Thought not.)

"Well, now," the "Bandit" said, "I know you must have Snead or Hogan for a partner."

"I'd like to try it just once more," Harvey said plaintively.

"Okay," said the "Bandit." "One o'clock at the Seminole Club. Bring your checkbook and your partner."

Harvey took his boy out there early and had him hit a few shots. Then they went over on the tee and waited for the "Bandit" and his partner. In due time their limousine showed. They stepped out of the car carrying their shoes and cashmeres and walked over to the tee where Harvey and his sleeper were waiting. Harvey introduced the "Bandit" and company to the young fellow.

The "Bandit" called Harvey to one side and whispered, "Now listen, you're not going out on the links with that poor fellow. He doesn't look as if he can walk eighteen holes, much less play them."

Feeling that the die had been cast and he might just as well go down swinging, Harvey said, "He'll not only walk eighteen holes but I think so much of our chances that I'll make it a thousand dollars nassau."

"Have you been drinking?" the "Bandit" asked.

"I haven't even had a smell," Harvey told him.

"And you're going to pay off if you lose?"

"Certainly. Don't I always?"

"Okay, then," the "Bandit" said. They went into the locker room, changed shoes, went back to the tee and the match began.

There were three reasonably good drives on the first hole, but the young fellow from Boston was twenty-five yards past the others. They played up to the green with two irons and the youngster took out a six-iron and whistled one up about six feet from the cup. The others putted and Harvey's partner knocked his in for a three.

Harvey and his pal were one up.

Shot-by-shot details of the match are unavailable. No golf historian covered the game, but the young fellow was out on thirty-four on the tough Seminole track on his own ball and he and Harvey stood three up. He came home in thirty-three, for a sixty-seven on himself. This performance required little aid from Harvey, so the two of them won all wagers, totaling four thousand dollars. Harvey was even for the season and out of his misery and the "Bandit" retired to the Keys to lick his wounds, to plan new and devious stratagems, and to lurk for new prey.

While the "Bandit" didn't realize it, Harvey's partner was one of the best golfers ever developed in New England. He had beaten more than one champion in eighteen-hole matches, and had won state and sectional events, but he wasn't well known since he had never won a major tournament due to his lung condition and his inability to play the thirty-six consecutive holes obligatory in the semifinals and the finals of any big amateur tournament. No less an authority than Francis Ouimet told me that he considered this fellow one of the finest strikers of the ball he'd ever seen.

To my knowledge, Harvey has never engaged the "Bandit" or his pal in a golf match again. He probably never will unless he can find his lank and talented friend once more. He'll have to wear his arm in a cast to interest the "Bandit."

Early in this chapter I observed that after the unfortunate real-estate fiasco, Harvey vowed never to work again. This must be amended because, now in his sere and yellow years, he is reclining on a small farm down in Virginia, which was a part of some of the properties belonging to his uncle's family. As a resident of the Old Dominion, he got himself appointed Postmaster of Baird, a small Virginia town of about three or four hundred souls, with the post office in back of a drug store and with a couple of wooden Indians out in front.

Harvey was proud of this appointment because, as he often boasted, he was the first Republican Postmaster that town had had since the Civil War. But, as might be imagined from his past-performance chart, Harvey's tenure of office was short-lived. He was never a great one for the details which confront any postmaster. He was accustomed to borrowing petty cash out of the drawer every once in a while and putting his personal check in to cover the shortage. A couple of postal inspectors came through town on a routine inspection trip and caught Harvey between checks. They were a little blunt about it and Harvey was so outraged that he wrote Postmaster General Frank Walker rather a sharp note. Mr. Walker answered it forthwith, indicating that if Harvey didn't like the Post Office Department's policy, he could resign. So Harvey again joined the ranks of the unemployed.

When Harvey was at Yale he was an able athlete but he never was able to make any of the teams. He was a good baseball player but his habitual lateness for practice and his other eccentricities kept him from earning a regular job. However, hearing that the team was booked for several games in the New York area with

Columbia, N.Y.U. and Fordham, Harvey really worked hard to get on the squad and to have an opportunity to show his ability in front of his New York, Long Island, and Meadowbrook buddies. He did make the squad and he was taken along on the trip, but the first day they played at Columbia, Harvey was unable to suit up because he'd brought along two shoes for the right foot. The disgusted coach sent him packing home.

During the war Harvey moved in to stay with his cousin, Raymond Guest, at Raymond's farm at Front Royal, Virginia. He had been a guest there before, in the early 1930's, when he came to spend the week end and had stayed for seven years. But this time he was to be the man in the house with Mrs. Guest, the small children, and the servants while Raymond was away doing his duty as an officer in the Navy.

After a month, Harvey came to Mrs. Guest and told her that he was forced to move. When she asked why, he said, "You make too much noise in the morning at five o'clock when you go downstairs to shake up the furnace."

Once Harvey and I were driving back from Meadowbrook after a round of golf. It was while the World's Fair was going on in New York; we saw Johnny Weissmuller billed as a star of the Aquacade there and I told Harvey that he was a pal of mine. "Why don't we go in and catch the show?" Harvey asked. I was agreeable, so we went in and saw the first show of the evening. There was a lot of swimming and water ballets, and comedy featuring the antic diving of Stubby Kruger and Weissmuller. Then, at a certain point in the show, Weissmuller took over as sort of an M.C. He described the different dives and introduced the personalities as they did their specialties from the sixty-five-foot board, or maybe it was a fifty-foot board, I don't know. Could have been a hundred-footer.

In an effort to impress Harvey, I told him I could do that kind of stuff, and added that there was nothing to it. He said, "You wouldn't go off that board at that height into that little shallow pool!"

I said, "I certainly would if someone would make it attractive enough to me financially."

"Will a hundred dollars interest you?" he asked.

"A hundred dollars absolutely fascinates me," I said, and I agreed to go off the board during the second show. After the first show we went back stage and visited Weissmuller and Kruger and the other boys we knew in the swimming dodge. I revealed my plan to Weissmuller, but to no one else.

He got me one of Stubby Kruger's comedy suits, one of those early 1900 bathing suits with the bloomers and the full sleeves and the guimpe-effect for a blouse, and a hat to match. I hid out backstage until I heard him call my name. He simply announced: "Bing Crosby of Hollywood, next diver."

I sprang blithely out on that board with my pipe in my mouth and took off. I had planned to do a plain front jack-knife but just as I left the board I fell to wondering what would happen to the pipe in my mouth—maybe when I hit the water the impact would drive it right through the back of my head—so I switched my plans in midair and went in feet first. I lost my pipe, however.

When I swam out I beat it back to Weissmuller's dressing room, where I was confronted by Billy Rose, the producer, who was in a positive snit. I imagine he had had visions of me getting hurt, Paramount suing him, unfavorable publicity, and other things of like nature.

I managed to calm him and I went on my way with Harvey, but he wouldn't pay me the hundred. He made the point that in his opinion, going in feet first didn't represent a dive, so he cut me down to sixty-five dollars. How he arrived at that precise figure I've never been able to figure out.

Now that Hope and I have got our honorable discharges from bond drives and Red Cross fund-raising, our golf still seems an easy way to earn money for worthy causes. Our game is just good enough not to make real golfers retch, and our miscues and flubs are funny enough to give non-golfers a laugh. In September of

1952 we played a match against two English opponents, Donald Peers and Ted Ray, at the Temple Golf Club in Maidenhead, England. The contest raised seven thousand and six hundred pounds for the English Playing Fields Fund.

After three or four holes the match turned into quite a block party. Maybe Hope reminded them of the loins of pork or the roasts of beef they don't see so much of these days, for when ten thousand or twelve thousand spectators planted themselves in front of us and we asked them, "How about giving us a little elbow-room; we'd like to shoot down your way," they yelled, "We don't want you to shoot! We want to look at you!"

As we ducked under and around the crush, and when we could get our breath and some attention, Hope and I essayed an occasional jocosity, but the most amusing remark of the day was made by one of our opponents, Ted Ray. Ray is an English comedian with a ready wit. At the sixth hole the gallery left us an alley only fifteen feet wide down which to drive. None of us were very expert and that sea of faces leaning over the ropes, peering down at the tee and watching us didn't make us feel more accurate.

Ray addressed his ball, waggled his club a few times and looked down the narrow lane of bodies. "Either stand back a little," he hollered, "or shut your mouths! I've had four balls swallowed today."

A London journalist, Charles Graves, wrote what seemed to me a funny story about our match. He treated it as if we were a party shooting grouse on the moors. "Hope got three," he wrote. "Crosby got a brace, but one of Crosby's was winged on the rise, which is a really sporting shot."

We did wing a few people, but, luckily, nobody was hurt. For one thing, we didn't hit the ball hard enough to injure anyone. Besides, it was a chilly day and almost everybody had on extra garments. You could fire a squirrel gun into the kind of coat called a British warm and never pink the wearer.

I think we got in eight or nine holes over a three-hour stretch, although the players were seldom simultaneously on the same hole. At the conclusion of the confusion it grieves me to record that Peers and Ray were one up, and the annual rout of the British Walker Cup team was partially avenged. My handmaiden and I want them again, though, alone and at Lakeside.

It did give me a warm feeling to know that such a great, good-natured crowd of well-wishers would journey far into the country to cheer and applaud actors from another land. Of course they say an Englishman will do practically anything to get out into the country.

That night we pulled another fifteen thousand pounds into the Playing Fields Fund with a show in a London theater. The theater deal was Hope's venture, but I did a guest appearance for him, sang a few songs and "hopped the buck" a little. Taken all in all, we thought it a pretty satisfactory day's work for a worthy cause. Every time I've even been in England, which is three, I've had a royal time, and the friendliness of the English people, their eagerness to let you know how glad they are to see you, is a very heart-warming thing to me. The hack drivers in London are just as colorful as our New York taxi jockeys, but whereas the latter are gabby and intrusive, the London jehus are taciturn and capable of remarkable understatement.

One rainy evening, on my way to dinner, I hailed a dilapidated brougham driven by a typical cockney, cloth cap pulled over his ears, a sleazy scarf knotted around his neck, a thin jacket covering his back and shoulders, and an unlit cigarette dangling from his lips. It was raining hard, the hack was leaking like a sieve, and the restaurant I sought was a far piece, so I broke the jump at one of the gentlemen's clubs en route. I told the driver I'd only be half a mo.

Well, I ran into David Niven and a few others, there were a few rounds of hot rum punch, some stories and group singing, and four hours elapsed before I emerged. I must admit, with great embarrassment, I'd forgotten all about Mr. Hack. It was still raining fiercely, and the driver was huddled morosely in his watery seat, his clothing soaked.

"Bit of a nasty evening, eh?" I said jauntily.

"Guvnor," he squeaked, "I ain't seen a bloody butterfly all evening." Such a spirited retort so impressed me I went right back in and got him a double rum punch.

I MIGHT AS WELL get my association with another sport off my chest. I don't see how I can tell my story without bringing in my passion for horseflesh. I took an unmerciful ribbing about it for years from Hope on the radio. The ribbing has abated, but I still own a few horses.

I've owned them ever since 1935. The first horse I owned was Zombie, a steed of peerless lineage but dubious ability that I bought from Jock Whitney when he was racing in California. I became interested in racing because I'd bought stock in the Santa Anita track.

A peculiar thing about the promotion of Santa Anita was that so far as I know Hal Roach, who was one of the founders, and myself were the only Hollywood or Los Angeles people who bought stock. Nobody could envision even a partial chance of success for such a venture, located in, of all places, far-away Arcadia. I don't know what inspired Hal's confidence, but I certainly can't claim to be clairvoyant. I only went in so I could be sure of a box seat on the finish line. They finally raised the greater part of the money in San Francisco or the East and, of course, the success achieved by this plant is now a fabulous legend. I think for a ten thousand dollar investment, I must have gotten back at least one hundred thousand dollars and the ten thousand dollar block of stock is now worth fifty thousand dollars. Call me lucky, indeed! And I still have a nice box on the finish line.

Also I met a famous ex-jock, Albert Johnson, from my part of the country—the Pacific Northwest. As a young jock, Johnson had gone East in the fabulous 1920's. A very popular, grinning, free-handed, cigar smoking kid, he more than held his own with Earl Sande and La Verne Fator, greatest riders in the country, then or since. He won the Kentucky Derby of 1922 with the California horse Morvich, many stakes with the immortal Exterminator, probably got his biggest thrill and certainly won a fortune the fall afternoon he won both parts of the 1922 Pimlico Futurity with E. R. Bradley's Blossom Time, and Sally's Alley, belonging to W. S. Kilmer.

But he'd retired from riding and wanted to go into the training end. I put him in charge of my one-horse stable. Only, like most one-horse stables, it ballooned to twenty-one horses before I was through.

I was to find out that even for people who put lots of money into it racing is a parlous thing—almost a pure gamble. Heavy financial outlay doesn't necessarily produce winners. One big manufacturing family is an example. They've had horses for years and years and have spent millions on the family stable, but as far as I know, they have never produced a truly great horse. Although it wasn't because they didn't buy the nucleus of a good stable or what seemed the foundation for a successful stud farm. On the other hand, a man named Charlie Howard claimed a horse named Seabiscuit for $7,500. It was one of racing's all-time bargains. Howard came East and bought him in August 1936, while the races were on at Saratoga. The horse was then three years old, and improved almost over-night. The next year he won $168,580; the total lifetime winnings were $437,730. His most sensational victory was when he beat Samuel Riddle's War Admiral in their match race at Pimlico in 1938. Seabiscuit proved to be one of the top money-winning horses of all time! That's how lucky you can be in racing.

On one occasion a friend of mine brought a horse out from New York called Black Forest. He was a well-bred horse from Colonel Bradley's Idle Hour Farm. He had been a stirring performer as a two-year-old but a training accident had led to his enforced retirement. When he arrived at Santa Anita as a four-year-old, he'd been inactive for about a year and a half. He had a pair of suspicious-looking knees, but my friend was convinced that he really could run. After watching several morning workouts, I was convinced that my friend knew what he was talking about.

I loaned my friend a couple of thousand dollars for a half-interest in the horse. We were going to wait for a spot with Black Forest and try to win a bundle the first time out. It was late in the year; the rainy season came on and for the rest of the Santa Anita meeting the track was muddy. My friend didn't want to take a chance on Black Forest's tricky knees in the mud; he was afraid that he might break down, so Black Forest never did get a chance to run at Santa Anita.

However, the Bay Meadows meeting was coming up near San Francisco. We figured we'd van Black Forest up there and see what we could do. If you've got a horse that runs good in the morning, it isn't long before all the clockers know it. The clockers tell the handicappers. The handicappers tell the tip sheets. And the first time your horse goes to the post, it's become a good thing and you don't get much of a price.

So we kept Black Forest over at the county fair grounds at Pleasanton. We hired an exercise boy and galloped our horse, cleaned him, and kept him in shape until a spot came up at Bay Meadows where we thought we could win a bet.

Our plan was to bring him over on race day and turn him loose. At last a race came up which suited our fancy. We had people betting for us in New York, New Jersey, Chicago, New Orleans—all over the country. The day of the race dawned bright and sunny. The track was fast. Everything was perfect for our coup. Black Forest won, all right, by about fifteen lengths, but he paid only ten cents on the dollar, the smallest price the mutuels are allowed to pay.

Pleasanton Fair Grounds had not been such a secluded training area as we'd thought. Somebody had gotten the word about our horse and had passed it on. I think everybody in the United States had something down on him that day.

After I went into a racing and training partnership with Lin Howard, the son of Charles Howard—we called our stable the Bing-Lin stable—we imported a sprinter named Preceptor from the Argentine.

He was a real handy horse at either three-quarters or seven-eighths of a mile. He'd carried big weights in the Argentine and had defeated the fastest sprinters in that country and in Brazil. We ran him a few times in California. He either won or came close, but actually he was under wraps most of the time.

Then we took him east to Baltimore for a big handicap at Pimlico and got Buddy Hass to ride him. We were prepared to make a sizable bet, because the field was made up of the best sprinters in the East. This meant that the winner would pay a big price.

There was, however, a catch. Our horse had a habit of lugging in. When he was about a sixteenth of a mile from the finish, if a horse came alongside him, between him and the rail, he tried to rest his weight on the other horse to keep him from getting by. This is one of the reasons why we had Buddy Hass ride him, for Buddy could whip with his left hand. If our horse tried to lug in, he could whip him on that side, pull away from the horse on the rail and prevent a foul.

Preceptor started at nine to one and took the lead at the eighth pole. At the sixteenth post another horse came up on his inside. Preceptor started to lug him when Hass, anticipating such a move, batted him a few left-handed ones with his whip, got him straightened out before any harm was done and he went on to win. To my amazement, the jockey on the other horse claimed a foul. Preceptor was placed down to second and we lost our money.

However this sort of thing can work both ways.

Two weeks later we took him up to Narragansett to run him in the Blackstone Valley handicap. The odds on Preceptor shaped up at about two or three to one, so we figured that because of his lugging in and the chance of a foul, we'd better not bet on him. Instead, we'd just run him for the purse, which was in the neighborhood of twenty-five thousand dollars.

This time at the eighth pole a horse named Olney went to the front. Preceptor started coming up along the inside and closing ground on him. Our jockey was an excitable Cuban, Ruperto Donoso, and as Preceptor ran up alongside of Olney, Olney crossed over in front of him. It wasn't a foul by any means, but Donoso stood straight up in his stirrups as if he'd been sloughed something awful by the other horse. Everybody in the stands laughed at Donoso's antics. It was obvious that Olney was the better horse, that he would have won easily anyhow, and that no foul had been committed. However, as soon as he had unsaddled and weighed in, Donoso went up to the judge's stand and raised a beef, claiming that he'd been fouled.

To our slack-jawed surprise, the judges took Olney's number down and declared Preceptor the winner.

I'd gotten into racing on the cheap side, which decreased my chances of having a notable array of winners. And when Hope began to kid me about it on the air, it became legend that my horses were dogs. I played along with this for laughs, since laughs are hard to come by. Hope is always short of good material, and if my horses supplied him with a little radio fodder it was all right with me. My horses co-operated too.

My partner, Lin, claimed Hope's bum raps for our horses hurt our market. We planned to sell the colts we raised, and Lin said bitterly, "It's hard to sell them if you and Hope go on the air week after week and laugh at them." Lin and I brought a four-year-old horse named Ligaroti from the Argentine and raced him at Santa Anita. But he was fresh from a seventy-seven-day trip on a slow freighter and he wasn't himself. The following summer we took him to Hollywood Park, where he won every stake that track offered for older horses—among them the Sunset Handicap and the American Handicap—and he knocked down prizes of twenty-five thousand to thirty-five thousand dollars.

Encouraged by his success, we imported more horses, among them a couple of pretty good mares. One of these lassies, Etolia II, won the Vanity Handicap at Hollywood Park. Our other feminine importee, Barrancosa, won two or three handicaps around California. Then we sent her East, where she dead-heated for first place in the Beldame Handicap with Mr. Woodward's Vagrancy, which was considered the best mare of that year. The Beldame is the top Eastern race for fillies and mares three years and up.

We also had Don Mike, who won two or three big handicaps in California. Ligaroti's half-brother, Don Bingo, won the big race at Belmont Park, the Suburban Handicap. But the non-racing public didn't hear much about these successes. Wins don't make for funny talk on the radio.

I liked to name horses after my friends. One was Madam La-Zonga, in honor of Jimmy Monaco's song of that title. Another was Midge, in honor of Midge Polesie, a valued friend of long standing of the Crosby family. When Midge Polesie and her husband, Herb, of "Twenty Questions" fame, heard that I was writhing in the throes of composing this autobiography, they rallied around with helpful hints and notes about anecdotes and incidents in my life they feared I'd forgotten.

The little filly Midge was very helpful to me, too. Albert Johnson thought she had a good chance when she was scheduled to run in a five-and-a-half-furlong race at Hollywood Park. The date was July 25, 1939. Although I was never given to large betting, I thought I'd splurge on this one. So I sent a good-sized bet out with a friend. But the friend developed a puncture driving out to the track and didn't get to the race in time.

You know the pay-off. Midge won and paid a hatful. With Lester Balaski in the saddle, she not only won but established a new track record by running the five and a half furlongs in 1:05:4. And I didn't have a dime on the nag.

Midge was never heard of after that. She was set out to foal a new generation of losers. I'm talking of Midge the filly, of course. Midge Polesie for whom the horse was named is still around and as I've said, is still a good friend, although she can't do five and a half furlongs any more.

Among other things, I genuinely tried to improve the breed of California racing. I bought and developed a ranch at Rancho Santa Fe and went at it earnestly until I sold my interest in the Del Mar race track, my home and ranch nearby, and almost all my horses.

I'd got interested in the front-office end of racing when Santa Anita opened in December of 1934. Bill Quigley, a California racing official, came to me and said that the directors of the Twenty-Second Agricultural District of San Diego County, California, wanted us to form a group to put on racing at Del Mar in San Diego County. It takes a lot of money to build a race track, but the Agricultural District people said they'd supply the coin and give us a lease on the plant.

Quigley and I formed a jockey club, made financial commitments and began to build a racing plant, only to find that the Agricultural District couldn't get up the money. We went in hock for it ourselves and eventually got the place built. The Agricultural District helped by taking a lease on it, and over a period of years that rent paid us back what we'd put into it.

However, at the outset, it was very tough going, and we lost money for a season and a half. Also, we were roundly criticized for our choice of a site. Actually, Del Mar isn't a very good site unless it can hold races in July and August, for, with the exception of those two months, not many people go there. In winter the track is a quagmire if it rains. When those Southern California monsoons come along, that part of the country gets so muddy at times that if only a few more drops of moisture are added, horses, jockeys, and spectators carry snorkels.

To add to our difficulties, it was hard to get good horses to ship there. When the Eastern horses were through at Santa Anita or Hollywood Park, they were sent East for the summer season at Saratoga and Belmont Park, Aqueduct, Jamaica, and Empire City. We were in a bit of a box. Without good horses, it was difficult to pull a big attendance. Without a sizable attendance, the mutuel handle looked like a dice game in the caddy yard.

But gradually we began to build interest and by slugging away on publicity gimmicks and other devices it began to be quite popular. Saturday nights we served big dinners and put on shows at the Turf Club. For those dinners we imported bands and such artists as Louis Armstrong and Wingy Manone, or maybe John Scott Trotter would portage in a Dixieland group.

And we brought down picture people from Hollywood like Charlie Butterworth, Pat O'Brien, Ken Murray, Bob Hope, Connee Boswell, Jerry Colonna and Phil Silvers. The shows were impromptu. Any of my buddies from tinsel town who happened to be on deck would get up and do his stuff ad lib. The fun might last four or five hours. It might go on till dawn. One morning about five o'clock Wingy Manone was playing "Muskrat Ramble" when a committee of trainers came over from the stables to complain that the strains of his horn were disturbing the horses. They were shagging and Lindy Hopping around their stalls and losing their rest, just like people.

Buster Keaton was one guest who got up and did an act for us. Being a comic of the old school, Buster had a routine of taking sensational falls from the piano or from anything handy, but he knew how to take them so it would look as if he were almost killing himself. Actually, he was breaking his falls with his wrists or his elbows, and was suffering no injury. Pat O'Brien decided to emulate Keaton and cut himself in on the applause.

Charlie Butterworth, whose dead-pan delivery and dehydrated wit made him—to me at least—one of the funniest actors who ever lived, watched him for a while, then said, "You'd better get that O'Brien out of here. He's breaking his falls with his veins."

A story about Phil Silvers has to do with an episode at the ranch when we Crosbys were located at Rancho Santa Fe and the four boys were scaled down in age from ten to six. They used to play softball all the time in the back yard. The house was a rambling Spanish adobe with a porch that went all around the place. There were always so many arguments during these ball games about who was out or safe or whose turn it was at bat or balls and strikes and one thing or another, that we finally established a rule that any one of them who become unmanageable or beefed too much would have to go sit in a dark corner on the porch with his back to the game until he'd served his time.

One afternoon we were having a big game in which Silvers was playing. He's a great baseball fan and rather fancies himself as an old one-old-cat player from Bronxville. I was called into the house for a long-distance telephone call. I was gone quite a while and when I came out the four younger Crosbys had Phil sitting in a dark corner on the porch. And the game was going merrily on without him. He emerged from that experience a thoroughly chastened man.

One of the greatest days we had at Del Mar was the match race between Seabiscuit and Ligaroti. Lin Howard and I owned Ligaroti and Lin's father owned Seabiscuit, and there was a great deal of argument back and forth about which was the better horse. Ligaroti had won five or six straight stake races at Hollywood Park. Seabiscuit had been East and hadn't participated in that particular meeting, so they hadn't met. We finally matched them at a mile and an eighth. There was no mutuel betting, but there was a purse and the customers could bet among themselves. Lin and I had a bet with his father and we had bets with other Seabiscuit backers.

Georgie Wolfe rode Seabiscuit and Speck Richardson was up on Ligaroti. They broke together and went by the stands head and head.

The crowd began to yell the moment the horses broke and they never stopped yelling all the way around. Lin and I had organized a rooting section with Ligaroti sweaters and little caps with Ligaroti printed on them and pennants bearing the same name. It was quite an affair.

They turned for home head and head, and they finished that way with both jockeys batting at each other with their whips and grabbing at each other's saddle cloths. At the wire the picture showed Seabiscuit a winner by a whisker. Although there has always been a dispute as to whether that picture was read properly.

Be that as it may, they broke every track record en route. They broke the record for the half mile, the three-quarter mile, the mile, and the mile and an eighth.

They both carried one hundred twenty-six pounds and it was a fabulous performance for two horses carrying that weight.

There was an awful stew about the jockeys' deportment and track manners. The judges claimed that our jockey was at fault. They ruled him off for thirty days and gave him a fine, which we paid. But they didn't know that I had had a movie of the race made and I ran it off for Mr. Howard. In the film it was clear that Richardson was no more to blame than Georgie Wolfe. Nothing will be gained by post morteming about which jock hit the other horse across the nose with his whip, thus starting the fracas. But once it started, they both grabbed clothing and saddle blankets, and from the sixteenth pole home it was a melee, a pier sixer on horseback.

We lost the race and lost the money. But to see two fine horses put on performances like that was worth the money. It is certainly one of my most treasured memories of Del Mar.

However, in the end the Del Mar deal became a burdensome chore. Bill Quigley passed away and much of his work—he was the one who had done most of it—fell on me. Never one to relish responsibility or work, my course was obvious. The chance came for me to get out, not only with the money I'd put in but with a profit, so I sold. My mother still has a little of that stock and my kids have some of it, a token amount, just enough to entitle them to a box in the grandstand and a Turf Club badge.

As it turned out, I would have made a lot more money if I'd waited. Del Mar has been more successful since I left than while I was a part-owner.

To me, a race track is for people who can afford to go there once in a while for an enjoyable afternoon of watching good horseflesh compete and who are reconciled to losing the kind of money they won't miss. If they win, good; they can buy dinner for the group. But anybody who goes to the races thinking he'll make money is kidding himself. If he continues to go day after day and bet day after day, he'll get clobbered.

Over the years I've met and known hundreds of horse-players. Keen fellows, smart fellows, who know every angle around the race tracks, and with access to any and all information. They have affluent periods, it's true, but most of the time they're flat broke. The percentage alone will eat the player up, even if he backs a reasonable amount of winners. Go to the races, yes, but go because you love the sport; don't go to make money. It can't be done.

Hope calls a race track a horse-drawn vacuum cleaner. And then there's the old truism: you can beat a race, but you can't beat the races.

I bet, of course, but I've backed my own horses and wagered just enough on them to make it interesting. But I never let myself get into the habit of "doubling up to get even." That's the route to insolvency.

I commend the following stories to those who are knuckle-headed enough to believe that racing results can be consistently figured with any degree of accuracy—even by "those in the know."

Most people think that because a man is a race-track official he "knows something." As president of Del Mar, "Where the turf meets the surf," I knew as little as anybody there. One day my father and mother were in my box. I gave them seven straight losers before they paid no more attention to my advice. Although they never bet more than two dollars on a horse, like all horse players they hated to lose. My mother was giving me "the solid eye," a look that meant "go away, you and your tips."

At this point, a friend of theirs, named Rocco Vocco, spotted a kid who knew his way around the race tracks. For a small fee the kid gave Roc a tip on a fifty-to-one shot named Star Simon, and Roc passed it along to Mother and Dad. When I heard about it I laughed loud and long and gave my folks the "logical winner." I bet on this horse myself, but my folks put their deuces on their tip.

After the race nobody laughed except Ma and Pa Crosby, for Star Simon won and paid one hundred eight dollars.

As I've said, my friend Harvey Shaeffer owns a little piece of ground in Virginia. On this Old Dominion farm he raised a horse or two. He got a brood mare from the Widem family and persuaded the owner of a local stallion to let him breed her. The result of this breeding was a horse he called Dreamboat. When Dreamboat was two years old, Harvey decided to ship him to California, along with some polo ponies which were traveling with members of the Meadowbrook Club to engage in contests with the Midwick Polo Team.

I was there when Dreamboat was unloaded from the horse car. A more cadaverous, jug-headed, fumble-footed bag of bones I've never seen. He hadn't stood the trip well. A hat thrown at him would have hung on any number of places. As I saw it, Harvey was wasting his money shipping the animal to Santa Anita and engaging stable room and paying for hay, exercise boys, and trainers' fees. But Harvey was supremely confident that the venture would turn out well. He put the horse in the hands of a Kentucky hardboot who was training a public stable at Santa Anita that year.

Harvey had graciously consented to make me a member of the syndicate he'd assembled to defray his horse's expenses. The syndicate would also participate in the profits, if any, of his racing venture. Needless to say, I consented *before* I saw Dreamboat unloaded from the train.

The horse arrived a couple of months before the Santa Anita opening. He was put in training, was given slow galloping every day and was finally brought up to breezes. He began to look as if he could run a bit but it was hard to find a race for him; that is, a race in which the conditions would be favorable enough to give him a chance. I thought Harvey ought to wait for a race consisting of the worst maidens at the track, so we could bet with confidence. But no such race was in the books and Harvey finally entered Dreamboat in a claiming race with horses worth three thousand dollars.

At that time, horses worth that much money were considered pretty shifty and hard to beat. So Dreamboat's assignment looked an impossible one.

Harvey had written to the other members of the syndicate in the East, telling them that when they saw the horse start to go ahead and bet on him. But the night before the race, one of those torrential California downpours inundated the countryside and the track was a quagmire. Dreamboat had never been asked to run in the mud in a workout. In fact, so far as we knew, he had never even stepped in a puddle. That, plus the fact that he was up against a difficult field, discouraged Harvey and me and we refrained from betting. We thought we'd watch Dreamboat run and we'd bet on him the next time if he showed promise.

The distance was a mile and an eighth, which is a long race to ask of a maiden on his first time out. Dreamboat broke sluggishly and as he came by the stands the first time he was approximately a sixteenth of a mile out of it. Going into the first turn he dropped a little further behind, but down the back stretch he picked up a horse or two and when the field turned toward home, there was Dreamboat splashing down the middle of the track, looking for all the world like Discovery.

While Harvey and I sat in the grandstand without a quarter

on him, he won by six or eight lengths and paid one hundred eighty-six dollars for a two dollar bet.

Trying to console Harvey, I told him, "We'll look for a soft spot next week. Although we won't get much of a price, we'll at least get the purse and we can bet on him a little." Harvey agreed, but to my surprise, a couple of weeks later I found Dreamboat entered in an even harder race than the first one. This time he was up against horses worth seven thousand five hundred dollars or five thousand dollars—horses that had been winning regularly at the track.

When Harvey came up into the grandstand box after saddling our horse I said, "Well, son, you've done it this time. You're going to break that horse's heart, running him with horses of this class."

"Don't worry," he said. "He'll break *their* hearts."

"You're not betting on him in this field, are you?" I asked.

"I'm going for fifty dollars across the board," he said firmly.

"Well," I said, "I can save you a long trip downstairs to the mutuel windows. Just put that one hundred fifty dollars in my pocket. I'll book it."

It sounds like the tag of a many-times-told horse-betting joke, I know, but Dreamboat just walked his beat and paid thirty-eight dollars. I had to pay off to Harvey. It was no joke.

As the meet went on, Dreamboat won two or three more races. They were always over a distance ground, and each time he jumped up in class to a point where I didn't consider it wise to back him. So I never cashed a ticket on him. He wound up running third in the San Juan Capistrano handicap, a race at a mile and five-eighths for handicap horses, behind two of the outstanding stake performers in the country. After that he became touched in the wind and Harvey was forced to retire him.

Dreamboat certainly fooled me. Even when he was racing his best he never looked any better than the day he arrived in California. He was a very unprepossessing horse but a horse who knew how to run through sheer instinct—or powered by some indefinable element called class.

Harvey had quite a few horses after Dreamboat. They were all of peerless lineage, coming from his uncle's mares and studs, but Harvey never raced them on the "big apple"—the major tracks. Instead, he preferred the "leaky roof" circuit—minor-league tracks where the going was a little easier. He had a steed named Oom Paul whom he campaigned around for several years with some success. One day he had Paul in a real good spot at Timonium, and, arriving late without his spectacles, and being reluctant to buy a program for one race, he asked a fellow what number Oom Paul was on the card.

"Number Five," was the reply.

Harvey hustled over and bought three one hundred dollar tickets on Number Five and then went down to the rail to watch his animal go to the post. What was his consternation when old Oom came prancing by with a big Number Two on his saddle cloth. Number Five was Boom All. Harvey swears Oom even winked at him. He rushed back to the mutuel window and tried to sell his tickets but it was a light day and no go. Of course, Oom walked in and paid nineteen dollars for two dollars.

One of the first colts I ever bought was sired by Mars, a son of Man o' War. Among my golfing friends in those days were Ford Palmer, who'd been a great end at Southern California, and Marshall Duffield, a great ex-USC quarterback. As a gesture of friendship to them, I named the colt Fight On, after the University of Southern California fight song.

Fight On worked well, but as luck would have it, the day of his first race—three furlongs—the track came up muddy. In the paddock, Albert Johnson, who'd trained him for me, told me that he wouldn't advise me to bet. He never worked the horse in the mud and didn't know if he could stand up in that kind of going. So I risked nothing on Fight On's chances. But Duffield and Palmer were with me, and although I did my best to dissuade them, they felt sentimentally obligated to have some kind of a bet. After all he *was* named after their school's song. So they each went for ten on the untried two-year-old.

Fight On got out of the gate on top and came down to the wire in a driving finish, leading a cluster of three or four other horses to the wire. He won by a distended nostril and paid two hundred forty-two dollars for two dollars. Like all race followers with a bet on a horse in a close one, Duffield and Palmer leaned instinctively toward the finish line and waved their arms in that direction to pull their horse in. After the race they told me accusingly that I'd applied my body English the other way, and that I'd waved Fight On back because I couldn't stand seeing him win with nothing on his nose. Since then, when I've been to the Coliseum to see a football game and the Trojan band breaks into the Fight Song, I wince.

Albert Johnson told me a story about Colonel Bradley that I've never forgotten. The Colonel had a sensational two-year-old. He brought this phenom back to New York for the spring racing season and entered him in an over-night allowance race for two-year-olds. He'd been telling his friend, Harry Sinclair, what a great horse he had, and Sinclair, thinking that he'd been let in on a good thing, arranged for large sums to be bet on the Colonel's hopeful all over the country.

While Johnson was with the Bradley horse in the paddock, the Colonel told him, "Mr. Sinclair's sitting in my box. He has sizable wagers on this horse and I'd like to give him a little thrill. Don't let the horse win too easily. You and I know he's probably the best two-year-old in the world and that there's no question but what he should win as he pleases in this field. But if Mr. Sinclair's going to make a killing, I'd like to see him sweat a little."

"O.K.," Johnson said, "I'll draw it a little fine."

The field was small. Only four or five horses were entered in it. It was a short race—six furlongs—and the Bradley horse went right to the front. After a quarter of a mile Johnson thought he'd let out a wrap and really let his mount run. As he did, another horse came up beside him and the other jockey let out a wrap too. At the half mile, Johnson let out some more wraps, but the second horse still stayed with him. When they turned for home, Albert went for his bat, but the other horse wouldn't be shaken loose. They thundered to the finish line as a team, with Albert shipping and doing his best and the other jockey doing the same.

There was a delay before the winner was announced, but the final decision was that the Bradley horse had finished first. Bradley sent for Johnson after the race and gave him a dressing down. "I asked you to make it close," he said, "but not that close. You might have blown the race. I thought Mr. Sinclair was going to have a stroke." Johnson tried to convince the Colonel that he had been doing his best and so had the horse, but he couldn't sell that idea then or afterward, no matter how hard he tried.

"How much was Mr. Sinclair betting?" Johnson asked Colonel Bradley.

The Colonel replied, "A quarter of a million dollars!" and it was Johnson's turn to almost have a stroke.

Johnson told me that it was the last time Colonel Bradley ever told him to "make it close." Whenever the Colonel put him up on a horse after that, his instructions were, "Go to the front and improve your position."

As most of the habitués of night clubs know, Joe Frisco, the stuttering comedian, is an inveterate, even an incurable, horse player. Once Joe and his buddy were rooming together in Hollywood in a furnished room. Their luck had gone from bad to worse. They were down to five dollars between them. It was nearing Christmas, and his buddy said, "We're not going to bet this five dollars on a horse race. Let's spend it on something with a little Christmas spirit. In the window of the delicatessen down the street there's a beautiful turkey with all the trimmings. It's cooked. It's ready to serve. It costs five dollars. You go down and get the turkey," he continued. "I'll get some plates and knives and forks from Mrs. O'Leary down the hall. I'll get a couple of bottles of beer from the saloon downstairs—they'll trust me—and we'll have a nice Christmas dinner."

Joe said, "O.K.," took the fin and departed for the delicatessen. But the store was six or seven blocks away, and en route he passed a room where they were betting horses. Entries from all over the country were posted on blackboards, and a loud-speaker was giving the results of each race. Joe stuck his head in to see if there was anybody in there he knew, and having done that, he stepped in to see what the prices were on the horses. Lo and behold, he found a horse entered at a Florida track which owed him a little money because of unhappy bets he'd made on him in the past.

The race was starting in five minutes. The horse would pay about five to one, and Joe had visions of a twenty-five-dollar profit. He couldn't resist. He bought a five-dollar-win ticket on this horse. It wasn't long before the loud-speaker said, "They're off in the fourth." Joe's horse was in front. He was in front down the back stretch. He was in front coming home. Then the loud-speaker said, "Here are the winners," and it announced three other horses. Joe's horse had quit at the wire. Joe went back to the apartment and opened the door.

His roommate looked at him and asked, "Where's the turkey?"

Joe said, "Th-th-th-the turkey's still in the stretch."

Not long ago Joe took a job in a San Mateo club. Knowing his affinity for the turf, I'm sure the big inducement was that he could be near the Bay Meadows Race Track. When he'd been there a few weeks, I talked to him on the phone and asked him how he was making out with the nags.

He said that it had been murder, and that he hadn't had a winning day since the meet opened, but yesterday he'd gone real good.

"What happened?" I asked.

"I g-g-got a ride home," he replied.

I've staked Joe quite a few times. Whenever he saw me at Santa Anita he touched me for five or ten. It always seemed worth while because I knew I'd get some laughs out of it. On one occasion I got to the track early to find Joe waiting for me at the Turf Club entrance.

"Bing," he asked, "can you l-l-let me ha-ha-have twenty bucks?"

"That's quite a large sum, Joe," I said. "Why so much this time?"

"I have the Singing Kid's markings," he said. "He never gave them to me before and he's been awful h-h-hot at this meet and I think I'm going to have a real good day if I just get a start, and I need about twenty bucks."

I gave him the twenty dollars, three or four races went by, and the news began to come up from the grandstand. "Joe Frisco is riding a big streak. He's had four straight winners. Parlayed them all. He's won six or seven hundred dollars and he's buying wine for everybody at the bar."

I thought I'd go down and see if this was true, but something interfered and two or three races went by before I started. On the way I bumped into a friend.

"That Frisco," he said, "he hasn't had a loser. He's had them all on the nose. He's parlaying them, relaying them every which way—round robins and everything else. He must have twelve or fifteen hundred dollars in his kick."

There he was in the grandstand bar, surrounded by thirty or forty admirers. Not only was he buying drinks, he was playing the big-hearted Otis and giving this pal five and that pal ten. I went up to him and eyed him suggestively, as if asking, "How about my twenty?" He looked at me, said, "Hi ya, kid," and went right ahead with his Mister Bountiful routine.

"Joe," I said, "how about—er—you know?"

He peeled off twenty, and said, "Here kid. Here's t-t-t-twenty dollars. Sing me a chorus of 'Melancholy Baby.'" I was so taken aback I sang it.

If I'm around when vaudeville actors, or show business people get together in the cool, cool, cool of the evening for a little anecdotal one-old-cat, I'm a cinch to hear still more stories about Joe. I offer here a couple of my favorite Frisco memorabilia which might not be too shop-worn, although—for a wonder—they have no bearing on horses or racing. I'll get back to horses later.

The first story has to do with The Paris-Louvre, a bistro in San Francisco. As its name implies, it features palatable provender in the shape of French cuisine. Crêpes Suzette are the *spécialité du maison*. They are served with flair and typical French showmanship. Their production features a Captain of Waiters and his chafing-dish, and two or three underlings, stoking and re-fueling the spirit lamps and carrying flaming delicacies from table to table.

I barged in there one night with Joe. Finding it crowded, we draped ourselves tastefully along the bar. The bartender asked what we would have.

"G-G-Gimme a Benedictine," Joe said, stutteringly, "and t-t-turn up the radio."

While we were having our drink, Joe watched the pyrotechnic display staged by the staff members who were serving the Crêpes Suzette. He seemed fascinated. Every few minutes a blue blaze broke out over some table. We heard the sizzling of brandy, the butter, and the pancakes. After a bit the Headwaiter came up to us and asked Joe if he wanted a table.

"N-N-No," said Joe, "I-I-I j-j-just came to get warm."

The second bit of Friscoiana is about another famous San Francisco restaurant, but since it is necessary to portray its proprietor as a little on the bibulous side, I'll call it Tom's place. The proprietor is of foreign extraction. He has a heavy accent, and an unquenchable thirst for the product his own bartender purveys. I've been going there since 1930, and I've always had a good time. It's a commodious place. There are always plenty of empty tables or booths and I don't have to wait. The food is good. The bar is stocked with excellent scotches and bourbons and there is a fine wine cellar. It's a spot where you can do as you please. You can wander about, visit the bar, dance a little, play the drums, sing, drop into the kitchen, watch chefs at work, or peer into the icebox and feel the meat, the turkeys, or the pheasant. In fact, it is a typical tavern of the *laissez faire* type. It's never necessary to make a reservation. Go there at any hour and Tom will take care of you—if he's still on his feet.

One evening I introduced a party of ten or twelve to Tom's place, including Joe Frisco. We had some drinks and a nice dinner. The clients that night were all the friendly type, and they wanted a song or two, so Joe and I put on a little floor show. I sang schottisches for Joe to dance, and Joe sang for me to dance. We sang duets, and told a lot of stories—I was Joe's straight man —and we managed to amuse ourselves wonderfully, with some encouragement from the other patrons.

After a while we went to the bar to quench the thirst our strenuous efforts had brought on. It wasn't long before Tom joined us. "Joe," he asked my erstwhile partner, "how you lika worka for me?"

"N-N-No thanks," said Joe, "I'm b-b-booked solid."

Tom was not to be so easily put off. "I give you engagement six weeks long," he told Joe.

"N-N-No, Tom," said Joe. "I just can't handle it right now— I got to get b-b-back to Los Angeles."

Tom pleaded for ten or fifteen minutes but Joe turned him down, with various excuses. Finally Tom pointed to me and said, "Joe, I tella you what—you come to work for me, I even take-a this other fella too."

Joe got a big jar out of this. He asked Tom if he knew who I was. Tom said, "No."

This really fractured Joe, and we left Tom standing bewildered by the bar and went back to the table to tell them of our little experience with Tom.

Some weeks later I was back in Hollywood and picked up one of the trade papers—*The Hollywood Reporter*—and saw an item where Joe Frisco had been booked into Tom's Rendezvous as a single. I shot Joe a wire immediately, as follows: "False friend, eh? You took it without me." I got a wire back from Joe the next day, saying, "After I told Tom who you were he weakened on you."

I've been back to Tom's Rendezvous several times since, but he gives no indication that he remembers any part of the whole deal. Maybe it's better that way—I might get an engagement there yet.

E VERY MAN'S LIFE is the result of what happens when his life touches the lives of others, and many people have influenced my life in one way or another. Sometimes, like Jack Kapp, of Decca Records, they've helped me achieve things I never would have accomplished otherwise. Others have made life more stimulating, and have run up the score on the lighter side instead of the somber side.

No story about me would be complete without some mention of five men whose lives have touched mine in one of those ways: Joe Venuti, the Fabulous Fiddler of Paul Whiteman's band; John Scott Trotter, the papa of my radio-musical family; Bill Morrow, who has guided my radio fortunes and has been my companion on many a junket; Tod Johnson, my tax-man, who handles the intricate and sometimes extremely delicate matters in this field; and John O'Melveny, who has kept me solvent and has thereby made possible Bob Hope's heavy-handed jesting about my being a human Fort Knox.

Everybody knows I've made a lot of money out of show business, but the fact that I've been able to save any of it is directly due to O'Melveny's guiding hand and his astute management. Jack is a genial and expansive Irishman. He's been at the helm of my fitfully tossing career ship for some twenty years now. Every penny I've made, after taxes, he has taken and has husbanded carefully. In some cases he has not only husbanded them but has increased them appreciably. For instance, he tells me that the income from my oil leases alone would take care of me comfortably for the rest of my life.

I have no intention of larding this story up with an interminable summary of my assorted business enterprises, even though they are extensive if not always successful. Among other things, I'm interested in a frozen orange-juice agency, a national ice cream-distributing setup, a production company turning out TV short films, and a project which is the brain child of Brother Everett and which bears the coy name, Bing's Things. There's also a corporation called the Bing Crosby Enterprises, set up as a catch-all for the capital gains made by the various endeavors in which I have a finger or to which I've lent my name. Some of these capers have made a little money, some have lost. I'm active also in two different partnerships: one with Pat Doheny, the other with R. Hope and Monty Moncrief (a Texas golfing pal) in the leasing and drilling of oil lands. Pat and Monty are oil men with long records of success in their field, and I leave my end of the oil business in their capable hands.

I even have business interests I know nothing about. For instance, Dennis O'Keefe, touring in Europe, sent me a card of the Ristorante "Bing Crosby" located in Firenze, Italy. He said the restaurant was so identified by a giant sign in front, and pictures of me, in various poses, around its walls. Next time I am abroad I must drop in the Ristorante "Bing Crosby" and try to get a cup of chianti on the cuff.

A lot of people in show business, and for all I know, other people as well, seem firm in their belief that I am one of the co-owners of the Decca Company or am at least a holder of a large block of stock. This is partially true. I once owned some stock in Decca, but not now. Sometime in the late 1930's—I don't recall the exact year—I had a brainstorm and decided I should own some stock in the outfit for which I was making so many records, so I bought quite a parcel at around thirty dollars a share. My advisers were horrified and not without cause because I disposed of it not too long ago at eight dollars a share, a considerable loss. In fact, about two hundred thousand dollars worth. But that's the way it goes. You make a little here and lose a little there. Candidly, my royalties from the company have amounted to a lot more than that, but that was my one and only adventure in the stock market, and I promise it'll be my last.

As long as I am mopping up the business department of my narrative, I might mention the Pittsburgh Pirates, in which club I've invested a bundle of what the financial lads call "venture money." It's my fervent hope that the Pittsburgh fans will be rewarded for their long-suffering patience with a team of which they can be proud. Hurry, day! In a careless moment I promised my four baseball-maniac sons that if Pittsburgh ever got into the World Series, I'd charter a private car and transport them and any number of their buddies eastward for the big event. I hope I'll have to spring for that train ride yet.

Maybe some of the luck I've had will rub off on the Pirates someday. Perhaps most people don't remember it, but when I started to make a picture called *Going My Way*, I put on the uniform of the lowly St. Louis Browns, and by the time the picture was released, they'd won the pennant! It seemed impossible, but it happened. Wouldn't it be wonderful if this could happen to the Pirates! Wonderful, but incredible.

The Whiteman outfit was loaded with characters who have become legendary to jazz lovers. Joe Venuti was one of the most fabulous of these. Wherever musicians lay down their instruments to take five during a jam session, the conversation turns to Joe, and someone always comes up with a story about him. I have contributed a few such bits of Venutiana myself.

Joe's a voluble, volatile, and violent Italian. He's very loud, very noisy, and very given to telling fantastic stories about himself and his family. Nevertheless, he's a great artist on the violin. I don't think his equal exists when it comes to playing popular music on his chosen instrument.

Joe has a beautiful classic tone on the violin which he never uses because it's too intimate; too refined. Joe likes everything with *beaucoup* volume. He told me once he would have liked to have been a tympanist but if he had, he would have had to use hatchets for whatever a tympanist uses for drumsticks.

When Joe and I were in Hollywood with the Whiteman orchestra in 1929, working on the Old Gold radio program, Charlie King was our guest star on one program. Charlie was an attraction because he'd been featured in one of the first musical talkies. The Old Gold show ran for a whole hour. We rehearsed for it afternoons at the old KHJ studio in downtown Los Angeles. In those days radio was regarded as a frighteningly technical medium and we approached it much more seriously than we did later in its development. We rehearsed and rehearsed to make sure everything would be perfect. The soloists had to learn their positions at the microphone; the section mikes had to balance; the opening had to come off with split-second precision. As part of this intensive preparation, we were rehearsing with Charlie King. Charlie was a singer of the old school. He was a great guy, but in the opinion of such irreverent individuals as myself, he was far better as a comedian and dancer than as a singer. He was what we call a ricky-tick singer today—meaning that his style was a little on the razzmataz side.

During rehearsal, when he began to give out with that "Just bring a sma-aile to Old Broadway" stuff, Venuti was fascinated and he kept his eyes on Charlie throughout the rehearsal. Before the show we had an hour break, and when we went out to find something to eat, Joe disappeared. He came back just before we went on the air.

As I've said, a radio program was more or less sacrosanct then, so we were nervous and Whiteman was in a swivet. He was getting money by the sackful from Old Gold and it would continue to jingle in—if things went smoothly. His music was the best in the land, and it had to sound that way. It wasn't transcribed. He had only one crack at it—when we were on the air. So there was much tension before the show. Then voom! the red light was on and the awful moment had arrived. The show started well, and presently it was time for Charlie King's solo. He stood up to

face the mike. As he took his place, Joe opened his violin case
and pulled out an old blunderbuss of the vintage of 1870, and
drew a bead on Charlie. We began to laugh. We didn't really
think that Joe would shoot King, but you never could be sure
with Venuti. He was wholly unpredictable, and I remember
thinking that King was in some slight jeopardy, even if the
weapon was loaded only with rock salt.

Joe kept the gun on him, as if daring him to send one more
corny note soaring from his larynx, and I thought Whiteman
would have a stroke. He'd lost control of the band; we were
laughing so hard we were *hors de combat* and Charlie King was
singing *a cappella*. But toward the end some of the more sedate
instrumentalists rallied and mustered enough breath to give
Charlie a finishing chord.

Undoubtedly Venuti helped age Whiteman. Paul once gave
him a violin-solo assignment. The occasion was a concert. For
the most part, the audience wore white ties, with only a sprinkling of the more *dégagé* black. When Joe came forward, he said
to Paul in front of the audience, "Let me use your violin." To
avoid unseemly argument, Paul handed it to Joe. Joe played a
number, then pretended to get his bow tangled in the strings.
Finally, in exasperation, while the audience went into hysterics
of mirth, he chewed up Whiteman's fiddle, crunching it with
his strong white teeth and spitting out pieces of wood.

One of my favorite Venuti stories has to do with the bass-
fiddle player he got "right off the boat from Italy." Joe had his
own band then and was working for Tommy Guinan, Texas
Guinan's brother, in a box bearing the gay name Tommy Guinan's Playground. When Tommy and I see each other nowadays, we laugh about that engagement Joe played for him. "That
buddy of yours put me out of the café business," Tommy says.
"I was going great until I signed him."

For years Joe had wanted to import a bass player direct from
Italy. It was his theory—an invalid one as far as I could see—
that such a musician would have a way of playing a bass fiddle

that would fit in ideally with a Dixieland combo. Finally, after much finagling, Joe went down to Ellis Island, fetched such a character back with him and put him in his band for the opening night at Guinan's Playground. There was a sell-out audience on hand and everything seemed to indicate that the joint was on its way to a long and successful operation. Joe played a couple of solos and the band went very big. Bix Beiderbecke showed up, carrying his cornet in a paper bag, and sat in with Joe's musicians. However, the freshly imported bass player became hungry. He'd been on the bandstand only an hour when he yelled at a waiter to bring him a steak. The waiter brushed him. He had other and more important things to do, such as waiting on people who were actually paying for their food, and also tipping.

The bass player got hungrier and madder. At last he said to Joe in Italian, "If that fellow don't bring me that steak quick, I'll kill him!"

Never at a loss for an uninhibited notion, Joe said, "The next time he comes near the bandstand, pick up your bass fiddle and hit him over the head with it. That'll teach the——."

The fiddle player with the steak yen nodded. When the waiter came by, he lifted his bass fiddle and—bong!

It started a riot. The waiters came out swinging and tore into the musicians. The patrons departed for calmer surroundings. Tommy Guinan's Playground opened and closed the same night.

Joe could never resist a spot of violence. He loved it more than music. On another occasion he was playing at a roadhouse night club near Cincinnati. It was a country-club type operation with a band and a floor show, but because of its spaciousness it was difficult to heat, and Joe complained that it wasn't warm enough. "I can state without fear of contradiction," he announced, "that I am no penguin." The manager kicked the heat up a degree or two, but it was still too frigid for Joe. He kept right on complaining, but the manager did nothing about it. One night

"I feel it coming on."

Joe brought a lot of apple boxes and packing cases with him
when he came to work, broke them up in the middle of the
dance floor, and started a bonfire on its waxed surface. The
owner summoned the fire department, who turned hoses on
everybody. When it was over, Joe was looking for a new job.

There's only one rule with Joe. If he says he's going to do a
thing, you'd better believe him, because it's a certainty, no matter how goofy it sounds.

I remember when we were with the Whiteman band and
playing concerts that we played an evening concert in San Diego
to a black-tie audience. We were arrayed on a big stage banked
with flowers. The program was almost entirely Gershwin, featuring the "Concerto" and the "Rhapsody." But for a change
of pace we were to give out with a melody of Victor Herbert
songs. I was sitting in the fiddle section cradling my prop violin,
the one with the rubber strings. I also had a little humming
called harmony-humming to do through a megaphone as a background for an instrumental solo.

Joe was seated next to me. They started the Victor Herbert
section and were going along swimmingly, playing things like
"Gypsy Sweetheart" and "Dance, Gypsies" and "Italian Street
Song." They were getting ready to play "When You're Away,
Dear," when Joe turned to me and whispered, "I think I'll sing
this chorus."

I told him, "You must be out of your mind."

"Anyhow," he said, "I think I'll sing. Hey Paul!"

Whiteman was busy conducting and following the score, but
he took time out to whisper to Joe, "What do you want?"

"I'm going to sing the next chorus," Joe said.

"Joe," Paul said, "you know I've got a weak heart. Don't be
silly. Play your violin."

But Joe was firm. "I've got to sing it, Paul!" he said. "I've got
to do it. I feel it coming on."

Paul was conducting the modulation and was getting closer
and closer to the melody. When it arrived Joe stood up, put his

fiddle on his chair, reared back and sang the whole chorus from start to finish with a real stale concert baritone type of delivery. He sings like Jerry Colonna, with long notes and hollering effects. When he got to the end, instead of hitting the last note vocally, he gave out the loudest razzberry I've ever heard.

It shook the rafters.

While he was singing, the audience didn't know whether to take it seriously or whether he was clowning. Coming as it did in the middle of a medley it was hard for them to believe that he was being comical. But when he gave out that razzberry, it removed any question from their minds. The applause almost atomized the theater.

Then Joe sat down. He seemed very happy. I thought Whiteman would have apoplexy, but he pulled himself together enough to conduct the rest of the Herbert medley.

When Joe left Whiteman, he assembled his own band. For the most part they played cafés. But as fate would have it, Joe and his outfit were booked to play dance music at the Texas centennial which Billy Rose helped stage some years ago. One band wasn't enough for Texas, or for Billy either, for that matter, so they booked Whiteman and his band, too, as the major attraction in the big auditorium, and to accompany the galaxy of star attractions booked for the function. Much of his show was done with the spotlight playing on the performers and Whiteman conducting the orchestra in the dark. But being every pound a showman, he had a baton about three and a half feet long constructed with an electric light bulb in its end so his musicians could watch it.

Joe's band served in a relief capacity on the opposite side of the dance floor. After Whiteman had played the show, his band took a fifteen-minute break and Joe's band played a little dance music until the Whiteman band was ready to resume. When the Venuti band had taken their seats, Joe came stalking out lugging a broom with a railroad lantern on the end of it and began to conduct with the broom and lantern as *his* baton.

A few more wisps of Paul's hair fell out then and there.

Joe was considerably better with the bow than with the cue. He thought he could shoot pool like a champion, but my old pal of the Whiteman days, Eddie Lang, used to take most of his salary away from him at the game. Like a lot of the other fellows Eddie hooked, Joe was never able to get rid of the illusion that he could beat him. He never did. More than once their games ended with Joe ripping up the green baize cloth with his pool cue, breaking the cue in half, throwing the balls through the window, and leaving in a huff, considerably poorer for his experience.

Before I call it a day on Joe—a theme which I admit has me under its spell—I'd like to mention his discovery, Hammerhead Jones. I heard of Hammerhead first when Joe came to our house one night for dinner. It was after our North Hollywood home had burned; we were living in a Beverly Hills house we'd rented from Marion Davies. Some of her living-room chairs had seats made of tough wicker. After Joe dug into some spaghetti smothered under a blanket of meat balls, we fell to discussing those chairs. Joe said that although they were made of very tough material, he'd bet that he could break one of them with his head. Over-confidence had given me nasty spills before, but I said, "Let's see you do it."

Joe took one of them, raised it, crashed it against his skull, and his head popped through.

I said stubbornly, "I bet you couldn't do it to a whole dozen."

"For how much?" he asked.

"For five dollars," I said.

Without a change of expression and while I sat transfixed, he did it to all of them. Then he told me, "That's nuthin'. I've got a guy in my orchestra called Hammerhead Jones who makes me look like an egg-head."

"What does he do?" I asked.

"He's a feature performer I picked up in an amateur contest down South," Joe said. "He's bald. He comes out and he reaches into his pocket and pulls out two ball peen hammers machinists use. Then he plays 'Nola' on his skull with them."

"How does he get the notes?" I inquired.

"He opens his mouth wide for the low notes and closes it tighter for the high notes," Joe said. "He plays 'Flapperette' as an encore. 'Flapperette' is very good on the skull. But if he takes two encores he gets a concussion and has to lay off for a week."

I'm afraid Hammerhead is only apocryphal. Joe swears he exists, but nobody has ever seen him. Joe explains this by saying, "We just use him when we're on the road. 'Fraid someone will steal his act. He travels in an army tank."

One of the reasons I use Joe Venuti so much on my radio program—in addition to his artistry with his chosen instrument—is because it's the only way I can stay even with him. One way to put it is to say that Joe is an improvident strolling player, and every so often I get a wire from some flag-stop or spa importuning me for money to get him out of town.

As I recall it, the last such occasion was a wire from Las Vegas and the bite was for five hundred. It took me a couple of days to find our radio writer-producer, Bill Morrow, who was on a bit of a ramble entertaining Henry McLemore, Bob Ruark, Bill Corum, or some other kindred souls from the Eastern writing fraternity, and query him on the possibility of using Joe on a show. The delay brought another wire from Joe—this time asking for seven hundred and fifty dollars. We finally went for that amount, so Morrow's unavailability cost me two hundred and fifty dollars. To keep this from being a total loss, we gave Joe two shots on the show, thus establishing a Venuti base rate of one show for five hundred dollars or two for seven hundred and fifty dollars.

John Scott Trotter joined my musical family at the beginning of my Kraft Music Hall series in the 1930's. He's been with me ever since. I'd known John in New York when he played piano and made arrangements for the Hal Kemp band. Both Hal and Johnny were products of the University of North Carolina. John —as everybody who's listened to our radio program knows—goes about two hundred and ninety-five pounds. For a band leader he has remarkable self-control. Never have I heard him resort to profanity during the long, tiresome rehearsals. Things can go wrong with an arrangement. Musicians are late or maybe hung a little. After five or six hours, they often get fidgety and restless, or their attention wanders. But I've never heard John raise his voice or upbraid his musicians. Once, when they really got out of line, he rapped with his baton and said, in cool, crisp tones, "Gentlemen!" The bandsmen were so shocked that he'd said anything at all that they calmed down and he had no more trouble with them.

Trotter is a real gourmet, dedicated to the pleasures of the table. He follows food the way some people follow the sun. Between 1937 and 1945 we went on the air live instead of as a transcription, and the only free time John had was between programs. But sometimes he'd do a few arrangements in advance, then fly from Los Angeles to New Orleans for oysters Rockefeller at Antoine's, or to San Francisco for cracked crab when it was in season, or to Olympia, Washington, for Olympia oysters. He'd go anywhere to get delicacies which couldn't be obtained in any other town or at any other time of the year.

On one occasion in the early 1940's he was serving terrapin he'd flown in from Baltimore. His whole dinner was planned as an overture for the *pièce de résistance*, and John was in a tizzy about it. He warned us that there would be no drinking at his party. "I will select a proper wine," he said, "but I won't have any cocktails or highballs. You're not going to cauterize your taste buds with red-eye before you eat my dinner." Some of the bandsmen reverted to their college days. They brought along flasks in their cars and sneaked out for an occasional *apéritif*.

John Scott's very precise about everything he does. He is even methodical at swimming, which is the only exercise he takes. He gets into the pool at the Racquet Club at one o'clock in the afternoon and swims until supper. He swims to one end, then back to the other, hangs onto the edge for a while and talks to people. Then he swims up and down a few more times. He says that this is the only thing that keeps him slimmed down to just under three hundred pounds.

Whenever men gather informally to bat the breeze a bit, conversation flows and tall tales follow one upon another. Inevitably it gets around to who knew the biggest eater or who witnessed him in action. Trotter is no mean trencherman, and I never fail to accord him full honors. But truthfully, his most prodigious feats are in the field of dessert.

On a good night at the Tour d'Argent in Paris, I've seen him eat four servings of Cherries Jubilee hand running. And once at a formal dinner party I saw him destroy five baked Alaskas without taking a long breath. But to qualify fully for championship recognition, a fellow must be able to handle all courses of a meal with equal facility. Trotter's a specialist and really cannot be considered when a dinner-table decathlon is discussed.

However, George Coleman, who is sometimes called "The Oklahoma Fork," can do a good job at the board. Nothing flashy, just a good, steady performer. And Mrs. Coleman—"La Forchette"—is quite good in the ladies' fight. She's outstanding because, despite her prowess with the viands, she is slender, graceful and petite.

Once, after dining sumptuously in the main dining room of the *Queen Mary*, I strolled out into the lounge with Mrs. C. and she plunged her hand into a bowl of what she thought were after-dinner mints. She popped a couple into her mouth only to discover that she'd bitten on some Bingo chips.

I knew a ranch superintendent who worked for Newt Crumley up in Elko who was better than an empty stall with the groceries, name of Al McGinnis. I've seen him eat two tins of home-made biscuits, one dozen to the tin, without visible dis-

tress, but my personal nomination for the all-time free-style title
is a fellow by the name of Ducky Yates. This boy weighed two
hundred and sixty pounds, was equipped with a fine physique,
and enjoyed the singular distinction of having attended both
Yale and Princeton. At one of these schools (or perhaps both)
he was on the weight-lifting team, but I'm convinced that his
real sport was eating.

Harvey Shaeffer, who attended Yale with Ducky, tells me
that on many occasions he's seen him dispose of two dozen eggs
at Child's restaurant in New York before retiring for the night.
Ducky was a golfer of sorts—in fact, a pretty good golfer—and I
think that at one time he was a scratch player. He was a participant in our golf tournament when we had it at Rancho Santa
Fe near Del Mar. The concluding evening of the tournament
was always featured by a dinner party given on the ranch
grounds for the contestants, officials and newspaper people.
The menu for the dinner included a T-bone steak, baked potato,
Mexican beans, salad, bread and butter, and apple pie à la
mode. Draught beer was available for those who fancied it.

Toward the middle of the evening Grantland Rice circulated
among the tables with Guy Kibbee in tow. He was challenging
all and sundry to an eating contest with his protégé, Mr. Kibbee,
who had something of a local reputation as a gastronome and
buffet bandit. When he passed Ducky Yates' table, Ducky
stopped him, saying, "I've had two dinners already but I figure
that's about the right handicap. Sit your man down here and
we'll 'head and head' it for a bit."

Rice plunked his entry down and the T-bones and the other
viands were brought forth. The contestants went through everything once and still looked fresh and unmarked and betrayed no
signs of distress.

Then the second dinner was brought on. At the conclusion
of the serving, Kibbee was puffing a bit, but Yates seemed un-
disturbed. A third helping was brought. When this had been
put away, Kibbee was breathing hard, his face was flushed, and

he was in obvious difficulty. Yates seemed serene. At this point Kibbee looked over at Yates' side of the table and gasped, "What are you doing with the bones?"

"What bones?" inquired Yates blandly.

At this, Kibbee threw his napkin up in the air, signalling a TKO. The match was over and Kibbee retired in confusion for the Bisodol.

A half hour later I was on the telephone when Yates came in the house and asked if he could borrow a windbreaker. "What for?" I asked.

"I want to run down to the beach at Del Mar," he said, "I understand there's a place down there that's got great hamburgers."

Another of the group Bob Hope once called "the slaves of the pot-bellied lamp" (meaning me), is my radio-script writer, Bill Morrow. Other radio writers consider him just about the best in the business. Bill's a little eccentric. He travels with more gear than any man I've ever heard of. He feels naked on a trip unless he carries cameras, typewriters, film, flash bulbs, fishing tackle, boots, waders and tripods. When he starts to the depot he looks like a foray moving out to harass the enemy. He's also hat-happy. He lugs a small haberdashery of assorted headgear with him—mostly Italian-made velours in winter and Panamas in the summer. Quite naturally, he's God's gift to the airplane lines, for the extra fare he pays for excess baggage must amount to a sweet sum annually.

I call him The Pack Rat. When he checks out of a hotel the management runs a bulldozer into his room to scoop out the accumulation of old paper, old bottle tops, old tin foil, and old sandwich crusts. When he rooms next to me, I can hear him digging in his things at all hours of the night. When he goes into a hotel room he takes all his gear and throws it at the wall. Then he spends the rest of his visit digging and scratching for the things he wants. No matter when he gets home at night he puts on his pajamas and robe and starts digging, scratching, and looking for something he needs, perhaps a little scrap of paper on which he's written a memorandum. Whatever it is, he's mysterious and vague about it when I query him on it in the morning.

I've never known anyone more horror-struck at the thought of being caught without a supply of what he regards as the necessities of life. When we headed for Paris together in 1950, Bill had heard there was a scotch scarcity in France; that you could get only an occasional bottle of it, and none of it very good. We blew into New York a week or so before sailing and since Bill is on good terms with various restaurateurs and bistro keepers around town, he confided his worriment to them. These jovial hosts were so appalled at his plight that when we reached our suite on the ship we found no less than twelve cases of scotch stacked there. And each traveler who enters France is allowed to bring *one* bottle of alcoholic beverage with him.

We had a bedroom apiece and a sitting room but there was hardly space in those three rooms for us to turn around. If I got out of bed carelessly I stepped on a piece of Bill's multifarious equipment or a bottle of scotch.

At Cherbourg a special launch was required to transport our belongings—or rather, Bill's belongings—to the customhouse.

There was a big circular table behind which the customs officers stood to examine luggage. Our luggage filled the whole table. We had recording equipment, tape machines and tape, reference books (all Bill's) and the scotch. Each person who visits France is allowed to bring in two cartons of cigarettes. We had two packing cases full, for it seemed that Bill figured there'd be none of his favorite brand available in Paris. I couldn't begin to describe the other things he had.

As for me, I had a change of clothing and my golf clubs.

I ducked into the gentlemen's room to let Bill handle things, but I couldn't stay there forever and after a while I reappeared. By that time they had made Bill remove all of our things from the table, had cleared the honest passengers and sent them on their way, and made Bill put all of our stuff back on the table again.

Then they began to work on us. They asked, "*Quelle est là!*" and Bill said, "Wheeskey."

They looked at the twelve cases and repeated unbelievingly, "Wheeskey?" Bill said, "Yeah."

Their faces grew red and their voices shrill. They choked and spluttered words which probably meant, "What are you trying to do—sabotage the whole French wine industry?"

Then came the cigarettes. Next the luggage. Then the tape-recording equipment. The entire caboodle was shipped to Paris and put under bond. But M. Moreau doesn't quit easily. He's an operator. He found out who was who around the customs office and eventually he got every bottle and every carton back. A little *pourboire* here and dropping a word to the right fellow there are wondrously effective when given with the Morrow touch. Of course we couldn't drink all of that whiskey so we made many fast friends in Paris by giving it to fellows like Paul Gallico (who happened to be there) and Wesley Ruggles, a former Hollywood director domiciled in Paris, and to various thirsty chaps we met at our Embassy.

Making ready for our trip to London from Paris en route to Scotland for the British Amateur Championship, I came face to face with the fact that Morrow is constitutionally averse to making trains on time. He's always late and generally settles for the next train.

On this occasion I told him sternly, "We're taking the twelve o'clock boat train. That is, I'm taking it. I don't know whether you'll be ready or not, but I'll be on it."

"Don't worry," he said, "I'll be with you."

The night before our departure I went one way and Bill went another. I came home about one o'clock to find him packing like mad. I went to bed but when I woke up some time during the night he was still scurrying back and forth, still digging for missing things, still pack-ratting around.

When I rose about nine he was shaved, had had his coffee, his bags were packed and labeled. He was smiling and exuding smugness. We had a little time to kill, so we went into a park and had more coffee under the trees.

Around eleven o'clock we summoned our hired charioteer and loaded our things into his auto. The car was a large one but Bill's impedimenta filled the rack on top, the turtle-back and the back seat from cushion to car roof. I sat with Bill and the chauffeur in the front seat. I had a little hand-bag with a few things in it, an extra pair of slacks, and my toilet articles, plus my golf bag with my golf shoes and a sweater pushed into it.

The chauffeur put the car in gear, pulled away from the curb and Morrow said, "Oh, my God!"

"What now?" I asked.

"My passport!" he said weakly.

He jumped out of the car, pulled the stuff from the rack, out of the turtle-back, and from the back seat of the car. Opening every bag he fell to digging again.

He dashed back into the rooms we'd just vacated, went through all the drawers and turned everything upside down. It was eleven-thirty, then twenty minutes to twelve, and we were fifteen or twenty minutes from the depot.

Whipping back to the street, he riffled through his baggage again.

Then a thought struck him; he felt his pocket, and there it was. He threw everything back on top of the car, into the turtle-back, into the back seat and we started once more. We'd gone about a half mile when he said, "Oh, my God!" again.

I asked, "What now?"

"My travelers' checks," he said in hollow tones.

Our driver turned, smiled and said, "I found them on the street."

We made the train.

As I've said, Bill's a brilliant radio writer, but he's also a dead-line writer. He never has his script ready until fifteen minutes before I go on the air. I've suggested, "Why don't you sit down at the typewriter and knock out a few scripts and get ahead of the game? If you do that, maybe the next time we get ready to do a show there won't be a mad rush with everybody in a hassle."

"Don't worry," he tells me. "I've got things in mind. There's no hurry. It'll be done." Three or four weeks later we've got two or three days to go, and I ask, "Have you got anything yet?"

He gives me his stock answer: "It's building. I don't know which direction it's taking as yet, and I don't want to put anything down because I may go off on another tangent." Finally my songs are set, I'm holding out my hand for the script, and Bill shows up at the studio—with nothing. Thirty minutes before we go on the air, his script starts coming in, a page at a time, from the mimeographers via runner from CBS.

Somehow it always comes out all right and the fact that his dizzy system works cools some of the heat out of my criticism. All I know is that being a Morrow-type writer would drive me crazy. He might have had his script in his head all along, but I doubt it. For one thing, he never tells it to me, and there's no reason to keep it a secret from the one who's going to say what he writes.

He drives his secretaries crazy, too. He has a five-room apartment in Hollywood where he always has an old mulligan stew or beans simmering in his kitchen. He pads around in a Japanese kimono and flip-flopping slippers, looking like a bald Shirley Booth, giving whatever's cooking a stir while his secretary sits alerted behind a typewriter. She comes in at nine o'clock and takes her place, her hands poised over the keys, ready to take down his gems.

Bill says crisply, "Page One, Crosby script. Crosby says—just a minute, I've got to go out to the kitchen." Then he disappears and fools around until the phone rings, and it's an old pal from out of town; perhaps it's Society Kid Hogan from Chicago. Bill tells the Society Kid to "come right up," and the resultant gab fest lasts until noon. Then Bill says, "I guess we'd better have lunch." After lunch somebody else like Bill Gargan or Groucho Marx drops in, and at five o'clock Bill's secretary is still poised. Then she goes home and another girl appears as his second shift. By then it's dinner time and she has to wait while he dines.

After five or six days of this, he still has on paper only the words: CROSBY SKETCH, PAGE ONE, CROSBY SAYS. This is my cue to drop in to look at him reproachfully, but I get so nervous waiting for him to write another sentence that I have to leave. He not only has a second secretary, he has a third one for pinch-hitting purposes, but none of them do anything until the last day, when a deadline's sitting in his lap. Then he fires stuff at them like a machine gun. He has one of them typing, another running to the mimeographers with the product, while the third works with John Scott Trotter on music cues. At the last moment, Morrow is as busy as a one-legged man at a pants-kicking contest.

His secretaries are all shell-shocked when they've been with him for six months. Very few of his girls last longer than that. They have to have stoical temperaments to survive even that long. That's Morrow, the traveling companion and calming influence of my radio moments.

On one occasion we had my four boys booked on my broadcast when Dennis came down with a little throat trouble, which resulted in an impending throat operation set for a certain date. Dixie had made all arrangements, but Morrow called Dr. Joel Pressman, Claudette Colbert's husband (who was going to perform the operation), and had the date set back two days so we could use Denny on the show.

Denny either neglected or didn't dare to tell Dixie about it.

She discovered what had been done when she called Dr. Pressman about some other matter, and you can imagine the tempest which broke around my head.

Morrow's social contacts go by fits and starts, too. On tour, he can be counted upon to pick up some very unusual travel pals. Once we were en route from Boston to New York on the early morning train, after a big night. Fortunately, a car attached to the train offered breakfast and a drink or two to restore our wasted tissues. We were having a little corned-beef hash and a bottle of ale laced with Worcestershire sauce and a raw egg, when Morrow noticed two girls in the car. Each of them was six feet tall and rugged in an opulent sort of way. They could have been very useful backing up the line for the Green Bay Packers.

It wasn't long before Bill engaged them in conversation. In an even shorter time he was jotting down their telephone numbers and addresses in his little black book. They downed an ale or two and were waxing gay when the conductor called, "New London"; and the two dolls grabbed their handbags—or their welding kits—and got off. When Bill came back from saying farewell to them, I asked, "Now what was that all about?"

"They're very nice girls," he replied.

"I know they were very nice girls," I said, "but why were you taking down their names? After all, they live in New London and you live in California."

"Yes, it's a shame, isn't it?" he said lightly.

"What do they do in New London?" I asked.

"They're clam openers," he said. "I may be through here some day and want some clams opened. You never know."

Never did Bill put me in worse jeopardy than the time when I had Dorothy Lamour on our broadcast as a guest. She did a song on the show and it was very good, too, but we had Hope on the show. He ad libbed all over the place, up and down the aisles, milking laughs until unconscious. The result was that the show ran over-long and something had to be edited out. Bill

Morrow did the cutting and the axe fell on Dotty's song. The night the show went on the air she had a dinner party. Included among the guests were a couple of people she'd been talking to about a night club tour and whom she wanted to hear the song. Dorothy is very easy to get along with but I must say that on this occasion she was really steamed and justifiably so.

We were shooting *The Road to Rio* at the time and I stayed away from the set until well after lunch time, until she had had a chance to cool out a little. Although it was Morrow's doing, she still jumps me out about it every once in a while.

We do a lot of radio broadcasts up San Francisco way and when we go there Morrow generally checks into the St. Francis Hotel, adding work and confusion to the already taxing tasks which engage Dan London, the personable manager of the hostelry.

If we're going to do two or three San Francisco shows there, Bill generally spends a week. Once, after the first show I returned to Pebble Beach and phoned Bill the next day at the St. Francis. The operator said his room didn't answer. I tried it again on succeeding days up to the end of the week and got the same response: "Mr. Morrow's room doesn't answer." I then called Los Angeles to see if I could find out what had happened and to my surprise I got Morrow on the phone. He'd merely forgotten to check out of the St. Francis. A nice little bill was piling up there against the Crosby Enterprises.

For the most part, Bill Morrow's companions are highly colorful like himself. He has a wide and contrasting group of friends. They range from Society Kid Hogan through Johnny Myers, Joe DiMaggio, Aly Khan, and many other interesting and volatile individuals. One such is named John Donovan, who was a commentator for the ECA and for the Marshall Plan when Bill and I were in Europe in 1950. Donovan had been a newspaperman and commentator and I've been told that he's now in Saigon doing the same kind of work for some American syndicate.

It so happened that when Morrow and I were in Brussels,

Donovan was there at the same time on an assignment for the ECA. Being an old pal of Morrow's from Third Avenue in New York, he tried to look us up. He took it for granted that we'd be checked in at the Metropole, which is where everyone in show business stays when they're in Brussels. Instead we had checked into the quieter and more sedate Plaza.

John phoned the Metropole and in his best Irish-French asked the phone operator if Monsieur Bing was registered there. She said, "*Oui, oui.*"

He told her, "I want to speak to Monsieur Morrow, who is with Monsieur Bing." The operator rang the room but there was no answer. John called several times. Each time he made sure that "Monsieur Bing" was registered, but he was never able to locate anyone.

Finally Donovan, who is quite a rib-steak artist, went over to the Metropole in person and asked what floor Monsieur Bing was on, after which he went upstairs and bribed the maid into letting him have access to the room for a few moments. The maid was a little dubious about the propriety of such a move but a handful of francs can work wonders and John was permitted ingress. No sooner was he alone and uninterrupted than he busied himself tacking signs up all over the room, signs which read: LEAVE BELGIUM IMMEDIATELY! YOUR LIFE IS IN DANGER! ! TONIGHT WE STRIKE! ! ! ! ! and BEWARE! ! ! ! ! ! and many other threats of a similar nature.

Then he ducked and a few hours later he phoned to find out the results of his interior-decorating caper and he asked to speak to Monsieur Bing. To his surprise the Monsieur Bing who answered the phone was not Monsieur Bing Crosby. It was Monsieur Rudolph Bing of the Metropolitan Opera Company. Donovan was a little shaken by this turn of events, as was Monsieur Rudolph Bing. In fact, he had called the police; they were fingerprinting everything and a full-scale investigation was under way.

Donovan hurried down to the hotel and presented his credentials. He identified himself satisfactorily and was able to convince the gendarmes that it had all been merely a prank. In the end the constabulary went away shaking their heads, unable to comprehend the inexplicable antics of "the crazy American."

I don't know whether John ever gave it any thought but I'm sure that his little prank probably cost me my chances of appearing at the Met. And I did *so* want to do the *Barber of Seville* someday—*if* they can dub in Pinza's voice.

Society Kid Hogan is one of Morrow's pals. Society Kid was a fighter of sorts about the era of Willie Ritchie, Pinky Mitchell and Charlie White. I don't know how good the Kid was but he did fight some of these boys and was a main eventer around and about the Middle West. Toward the end of his career, the Kid was forced into a fight in an effort to solve some of his economic difficulties. He probably shouldn't have taken the bout for he was over the hill a little.

It was a six-round contest. The Kid was taking an awful pasting in each round, catching everything the other fellow threw. Seeking to bolster the Kid's confidence, his manager told him after each round that he was doing all right, that he had nothing to fear, and that the other guy wasn't hurting him. At the end of the fourth round, the Kid staggered to his corner and flopped in his seat in dire distress. His manager, sensing his mental condition, said, "Kid, you're going great. You've won every one of the first four rounds." The Kid extended his hands and said, "Well, take these gloves off and give him the other two rounds."

I hope I'll be pardoned if I digress a moment for a spot of reminiscing about Jimmy McLarnin, a golfing pal of mine at Lakeside who was one of the greatest fighters who ever lived. He was once booked in England to fight a British lightweight, Nel Tarleton, who had achieved some prominence and was thought entitled to international consideration in lightweight ranks.

It was a bad match from the beginning. Jimmy carried too

many guns for this boy, but they were hopeful of getting some money from the sale of the motion picture rights, so Jimmy was trying to carry his opponent. As *aficionados* of the fancy know, in England at the National Sporting Club most of the audience wear dinner jacket and black tie, and there's very little yelling or screaming at the contestants. Everything is orderly and under control.

Jimmy came out for the first round, sparred a little, and crossed a stinging right to Tarleton's chops. Tarleton's knees sagged, and Jimmy had to act quickly to keep him from reaching the deck. He held him up for a minute or two, waltzed around until Tarleton regained his equilibrium, and confined himself to light sparring for the remainder of that round—and for the next two or three rounds as well. A fellow in a dinner jacket who'd obviously bet a considerable sum of money on Tarleton at the very attractive odds the bookmakers had offered was seated in the second or third row. At intervals he hollered, "Avoid him, Nel, avoid him."

Jimmy was having a hard time making it look like a fight, so occasionally he stung Nel a little with a sharp left or right, or threw one into his stomach. Whenever he did that, it would take Nel a minute or two to recover. Jimmy supported him in a clinch and waltzed around a little more, while the chap in the third row kept yelling, "Avoid him, Nel, avoid him!"

This went on for eight or nine rounds and Nel was getting weary of Jimmy's incessant left jabs. Finally, in a clinch while Nel was leaning over Jimmy's shoulder, the fellow in the audience yelled once more, "Avoid him, Nel, avoid him!"

Nel grunted back at the spectator, "Avoid him? I'd have to leave the bloody city!"

Awhile back I mentioned that Groucho Marx is one of those who is likely to drop in to pass the time of day with Morrow. Anyone who's ever kicked around much with Groucho Marx has had a plethora of laughs for his share. I've been lucky in that respect. A tome like this would be incomplete without including something about the garrulous Groucho, who's a colorful and highly quotable character. During the wartime Victory Caravan tour—the same being a hegira cooked up by the Government to transport actors all over the United States in the interest of War Bond sales—a group of us were being shown around the White House by Mrs. Roosevelt. We came to the gallery containing the portraits of the Presidents and, pointing to a portrait of General Grant, Groucho said to Mrs. Roosevelt, "Tell me, did General Grant wear a Vandyke, or did Van Dyck wear a General Grant?"

After a moment's study, Mrs. Roosevelt replied vaguely, "I really don't know."

In 1948 Groucho was doing a show with me in Chicago when our radio troupe was touring in that area. It happened to be opening day of the National League baseball season. It was a cold and blustery spring afternoon, with the wind whipping off Lake Michigan. But the Pittsburgh Pirates were engaging the Cubs just the same and we were determined to see the game. With a view to the threatening temperature, all members of our gang put on plenty of extra warm clothing except Groucho. He turned down my offer of a suit of long-handle underwear. He gave a five-minute monologue covering his reasons for doing this, although at the time he didn't even sport a mustache for added warmth.

He soon regretted declining the woolies because it was really cold at the ball park, and he was even more vociferous in bemoaning his congealed condition than he'd been in turning down my offer of clothing. His body was cold but his jokes were sizzling. A big fellow sat in front of us wearing one of those luxuriously thick, cashmere-soft, three-hundred-dollar camels-hair overcoats, or maybe it was a vicuña. Groucho tapped this fellow on the shoulder and said, "Would you mind removing your overcoat? I can't see the game."

He really broke up the box with his sallies, his observations about Chicago, the weather, and the Pirates. He even made a bonfire of our programs to keep warm. Finally he gave up, shivered his way out to a taxi, and went back to the Ambassador East to catch the rest of the ball game on the radio.

My next tidbit of Marxiana concerns Monsieur Marx and another interesting and highly combustible type, the New York taxi driver. As can be imagined, a number of hilarious chemical reactions take place when these two ingredients are mixed. One summer in New York Groucho and I headed for Ebbets Field to watch the Pirates play Brooklyn. Perhaps I'd better point out to hinterlanders that New York hack drivers hate driving fares to the Brooklyn ball park because it's a long way and they run a risk of cruising back to Manhattan empty—"deadheading" as they call it in railroading. However, we merrily hailed a taxi on Fifth Avenue, and boarded it bearing with us a package of sandwiches and other delicacies, including a bottle of cognac which had been presented to us by a friend, Leo Lindy, the genial Broadway restaurateur.

"Where to?" the driver asked pleasantly.

To disguise the real blow, Groucho replied, "Chicago!"

"Chicago!" screamed the driver.

"You heard me," said Groucho, "but just to show you we're nice people, we'll go to Ebbets Field instead."

"I'd rather drive to Chicago," groaned the driver.

"That's impossible," said Groucho. "Pittsburgh isn't playing there."

"Are you from Pittsburgh?" asked the driver.

"I don't know if that's any of your business," replied Groucho. The driver mumbled and grumbled a bit. Finally he turned around and surveyed Groucho quizzically. "Say," he said, "you look like one of the Marx brothers."

"So do you," snarled Groucho.

This sort of thing went on and on till we reached Brooklyn, where the driver got lost and had to make several stops to inquire the route to Ebbets Field. Of course, each time he came back to the cab he was a clay pigeon for Groucho's taunts.

"Look, why don't we stop this arguing," begged the driver.

"You should have stuck to Chicago," said Groucho. "We'd have been there by now."

"It wasn't my idea to come here," the driver shot back.

"Well, it's lucky we've got our lunch," mumbled Groucho. "We may be lost but we won't starve." So it went that way back and forth, and around and about, until we pulled up to the ball park.

Even then, while Groucho was paying the driver, the quips were still flying back and forth. Once we were inside the park and comfortably seated, like all baseball fans we decided to eat. Chatting happily about the repast we were about to enjoy, we found that we'd left our lunch in the taxi. This gave rise to a moment of dismay but it was a warm summer afternoon and we were at the ball park, so we feasted philosophically on hot dogs and cokes, and speculated calmly concerning the possible whereabouts and doings of our friend the cabbie. Undoubtedly in the cool evening his blood pressure would return to normal and he would have a picnic lunch with his fair lady in Prospect Park. Or, if he'd returned to New York (and I'm sure he did) he'd indulge in a light collation in Central Park consisting of sipping away at the excellent cognac of our friend, Leo Lindy, and tasting the delicacies he had provided.

The whole thing might be summed up as THE CASE OF THE TAXI DRIVER'S REVENGE.

Speaking of taxis, for many years Groucho and I have harmonized the old songs at parties and restaurants and even in cabs. Our two favorites are *circa* 1914. One is called "Night Time in Little Italy" (author unknown but I believe Berlin), the other, "Play a Simple Melody," which I'm sure is by Berlin. Crossing from Europe in the summer of 1950 on the *Queen Elizabeth*, I was invited to take cocktails with the captain along with Irving Berlin, Mischa Elman, the violinist, and others. In such a group the conversation naturally got around to music and songs and I told Irving how much Groucho and I enjoyed "A Simple

Melody." I knew of course that Elman is an authority on classical music, but I didn't know that he also knows considerable about popular music. However, he said that he didn't remember ever hearing "A Simple Melody." With that opening Irving and I sang it for Mr. Elman and the rest of the assemblage, our rendering being heavily laced with harmonic decorative effects. Someone remarked what a wonderful duet-tune it was, and when I returned home, the same thought struck me and I recorded the number with my son Gary, as his first venture as a recording artist, more of which later.

Right here I'd like to toss in another story about a New York cab driver—one who picked me up downtown in Wall Street where I'd been to see some attorney on some business. After I got in the cab and sat down and we were en route uptown, he turned to me and said, "Anybody ever tell you you looked like Bing Crosby?"

"Yes, occasionally," I said, "but Crosby's much older, much fatter than I am."

"Yes, I guess so," he said, and turned back to his driving. A few minutes later he turned to me again and said, "You wouldn't mind looking like him if you had his money."

I said, "Is he pretty wealthy?"

"Loaded," he said, "just loaded."

"I didn't know that," I said.

"Yes," he said. "You know Jock Whitney and Alfred Vanderbilt and Winthrop Rockefeller and all those fellows?"

I said, "Yes, I've heard of them."

"He can buy and sell them bums any time he wants," he said.

When we arrived at the hotel uptown I gave him much too big a tip.

EN ROUTE up and down and around and about, I've had a few misadventures—but I have taken no more of a jerking around by hotel people and the constabulary than most people who travel a lot. However I have jounced over a few such thank-you-marms which the press has thought newsworthy. Why they thought so, I don't know.

On a visit to Vancouver a room clerk at a hotel didn't want to let me in, and it was blown up into a front page story. I'd been fishing in the Rockies with Bill Morrow. We reached Vancouver with a substantial stubble on our faces. We had on clothes we'd worn for three or four days and we must have looked like a couple of loggers coming to town lonely and loaded, seeking a skid-row flop.

The Vancouver Hotel is a fine hotel and it does such a big business it's generally hard to get a room there. But I thought it was so late in the season that we wouldn't have much trouble. We drove up, got out of our car, went into the lobby, approached the clerk at the desk, and asked for a room. He looked us over with halibut eyes and asked incredulously, "You want a room *here?*"

"That's why we're here," we said.

"I don't think we have anything available," he said.

I began to steam a little. I said, "There should be no doubt in your mind. Either you have something or you haven't."

"We run a very exclusive hotel here, you know," he said.

I said to Morrow, "Let's blow."

Walking out we passed a bellboy at the door who had been

there when we'd stayed there the year before. Remembering Morrow and how lavishly he'd tipped, he was loath to see us leave, so while we walked to our car, he ran quickly to the manager's office. Apparently he told him that a human Comstock Lode was making his departure, for the manager came out with the bellboy, apologized, and took us back and got us a room.

That was all there was to it, but when the newspapers and the press associations got through with it, it took on the proportions of an international incident. You couldn't tell who had insulted whom or why, but it all blew over without the U.N. taking it up.

Then there was the time I decided to take a nap on a patch of grass in Paris. I'd had a big night. I'd been out with friends from New York, had gotten little sleep, and somehow it seemed noisy around the hotel that morning. There seemed to be cats stomping up and down on the carpet outside my door, so I figured maybe I'd take a few magazines and papers out into the park and catch a little rest there before a luncheon appointment.

I wandered over to a place called the Rond-Pont, near the Champs Élysées. It's a very small park—really a grassy plot with little walks going through it, a few benches, and some trees. I didn't know it but there was a sign there which said in French that it was forbidden to sit or lie down. I sat down a while, started to read a paper and got sleepy. I put the newspaper over my face, took off my shoes, lay back on the grass and tried to grab a little shut-eye.

It wasn't long before there was a rap on the soles of my feet and I rar'd up to find a couple of Paris cops swishing their policemen's billys. They upbraided me in French for being there and I tried to tell them in pidgin French why I was there, but my story boiled down to the fact that I was tired. Of course that was no excuse. They took me by the arms and walked me down the street.

"Where are we going?" I asked.

"We're going to the police station," they said.

I tried reasoning with them. "I'm an American singer," I said. "I'm over here on a vacation. What I did wouldn't hurt anyone and I'd like to clear this thing up before we get to the station house." They didn't know what American singer I was, and if they *had* known, it would have meant nothing to them. I showed them the label in my jacket. It read: "This coat was made by Eddie Schmidt of Hollywood in 1950 for Bing Crosby."

It didn't register.

I kept talking, but all the while we were walking down the street I didn't feel good. Which made the prospect of being in a French pokey for a day or two until I could get hold of somebody to spring me seem even more distasteful. Yet it was clear that that was where I was bound. There was no question about their attitude about an American dozing on their sacred plot of grass.

By this time we had picked up a little gallery, in fact quite a crowd.

Finally I pulled out a bill clip which the Professional Golfers Association of America had given me for a job or two I'd done for them during the war. It had a jewel on its golden front, and under that was PGA in big white enamel letters; and under that in small print was: "For Bing Crosby for his efforts on behalf of golf and on behalf of the Red Cross," or words to that effect.

"What does 'PGA' stand for?" the cops asked.

It was then that I had a flash of inspiration. "Police Guarde Americaine," I said.

"You a policeman?" they said, raising their eyebrows, "and on vacation here from New York. We thought you said you are a singer?"

"I'm a singing policeman," I told them.

"How can a policeman have enough money to afford a vacation in Paris?" they asked.

"Well, now," I said, "a policeman in America has many ways of making money which are not available to French policemen."

They looked very knowing at that. They said, "*Mais naturelle-ment*," and added a sentence or two which seemed to indicate that they understood fully because "one saw that sort of thing all the time in the cinema Americaine."

Since I was a fellow cop, they weakened a little. We stopped our progress stationward and we were joined by another cop, higher rank. They told him the whole tale. He shook hands with me and although the name Bing Crosby meant nothing to him, he was glad to meet me because I was an American cop. He said, "You can go along now. But never again. *Jamais encore*." I said fervently, "*Non, jamais encore*," and that was the end of it.

Being a boy from the Pacific Northwest, I'm very fond of that particular part of the country and I return there whenever I can. Especially do I like to go back to Idaho, where I do a lot of hunting and fishing. I have many good friends and ex-school chums there. It's a great state, offering many advantages, but candidly, its roads and highways are not very much like the Pennsylvania Turnpike. The state government, of course, can cop a plea because the population of Idaho is small. It's a big state with tremendous mountain ranges and the tax money available isn't sufficient to do any better road-building job than they do.

During the war, I was driving through on synthetic tires, which were all I could get. In one day I blew four tires jouncing over the numerous potholes between Twin Falls and Lewiston. Some newspaperman interviewed me on arrival and, being a little more slack-jawed than I am normally, I said, "O.K.," when he asked me how my trip was, "but the roads are a little rough. In fact, I don't think Lewis and Clark could make it now."

When this flip observation made its appearance in the Boise *Statesman* it stirred up quite a storm, which almost cost me a little money. The commissioner of highways in Idaho at that time was Matt Halley, an ex-Gonzagan of the same vintage as myself. Matt had run the hamburger stand at school and he was able to produce records which clearly proved that I left the institution owing his Bisodol Bistro eighteen dollars and twenty-five cents. He announced jokingly that unless I prepared a retraction, he would press suit for the debt. I hastily made proper public amends, but I'm going to wait until things get a little better to pay the bill.

But once more an incident which might have happened to anybody made the front pages. While the necessity for such coverage eludes me, I've been very lucky with the press. They've been more than fair with me in every way, and I have some very good friends among the craft.

Elko, Nevada, is a little town of about five thousand souls, situated in Elko County, which is—if I may say so without being accused of shilling for my favorite corner of the globe—the second-largest cattle-producing county in the United States.

It should be obvious that my reason for buying the ranch in Elko and a summer home at Hayden Lake, Idaho, had to do with a search for seclusion and remoteness. I wanted my family to have a chance to lead a normal life away from the limelight which is inescapably their portion because of their dad's way of earning his daily bread.

But, despite their remoteness, I get all kinds of drop-ins. For instance, unencouraged by me, an utter stranger arrived one summer at Hayden Lake with his family in a travel-stained auto. He had written some songs and, feeling that the words and music which had "come right out of his head" and which he had put down on paper were sure hits which would make him wealthy if I would sing them over the air or make recordings of them, he'd sold his successful ice-cream business to pay for the trip to Idaho and to finance him while he was competing with Rodgers and Hammerstein.

I listened to his portfolio of songs, but they had no chance of becoming hits or even being published. And having to tell him that depressed me for several days after I'd broken the news to him as gently as I knew how.

There are other hopeful folk who call me on the phone wherever I happen to be to sing me a song they've written. How they run me down and find out my whereabouts beats me. Some of them have written words for which they want me to write the melody. I was staying in a San Francisco hotel when a woman reached me on the phone and sang me a song. When she'd finished I said, "Leave a copy of it at the desk. I'll take a look at it and send you my reaction."

"What desk?" she asked.

"The desk downstairs," I said.

There was a long pause. Then she said, "But I'm in Baltimore."

I guess this is as good a spot as any to make my pitch-warning to just ordinary, everyday people who write songs and who, having done so, think they'll live happily ever after on their take from Tin Pan Alley if they can get me or anyone else to sing them. That is a snare and a delusion. People are always approaching me with that notion and it always makes me feel bad. The chances against an amateur song writer getting anywhere in a profession which is already overcrowded is a million to one. There are five thousand song writers with hit songs to their credit already in the American Society of Composers, Authors, and Publishers, and ninety-nine and ninety-nine one-hundredths of these song writers don't average one hit a year.

Any self-appointed successor to Jerome Kern should proceed cautiously and take his work to someone in his community who knows music and will give him honest advice. It is useless to send such material to me. I don't have time to examine it and anyhow, my opinion is far from dependable. My judgment has been very wet on many songs in the past.

There are a lot of fly-by-night publishing companies—at least they *call* themselves publishing companies—who promise to get action on songs for such innocents for a fee. They talk largely about publishing them and getting singers to sing them and bands to record them. Once they've seen the color of their victims' money, they keep on encouraging them and bleeding them, when there's no earthly chance of their victims' songs ever becoming even a scratch hit. After a while, when the writer runs out of cash, the "publisher" loses interest and finds a new sucker. A picture, *Just For You,* I made in 1952 covers this point. The script tells how a couple of young fellows are mulcted by a bogus publishing company, an outfit similar to the ones I've just described. This type of publishing house accepts material from amateur writers all over the United States, then sends them form letters and encourages them to believe they're getting somewhere when actually the songs they've published are sitting on their shelves and will remain there.

I suggest to such writers that before they spend their money they take their song to somebody in their home town who's a musician, someone who's playing in a band, in a café, or hotel, ask him to listen to it and get an opinion from him. His opinion is just as expert as mine. He can tell at the beginning whether or not it would be wise for them to begin breathing down Irving Berlin's neck—or save their hard-earned cash.

I can never tell who's going to pop up. In the life I've led, there've been old pals who occasionally reappear like Rip van Winkle drifting down out of the Catskills. One figure out of my past who blew into Elko unexpectedly was Pants Donnegan. At least, that's the name I'll give him here. In the old days, Pants was a great musician and an asset to any band. He still works now and then, but he's a little unreliable. He goes from job to job, but if he gets bored, he just stops showing up. I hadn't seen Pants for a long time when these events took place. One summer the help was having breakfast at six-thirty before going haying, when up drove a taxicab and the cabbie poured Pants out of it in a state of alcoholic shock.

"Where'd you come from?" I asked.

"I drove over from Reno," he said.

This in itself was fairly startling, since Reno was almost three hundred miles away. But I told the cabbie to wait, injected a drink into Pants to rid him of his shakes, and set some ham and eggs before him which he eyed distastefully.

He demanded more shake cure, and was beginning to get stoned all over again. He was talking loudly and throwing his weight around, and I tried to keep him out of sight until everybody got off to work. I didn't want the help to get the idea that I countenanced drinking at that time of day. It turned out that the reason for Pants' visit to me was that he needed money for a ticket to Chicago. He said that he had a job waiting for him there with a band.

I had a talk with the cabbie and found out what Pants' bill was. It came to one hundred and eighty-two dollars. I made a deal with him. He settled for one hundred dollars. He figured he'd better take that, since he could see he was going to get nothing from Pants. So he took it and drove away. I phoned the Elko Airport and reserved a seat for Pants on an eastbound plane. Then I gave my foreman one hundred dollars and told him to hold onto it, and also to hold onto the plane ticket, and not to give either to Pants until he saw him going up the ramp into the plane. I knew if he hit an Elko saloon with one hundred dollars in his kick, he'd spend it, and sell the airplane ticket and blow the proceeds of that sale too. Then he'd be back freeloading with me once more.

When I bundled Pants and the foreman into the car, Pants was getting a little touchy. Somehow he'd got it into his head that I didn't want him as my permanent guest. As they drove off, he shouted from the window in abused tones, "This is the biggest brush-off I've ever had!"

I wasn't braced for Pants' call, but when my omnipresent twin-girl fans arrived at my Elko front door I was not surprised. They're likely to pop up anywhere. I've gone to Washington, D.C., to play a golf match and have looked up to see them in the gallery. I've visited Chicago to make a personal appearance and they're there. They live somewhere in New York State, but they get around.

They must be twenty-two or twenty-three years old by now,

but when I first noticed them they were about sixteen. For the first two years of their twin-fans-trailing-crooner routine, they peeked around the corners of buildings at me, and when I saw them, they giggled and ran. As the years rolled by, they came a little closer. One day I grabbed them and bought them a sandwich at a restaurant. They were nicely dressed, well-mannered, pleasant. They're through college now, but I still hear from them from time to time.

One day I was sitting on the front porch at the ranch and I happened to look up. Trudging down the road they came. They'd hitch-hiked from Elko, sixty miles away. There's no bus service from Elko out to my place. I brought tea and sandwiches out to them, and we had a chat. I offered to drive them back to Elko, but they said that would spoil their adventure, and when they'd had their tea, they went down to the main road and hitched a ride into Elko. From there I suppose they got on a train and went back to New York.

By and large, the fans have been good to me. When they see me on the street, in an elevator, or in a hotel lobby, their first reaction is, "Why, here's somebody I know." They smile and I smile back. Some of them say, "How are you?" and when I say "Fine," they say, "That's good," and walk on a few feet farther. Then they stop, do a double take and I can see them saying to themselves, "No, it couldn't have been." Then they walk on, looking a little puzzled.

Other people come up to me and say, "Hello. I've enjoyed seeing you on the screen." I say, "I'm glad you feel that way," and we shake hands.

Some of them want autographs, but in spite of stories of stars being chivvied by ravening hordes of autograph hounds, many of them aren't so pursued. However, I do run into the hard-to-please who criticize my handwriting and ask scornfully, "Is that the best you can do?"

When I protest, "I'm sorry; I can't write any better than that," they go away disgustedly. "Well, nobody'll ever recognize this." Then there're the ones with the leaky pens.

Once in a while I've been asked what has been the most satisfying and rewarding experience in my career. The answer is readily available. Nothing I've ever done stands out like my trip overseas to entertain the troops in England and France during the last war. If I never do anything else, I'll always take satisfaction in knowing that I helped some of our soldiers relax for a few moments when they needed amusement and entertainment.

If there were enough lads in Uncle Sam's army of the same kidney as the paratrooper I met on the *Ile de France* on my way overseas, it's small wonder we Americans helped our Allies win the last war. He was a very determined character, indeed.

The *Ile de France* had been converted into a troopship. In peacetime it carried between twelve and fifteen hundred passengers, but on this particular crossing they were packed together like a bride's spoons. They slept in relays. They'd sleep eight hours, then get out of their bunks, go up on deck, and let somebody else hit their sacks for eight hours. I had a little cubicle in which I slept. It was just big enough for a bed. My door opened onto a space where paratroopers were quartered—about a regiment of them. They were a rugged-looking bunch, with crew haircuts and polished high boots. Most of them bore scars acquired during their training period. They worked off their excess energy by getting into fights nearly every day. Two or three of them climbed up into the crow's nest and wouldn't come down until they had seen their fill of the sea, orders or no orders. A big, blond, tough, Boston-Irish paratrooper, with a chin like a landing barge, stationed himself outside my door and waylaid me.

When I came out, he said, "Sing me a song!"

"I haven't got any accompaniment here," I said. "I ought to have at least a guitar."

"Oh yeah?" he said. "You don't want to sing me a song. The hell with you."

Our troupe was made up of a comedian, a girl singer, a girl dancer, an accordion and guitar player, and me. We did five shows a day on five different decks. We started mornings and worked through until dinner, with time out for meals. But every time I came out of my cubicle, the blond rock from Boston was waiting for me and saying, "Come on and sing me the song!"

Each time I said, "Why don't you catch me later when my troupe is all together and we're doing a show?" On the last night, just before we were to land, I got hold of a guitar player, found the Boston strong-boy, got him out in the hall, the guitar player struck a few chords, and I sang him a solo. I selected "Sweet Leilani" for the occasion. When I was done, he harrymped, "Not bad," turned on his heel and went back to join the crap game.

Evidently he'd been trained not to give up until he'd obtained his objective. I'll say for him he had Situation Crosby well under control.

When we landed in England, we did a few transcriptions for the troops with Glenn Miller's band at the Air Force Command. Then we toured the English air bases, all the American installations, the bomber groups, and the fighter groups.

In the years before Hitler pounded into German noodles the idea that they were supermen, the Germans had nicknamed me Der Bingle and I had given a little fellow named Hen Michelmans a run for the loose marks kicking around in the Rhineland. When I got to London, the Office of Strategic Services thought it might be a good idea if I broadcast direct to the German people. Buzz bombs were falling all over London at the time, and its citizenry took a dim view of Kraut *Kultur*, to say the least. When the time for the broadcast came and I walked into the studio some of my English fans showed up and there was a certain amount of commotion outside. An English stenographer passing by asked, "What's going on in there?"

"Bing Crosby's broadcasting to the Germans," she was told.

She was outraged. To her, it didn't seem punishment enough.

The inhabitants of the British Isles are a stanch and sturdy—but to Yanks, an incomprehensible—breed. When I arrived at Greenock, a troop-debarkation town in Scotland, I ran into Fred Astaire, and we went to Glasgow together to take a train for London. Glasgow is off the beaten path for ordinary trans-Atlantic travel. Even in peacetime it's unusual for anyone in show business to go through that city on the way to London, Paris, or Rome. So our appearance in Glasgow—if I may be so immodest—was a sensation. I can only conclude that the last American actor seen there before Fred and I hit the town was Tom Mix or John Bunny. It seemed to us that people came out of the braes and glens who hadn't been in Glasgow for years.

The police estimated that there were thirty-five thousand or forty thousand people milling around the depot where we made our stopover. It wasn't a big depot, and because of the pushing and crowding, Fred was afraid someone might get hurt, so we got the police to lock us in the baggage room for protection until the train left. The crowd grew more demonstrative and announced that they wanted me to sing and Fred to dance, but they filled every inch of space and there was no room for us to do either. The train was made up and ready to go, but we couldn't board it because we couldn't shove through the press. The policemen waggled reproving pinkies, but although a bobbie's slightest wish is usually law in Great Britain, it made no difference in this case.

The crowd continued to surge around the baggage room for forty-five minutes. Fred and I were desperate. We had performance dates in London; it was important for us to take the train, and it couldn't be held for us much longer.

In the crisis, I peered through a window to see a figure striding down a ramp. He was dressed in striped trousers, a frock coat, a wing collar, the inevitable Ascot scarf and a high silk hat.

Confronting the crowd, he said, "Stand clear! Do you hear me? Stand clear!" He pronounced it "cle-ah."

An amazing thing happened. The crowd fell back like a receding wave. We made our exit from the baggage room and walked down a ramp while our guardian in the high hat held up his hand portentously, like Moses giving the word to the Red Sea. When the train pulled out, and the conductor came through, Fred and I asked, "Who was the fellow who had such a phenomenal control over the crowd? Was he the Minister of Transport?"

"That," the conductor said, "was the stytion mawster!"

I don't know how that stationmaster rates with his wife, but I know one thing: to everyone else he's the most important fellow in Glasgow.

After the slight delay in Glasgow, our troupe flew to Cherbourg. We landed there a month and a half after D-day and worked our way up the peninsula, following our armed forces to Paris. Then we went on to Nancy and Metz, where the fighting was still going on. We did three shows a day. Between shows we visited field hospitals or other places where the wounded were cared for.

We were on the tour four or five weeks, but it seemed only four or five days to me; we were always on the move and there was so much excitement. The look on the faces of the men we entertained was better than money from Paramount. They were so glad to see us. Despite the mud and the jouncing equipment we rode in, the girls in our troupe always managed to put themselves into an exciting-looking gown for each show and to do their hair real pretty.

My big song was "White Christmas." Christmas wasn't far away, and the chances of anyone in our audiences getting home for it were so remote that it was a tough song to sing, but it was asked for wherever we worked.

At one point in my tour I worked out of General Bradley's headquarters. In addition to appearing before GI audiences in the various encampments, it was considered important to entertain the smaller groups in the outposts. So at the start of a day I'd get into a jeep and go around to the outposts, putting on little shows and talking to the boys.

Fred Astaire had given me two warnings. "Don't sleep near a bridge, and when you're out in a jeep, watch the telephone wires. When you can't see them any more, you're in trouble." Since Fred had almost lost his life not following the first of these warnings, I figured to pay them some heed.

When I came back to headquarters after my first day out, the lieutenant in charge showed me to what was supposed to be my barracks. The sleeping quarters were very comfortable and I was just about to tell him how fine I thought they were when I looked out a window and saw—a bridge! I walked to the door and pointed to a lonely shack on a hill some distance away.

"That's where I'd like to sleep," I told him. "Is it possible?"

"Of course," said the lieutenant, "but it's kind of lonely up there and the facilities aren't what they are over here."

Luckily I had my way, for during the night the bridge and everything near it was blown up.

Another morning I set out in a jeep with a lieutenant who was armed to the teeth. He had a gun, side arms, and plenty of ammunition. As the jeep rolled along the dusty road, I kept my eye on the telephone wires. We rode and rode and pretty soon the telephone wires were no more. I looked at the lieutenant, who didn't seem sure where he was going himself. Presently the patrols along the road began to look less friendly as they whizzed by. I glanced at the young officer and said, "I think we'd better turn around, don't you?"

The lieutenant agreed that we might be cruising around in No Man's Land and we turned back real fast. That night after dinner, I was invited to General Bradley's quarters. The General stood behind his desk in front of a tremendous map of France. It covered an entire wall.

"How did you do today?" he asked.

"Pretty good, General," I said. "We covered all the spots we intended to. We even got to the town of Saint Mère Eglise." At least, I think that's the way it's spelled.

The general looked at the map, then turned to me quizzically, "Saint Mère Eglise? We haven't taken that town yet!"

For a second my stomach felt as if it were making a non-stop down trip from the top of the Eiffel Tower to the bottom. Then I pulled myself together and tried to give it the light touch, the way Danny Kaye as Walter Mitty might have done it.

"We had it for a little while this afternoon," I said with hollow gaiety.

Shortly before my tour was over, I visited General Eisenhower's headquarters at Versailles. I'd found a memorandum in my hotel mailbox which said: "A Colonel Galt wants to see you. Please call him." I was so busy I didn't have a chance to call back right away, but when I mentioned the message to a friend, he asked, "Do you know who Colonel Galt is?" When I said, "No," he told me, "He's one of Eisenhower's aides. Chances are the General wants to see you."

"I'd like to see him too," I said, "but he must be very busy and I don't want him to think he has to entertain every itinerant minstrel who happens along."

"If you do see him," my friend said, "and he asks if there's anything he can do for you, why not see if he'll lend you an automobile for a couple of days?"

Automobiles were at a premium. Civilians couldn't get them. The subways had broken down and the French were all on bicycles. Colonels drove up to the Ritz in small cars, took out chains with links as big as horseshoes and a giant lock and locked their cars to hydrants before going in for lunch. I got in touch with Colonel Galt, and the upshot was that our troupe went out to Versailles and did some shows. Then we had luncheon with General Ike and his staff, and since he liked to sing barbershop harmony, we got up a quartet. Ike sang baritone.

When I was leaving, he asked, "Is there anything I can do for you?"

"You could let me have an automobile for a couple of days if you've got one handy," I said. I told him I wanted to go to Fontainebleau to see a friend from California who'd married a Frenchman and who'd been stranded there since the war began. It was true enough.

"Take my car and driver," he said.

"When do you want them back?" I asked him.

"When you're through with them," he said.

That was on a Wednesday. The General got his car back on Saturday. Of course it had five stars painted on it, and I'm afraid that those five stars were parked in front of a few gay spots where the General wouldn't normally have been featured. I bumped into General Ike at the Celebrities' Golf Tournament in Washington, D.C., around 1947 or '48 and he looked at me slyly and asked with a smile, "Are they taking good care of your transportation here?"

When I returned the car, I asked, "Is there anything I can do for you when I get home?"

"Yes," he said, "you might send me some hominy grits. I can't seem to get any over here." When I returned to New York, I mentioned those grits at a press conference. A month later I got a cablegram from Eisenhower, "Call off the grits," it said. "I've got grits spilling over all this area."

Kind-hearted ladies from the South had responded—some of it was cooked, some of it was raw, some of it had sauce, some even had red gravy on it. I hate to think what those cooked, sauced, and gravied grits must have looked like and smelled like after days or weeks en route from Dixie to Versailles. I don't think Ike has eaten a grit since.

In 1947 or '48, the General was in Los Angeles. I got a call from him. He said, half in jest, "I don't want to see you. I've seen enough of you, but I would like to see those four boys of yours." So they went to his hotel and he spent an hour with them. To me this only proved what I already knew—this man has great humanness.

THE BIGGEST MISTAKE I've ever made with my boys was giving Gary a car as a high school graduation present. It did him no good at Stanford. I guess it's too much to expect of a college freshman that he'll hit the books when there's a car outside the dormitory and opportunity to use it up and down a shore highway. Gary had eight years of grade school with the sisters and four years of high school with the Jesuit fathers. A considerable amount of restraint is a part of both these educational systems. They go in for supervised study at night, and no freedom except on Saturdays and Sundays—even then only until ten P.M.

But when Gary reached Stanford with an automobile at his beck and call, he fell apart. Like any other university, Stanford expects its students to be self-reliant and to face up to responsibilities when they enter college. Sooner or later a fellow has to accept the restrictions of maturity, and he might as well start when he's a college freshman. A good way to begin is to realize that nobody's going to take him by the ear and make him study.

I didn't know how serious Gary's situation was until he came home at Thanksgiving and I heard him telling one of his pals how easy it was at Stanford; nobody cared whether you went to class or not, and everything was a cinch. That wasn't what I'd heard about Stanford. I began to worry, and after he went back to Palo Alto, I took a week end off and went up to talk to his professors—particularly to the Dean of Men—to find out what was going on.

When I asked the Dean how Gary was doing, he said, "You

won't have to worry about him, because he won't be here after Christmas."

"Where'll he be?" I asked.

"I don't know," the Dean said, "but he won't be here."

I got hold of Gary, and had a talk with him. I pointed out the seriousness of the situation, took his car away from him, put it in a garage and went home to talk to his mother. Quite naturally, Dixie was upset. "I think we ought to write him a strong letter," she said.

"You write him a letter," I suggested.

She did. She told him that if he hadn't made up his grades by Christmas, that if he was bounced by Stanford, we'd arrange for him to work digging ditches for the city when he came home. It was no empty, blustering, parental threat. When it came to discipline, Dixie didn't fool, and Gary knew it. She added that she didn't think he'd have to dig ditches very long, for she was sure the Army would reach out and tag him shortly after he left Palo Alto.

Her letter must have carried impact. He knuckled down, survived the weeding out of the lamer brains after Christmas, and made a really good showing in the spring quarter.

My situation as a father is maybe a bit more complicated than that which faces most dads. Raising the sons of a movie star presents special problems. When the children of people prominent in show business go to school or to entertainments or to parties, the solid, well-grounded kids they meet at those places pay them no special attention, but there's always a bunch of bubble-heads who make a fuss over a boy whose father or mother's name is known in the entertainment world. "With all the money your old man's got, you'll never have to work," they tell him. Or, "You mean you've got only one car?" and they ladle out the old goo. If the kid who gets this treatment is a little susceptible—as some of mine are—such guff can spoil them.

My slant on such buttering-up is this: there's an old Italian proverb which says, "Never kiss a baby unless he's asleep." This

should apply not only to babies but to teen-agers until they've
reached an age where their judgment tells whether the "you're-
so-wonderful" line tossed in their direction is flattery or not.
Even if it's not, I don't think kids can handle that kind of praise.
When I want to be especially flattering to one of my offspring, I
say, "Nice goin' " and let it go at that.

It was easier to instill a sense of proportion and values into
them before they began to grow up. One of the things I liked
about my kids when they were younger was that they had fun
standing outside of our house at Pebble Beach making disparaging comments about our dwelling when strangers passed.
They said, "Wouldn't you think Crosby would have a better
house!" or "They say the guy who lives there is a terrible tight-
wad."

And they told me happily afterwards, "Some of the strangers
who heard us looked very interested, Dad."

When they were young enough to be driven to school, they
never let our chauffeur take them all the way up to the school.
They'd make him let them out a block before they got there and
walked the rest of the way.

It got tougher to keep them on an even keel later. Dixie and I
were never very anxious to get our boys too deeply enmeshed
in show business. Dixie insisted they get their education first,
and it was with considerable trepidation that I asked Gary to
make a record with me, as a kind of change of pace. What if the
thing were a big hit? What if it catapulted Gary into the spotlight? What if it made him a bobby-sox favorite? How would we
ever be able to control him if it did?

All these things are just what happened. The songs we recorded were "Sam's Song" and "A Simple Melody." The label
read, "Gary Crosby and friend." I never dreamed it would hit
with such impact. But as luck would have it, the record caught
on in the juke boxes and landed Gary on the cover of a national
magazine, to say nothing of the money that rolled in.

The "Sam" in "Sam's Song" is really Sam Weiss, a music publisher and an old-time friend of mine. After I heard the test pressings, I said to Sam, "Get a barrel! Gary'll need one for the loot that'll be coming his way." I was right. He needed one to pick up his royalties.

Some of my friends think I'm too tough a disciplinarian with my sons. I'm particularly well known for this at Hayden Lake, where I take my four boys each August for a month of recreation when they're done working on our ranch in Elko. When the twins, Dennis and Philip, were seventeen and Gary was eighteen, I set up a few rules to govern their checking-in-with-the-old-man hours while they were at Hayden. The twins had to be in by ten o'clock at night and Gary had to show at eleven. Those rules held good every night unless there was a party or a dance for young people at a neighbor's home with the parents present. In that case, they could stay out as long as the party lasted or as long as the parents were on deck.

Not everyone else at Hayden—meaning parents—went along with my kind of regulation. Nor does this apply to Hayden Lake alone. It's true in Beverly Hills. As a result, I've had some bitter arguments with my sons. They've come home at ten o'clock wearing a lip on them that would trip a pig, disgruntled at having to fall in with my fuddy-duddy notions, forced to leave while the fun was still going on and fifteen- and fourteen-year-olds were staying up. This made them feel embarrassed. But it's my claim that no kid that young has any business out after ten o'clock, fooling around in an automobile or laughing it up in beer parlors. A growing boy ought to get nine or ten hours' sleep, but my main concern is the trouble they might get into. Any dad who expects a group of seventeen- or eighteen-year-olds to wander around loose as ashes at two or three o'clock in the morning and not get into mischief once in a while is leading with his soft head. I tried teen-age psychology by reminding them that a manager of a big-league ball club like the Pittsburgh

Pirates insists on curfew regulations, too. I thought they'd go for that, since each one of the four young Crosbys is a self-appointed Pirate manager, coach and scout.

To some dads, home is a place where he can retire to the peace and quiet of the family hearthstone. Not me. Home is where I catch such questions batted at me as "Why isn't So-and-So a starting pitcher?" "Why was that fellow taken out in the sixth?" "Why was that other fellow allowed to finish the ninth?" "Why don't we put So-and-So on first and get some left-handed power in the outfield?" "Why don't we buy Stan Musial, Jackie Robinson, and Robin Roberts?" "Why didn't you buy into the Phils . . . the Giants . . . the Yanks . . . the Cards?" "What's the matter with the Pirates anyhow?"

These are only a few of the queries, pleas, and plaints aimed at a target called "Dad." Great second guessers are the four junior Crosbys, as well as scouts without portfolio. Not a day passes in which they don't try to sell me on the potentialities of some youth they've caught on a sandlot, on a public playground, or in a semi-pro league. Candor compels me to admit that the Pirates have signed a couple such at their suggestion.

But my athletes-should-be-in-early-at-night dodge doesn't seem to go over so big. Looking squinch-eyed at their activities has made me quite a heavy, not only with my own boys but with other folks' kids. My sons tell me I'm considered the big bad wolf at Hayden Lake; that the other kids run when I come around; and that I'm supposed to be a tough jailer.

This has put me squarely in the middle. There have been times when I couldn't tell whether I was Captain Bligh in a Hawaiian sport shirt or the cream puff of the world, for Dixie used to tell me that I was too lax, that I wasn't strict enough, and that I forgot our boys' transgressions too soon. She used to reproach me with, "You punish them; then ten minutes later you're taking them to a movie. That's bad. You should let the memory of their punishment linger so they'll remember it."

302

Lax or not, I'll bet they remember the spankings they got when they were younger. I laid in a big leather belt—similar to the one I'd backed up to at Gonzaga in the hand of Father Sharp—and when they did something particularly outrageous—for example, going into Dixie's room, taking her canary out of its cage, and giving it what they called "a summer suit" by plucking its feathers—I summer-suited them by taking their pants down and fanning their rears. They remember that all right. But I admit I haven't licked them for several years. They've grown too big. I don't duck too good any more, and they might wheel and duck me. I could out-shuffle Lin, but Gary and the twins carry too much thunder. So when punishment is indicated, I take their liberties away from them. If the infraction is a minor one, I lock up the TV set for a week, or ban the movies, or call off baseball games. If it's big, I ground them for a fortnight. No nothin'. Coventry!

The things Dixie argued with me about in connection with our children were threefold: she said that I didn't watch their table manners; that I didn't make them observe the social graces; that I didn't make them dress properly. As far as their deportment at the table was concerned, she fought a losing fight.

She was an ace private eye when it came to keeping up with their peccadilloes. It was in 1949 and we were residing in Pebble Beach. It was a Saturday. Linny was going to school in near-by Carmel. Gary and the twins were down from Bellarmine Academy in San Jose. I was in L.A. making a picture and Dixie was running the roost. The roost being a two-story modern California-type house overlooking the Pacific on the thirteenth hole of the Pebble Beach Golf Club. Being Saturday afternoon, the boys were restless to get to the local movie in Carmel and see the picture which featured their favorite horse, Seabiscuit.

BUT—and this was a large BUT—Dixie had ruled no movies this day. So the boys concocted a story that they would be playing basketball. They picked basketball because there were sev-

eral courts in Carmel and it would have been difficult to trace
them. A friend, visiting from the East, was cajoled into driving
them to the theater in the station wagon.

As one of the boys said, "If Georgie (the housekeeper) comes
looking for us at one court, we can say we were at another." This
seemed air-tight until they got home.

"We're going to have dinner soon," Dixie said. "Let's see your
hands."

They turned up their hands.

"How was the movie?" asked Dixie.

"Fine," they answered. Then they did a take. How did she
know they were at the movies?

"Your hands," said Dixie, with her characteristic squint.
"They'd never stay that clean playing basketball!"

She never gave up. She also fought them tooth and nail on
their clothing, their behavior, and writing thank-you letters
promptly and with reasonable literacy. I failed her in these matters because I don't know enough about them myself to notice
the violations. When Dixie saw the boys sitting around in slacks,
sweaters, and moccasins when we had company, she ran a slow
burn. They looked good to me, garbed in that fashion, because
that's the way I dress myself.

I'm afraid my four chaps will never be sartorial followers of
Lucius Beebe, or even very adept in the graces as recommended
by Emily Post. They're a little lax in this department. I recall
once when Gary was about fourteen, Dixie and I were up at
Pebble Beach with him. We were asked to a formal dinner party.
When I mentioned that Gary was with us the host said, "Bring
him too." So I let him use one of my black bow ties and fixed up
a double-breasted blue for him and along he went.

Dinner went smoothly enough and when the dessert was finished, the ladies, as is the custom, arose to go into the drawing
room, leaving the men to their brandy and cigars. Gary watched
this feminine exodus wonderingly and then, turning to me,

asked, "What's the matter? Did somebody say something out of line?"

At another such party, when the butler asked son Denny if he'd like white wine or burgundy, Denny broke up the whole place by saying, "Hit me with a little burgey."

While golf has provided me with a series of three- or four-hour rest cures, it has not made me any Anthony Eden or Lucius Beebe so far as male plumage is concerned. I'm afraid it has had a disorganizing influence upon my dress. I carry a bag of practice balls and golf clubs with me in my car wherever I go, for I never know when I'll want to jump out and hit a few. With this in mind, I wear loose-fitting sweaters or shirts which don't impede the swing—a swing which has become, yearly, more of a jerk.

There's no blinking the fact that I'm famous—perhaps "notorious" would be a better word—for the casualness of my clothing. My clothes ought to be good. They cost enough. I spend as much as anyone for them. But I don't blend them well. My garb may seem excessively casual, but I really spend a lot of time picking materials and selecting styles; and I patronize the same tailor M. Menjou uses. Of course, a figure like mine, a little on the stumpy side, is pretty tough for any tailor to drape. In tails I look like "Snuffy the Cabman."

Could be that some of my sartorial color combinations are due to my color blindness. My sons have a lot of fun with this visual failing of mine. It delights them if they can trap me into some cockeyed color combination. They've gone so far as to lay out a gray sock and a blue sock for me in the morning, and I've put them on without noticing the difference.

As a result, I sometimes go around in ensembles that are frightening. Not long ago, I was playing golf near London dressed in beige slacks, a sports coat, a plaid sweater, a cap, socks of outrageous hue and moccasin shoes. I decided to drop in at an exclusive gentlemen's tailor to buy some of those good English woolen suitings. I wanted to take them home and have my tailor make them up for me. When I drove up to the shop and walked in, they took one look at me and whisked me into an inner room, a cubicle in the back. Obviously they didn't want their clients to see such a gauche derelict in their shop.

I said that I wanted to see some material. The salesman who waited on me was formal and starchy. He had on a wing collar, an Ascot tie, and a cutaway. He began to lift down bolts of cloth and as he unwound a big bolt, a moth flew out.

"Consternation" is a weak word for what ensued. People rushed from all parts of the store and went after the fluttering interloper with rolled-up copies of the *Times.* I think that they were more perturbed than they'd ever been during the German blitzes. A moth invading a Bond Street tailoring establishment is nothing less than un-British. They were still spluttering and thinking up explanations when I left. I was embarrassed for them and glad to get away.

So far as my oldest, Gary, is concerned, I've had still another filial tendency to try to curb, for in addition to his propensity for casual apparel, Gary has a low boiling point. I suppose he gets that from his Grandpa Wyatt, who is a Southern gentleman of considerable choler and asperity. Certainly he didn't get it from his phlegmatic father, Bing, who once heaved a leg of lamb at his Uncle Larry across a dinner table in Spokane, and left Paul Whiteman in a fit of pique. I noticed this tendency of Gary's last summer when we were up at the Elko ranch. He didn't want to do certain things he was expected to do, and when he had to do them, there was a rush of blood to his neck. He worked alongside Leslie Gargan—the son of my old side-kick, Bill Gargan—who was at the ranch with my kids. Leslie has a Hibernian sense of humor, and after studying Gary in one of his tantrums, he nicknamed him the Puff Adder. A puff adder is a snake whose jowls swell up when he's angry or excited. Each time Gary lost his emotional equilibrium, Leslie said reprovingly, "Gary, your wattles are showing." This broke Gary up, diluted his ire, and restored peace and quiet.

None of the three other boys have such combustible tempers. Denny's easy-going. Everything rolls off his back without ruffling his feathers. He's an average student, but there are times, when it comes to ordinary, everyday matters, that he seems pretty vague about the score. I don't think he'll mind my telling this one on him. The band leader, Horace Heidt, once gave me a clock, and I said to Denny, "This is a four-hundred-day clock. It'll run for four hundred days without winding."

"Almost a year, hey," Denny replied. Freshman in college, too.

However, I mustn't let Denny bear all the burden as our principal knot-head. In reality, he's just as smart as the others only he doesn't spend too much time thinking. Linny, for instance, pulled one that ought to qualify him for passing comment. I used to hold a small seminar at the dinner table. When the boys fell to talking too much about athletics and other unimportant subjects, I'd quiz them on history or current events, or music, or any other subject I thought they ought to know about. When I asked Linny to tell me where the surrender of Robert E. Lee to General Grant took place, he thought a moment, then said, "Approximate Court House."

I found it a little difficult to grade his answer.

Lin gets good marks in school. He works hard to get them, but there are times when study gives him the pip. Not long ago, when I was away from the country on location, he sent me a letter. He gave me a full report of the World Series and of the pre-season football forecasts. He included his advance nominations for the All-American team from the East, the Mid-west and the Coast. He caught me up to date on the big fights. In fact, he covered the whole sporting scene for me. Then he added: "p.s. Greek is for the birds."

One thing I know: I'm going to keep yipping at these little scoundrels until they're twenty-one, and I'm going to demand that they have a goal in life, a purpose. The most tragic spectacle I can think of is that of a young man slipping aimlessly through school, then life, secure in the belief that affluence means happiness. I'm not going to let up on them. Dixie didn't. She felt the same way I do about that. We discussed it at length before I left for Europe last September.

It's not easy. It makes me feel like a heel to be jumping them out all the time, and the endless pleading, the coaxing and bawling out grow tiresome. I've had so many heart-to-heart talks with Gary I'm embarrassed when I say, "Sit down, Gary. I want to have a few words with you." I feel hammy and I'm beginning to fear that my "sage counsel" is only arousing apathy. But something seems to come up all the time that I have to talk to him about. And even though I feel as if I've been on too long, we go around again.

I don't claim I'm any prize as a parent. I know I overlook things I should take care of. In the past ten or twelve years, both during and after the war, I've been on the road a lot. I'm tired when I get home from the studio at night, and there are things I should do about my kids' discipline and studies that I've let slide. But I try. Dixie tried too. Maybe we've had the wrong approach, but we've done the best we could.

Some years ago Dixie and I set up a trust fund for our boys as an irrevocable gift. It represented our bundle at the time. Jack O'Melveny is the administrator of that fund. What with the money they've earned through investments that O'Melveny has made for them, this sum has had a healthy and, with one exception, an even growth. Gary has made more than the others from record royalties and radio appearances, so his trust fund is larger than those being held for the three other boys.

When they appear on radio shows with me they're paid the same amount paid any other guest of comparable drawing power. My sons never see these checks. They go directly to O'Melveny and are placed in their trust funds. When they read in this book—if they read it—that they've been paid two thousand dollars as a unit (five hundred dollars apiece) for a single guest shot, this will be the first they knew of it. Maybe it's time they were learning such things. It won't be long until the three older boys are twenty-one, and it's high time that they were beginning to give serious thought to what they'll have and how to take care of it.

I don't suppose that it's reasonable to expect a youngster to appreciate money that's handed to him without his doing much of anything to earn it. I've noticed that the only money my sons take care of is the money they earn at the ranch for the six or seven weeks' work they do each summer. They are paid just what the other ranch employees get per day, the rate being governed by what they're doing. Our arrival there early in June coincides with a lot of work with the cattle—cutting out cows and calves, moving steers up to the summer range. Then there's a day or two of branding.

As this work thins out, the boys are given other tasks, such as dipping posts for fences, for on a big ranch fencing never stops. Treating posts this way is a dirty chore. It means building a fire under a giant tub of creosote; the posts are dipped into the tub, held there for five minutes, and then they're stacked. Then they are put to tearing down stack yards—yards built in the middle of the meadows in which hay is stacked so the cattle can't get into them during winter. Before haying starts, the fronts of these yards have to be torn down, so that when the new hay is moved in and stacked, there'll be room for the equipment to move in and out.

While haying is going on, their pay is between eight and nine dollars a day—if they also stack. Stacking is the hardest job and it pays the most. The boys do every job done in the hay field—mowing, raking, driving buck rakes, driving the roustabout truck. There're other jobs, too—irrigating, which involves digging ditches and shifting watercourses, and a couple of days' work putting out salt. This is done by loading pack horses with blocks of salt, riding up into the range near the mountains and leaving the salt at licks best situated for the cattle's use.

Some of those who read this might be interested in how a cattle ranch like mine operates. It's called a cow-and-calf deal—we raise calves and keep our cows. Sometime in early April, we turn out about seven hundred and fifty cows and calves on what is known as the Taylor grazing, depending on how long winter is and how soon the grass starts to grow on the range. This particular Taylor grazing is forty or fifty miles square, is unfenced, and belongs to the Government. Each rancher is charged so much a head for its use. Five or six of my neighbors also turn out on the Taylor tract.

Back of the range, up on the North Fork Mountains, are the Forest grazing rights. This is also a Government-owned privilege and is leased to the ranchers at so much a head. Here I put up another seven hundred and fifty cows. With both sets of cows, we put out enough bulls to take care of breeding. Our total herd this year is three thousand six hundred head.

About the middle of June the yearling steers are driven to Gold Crick forest range, a two-day drive twenty miles or so north of us. There are generally about five hundred or five hundred and fifty of these. They stay on the Gold Crick until October.

Then, in October the yearling steers are brought back from Gold Crick to the ranch. The cattle buyers look them over and buy them right there. The yearling heifers are retained for breeding purposes. After being bought, the steers are shipped to Elko and then to California. There the feeder takes them for a hundred and twenty days or more, until they're ready to be sold to the markets. These steers weigh about four hundred pounds when they go on the Gold Crick range. They come off the range weighing an average of six twenty-five to six forty.

The cows come down off the range behind the ranch early in October—particularly the old cows who feel the cold weather coming on and want to get down in the meadow. The younger ones, feeling brash and bold and not having much sense, have to be gathered in and brought back.

The five or six different outfits operating on the Taylor range have what we call a "rodeur." Each rancher sends a man out on a chuck-wagon and they cover that area for a week or ten days, gathering the cattle. Then each rancher brings his own in. Sometimes on this rodeur we find cattle which belong to ranchers seventy or eighty miles away and who have drifted in on our range. Then, too, we sometimes get phone calls from ranchers down near Elko, sixty miles away, saying that they've picked up some strays of ours which have traveled sixty, seventy or even eighty miles during the summer.

During the summer we put up the hay while the cattle are out. This is a sixty-day operation. It involves the labor of forty-five or fifty men. Last year we put up sixty-one hundred tons of hay. It's wild hay. It's stacked loosely in the stack yards in stacks of forty or fifty tons each, sometimes more.

The cattle are brought in off the range and are fed all winter from these stacks by men working in pairs. They go out either in a hay wagon or a sled, rip into a stack, load the sled, then drive down the meadowland, spreading the hay on the snow for the cattle. Sometimes the stacks freeze and the men work until noon or better to open them up so they can get the loose hay out of the stack and onto a hay wagon or sled.

It's a tough job in below-zero weather. Next year we're going to try out a new type of hydraulic loader. It will operate from a tractor and will go in up against those stacks and throw the hay up on the rick. It should make the problem of frozen stacks and winter feeding much easier.

Branding the new calves takes place in the fall, after the rodeur, and in the spring before the turn-out.

It is necessary for us to buy forty or fifty new bulls each year, since the bulls are sold off after they've been in service three years. Otherwise we would soon be inbreeding too deeply and we'd probably get a lot of one-eyed cattle.

We raise a little grain, just enough for the horses and for sick calves. We generally maintain a flock of thirty-five or forty sheep for table. Mrs. Eacret, the foreman's wife, has some chickens, and we keep about nine or ten milk cows for milk, cream, and butter. In normal periods eight or ten men work on the place, but at special times such as haying or irrigating, there are many more. A two- or three-man fence-crew operates all the time fixing fence except during the months when there's so much snow they can't get out.

The ranch and the Elko back country abound with deer. Every male citizen of Elko County likes to get his buck each year and most of them do. And they all fish. The mountains—the Ruby Mountains, twelve thousand feet high back of Elko—are full of streams and lakes jumping with hungry, solid trout. There're other ranges of mountains, all in the county: the Independence Mountains, the North Fork Mountains, the Jarbidge Mountains. These, too, are laced with good fishing streams and are full of deer.

Although I haven't hunted deer widely, I sometimes think that Elko must have more deer than any other county in the U.S.A. While riding back of our place in the North Fork Mountains, I've seen as many as fifty or sixty deer in a single day's ride. Twenty-five per cent of them were buck. And a half dozen of them live in our meadows every summer and give our grain a going over.

Elko is also one of the last bastions of the Old West. I should know. I'm quite a fancier of Old West bastions. I've been going there for more than ten years now, and I haven't been asked for an autograph or to do a benefit show, or contribute to a charity, or to do anything but mind my own business, by any resident of the county. As nearly as I can figure it, if I'm known at all, it is simply as that fellow from California with a pretty nice cattle—cow-and-calf—outfit up near Wild Horse.

There are some palaces of chance in Elko; some long bars and densely populated saloons. But if you take your wife or a daughter into one of those places there is never anything which will give them offense. A nice woman is treated with respect at Elko, no matter what place she's in. Sometimes, of course, a buckaroo may get a little exuberant and too full of flit and start a ruckus. But the big Elko casinos have bouncers who do a job on anybody who starts trouble. There are two large characters at the Commercial Hotel—Pongo and Big George—who rule with an iron hand, and if anybody gets out of line he finds himself out on the street.

I happened in one day at noon when Pongo and Big George were just coming to work. To my amazement, I noticed that they were marked up. Pongo had a mouse over one eye; George was shy a couple of teeth. I asked them what had happened; their story sounded like Damon Runyon with Wild West trimmings.

"Wild Horse Charley was in here raising a little trouble last night," they said, "and we had to throw him out." Wild Horse Charley is part Indian. He comes from my part of the county. When the grape is in him he's a very tough dude indeed.

"How did you get so mussed up?" I asked.

"He threw us back in," they told me.

But the principal feature of Elko County is its neighborliness. One winter our phone line went down during a raging blizzard and cut off our communication with Elko. Suddenly the service came back on. Two or three days later I ran into a neighbor, Johnny Oldham. He said that he'd tried to call me, and when he'd found that our line was down, he'd ridden the whole length of it through snowdrifts till he discovered the break and had repaired it for us. It had taken him the better part of a day, but he said he wasn't doing anything much; he figured I might have some important calls coming in and he thought he might as well fix the line for me.

If we're going to brand or move cattle or engage in any activity which requires a few extra men, the neighbors volunteer their services, even if it takes two or three days. We do the same for them.

Some of our crew at Elko are regulars who return to Nevada

every year for the haying. Three or four of the fellows have been with me six or seven successive seasons, and they and the boys are great pals.

Phil is particularly fond of a little guy named Screamin' Shortie. Shortie's about five-foot-two, seventy-five years old, hasn't got a tooth in his head, and is very voluble and excitable. Phil gets a tremendous jar out of him. The topper was the time he was showing Phil how to drive a tractor and rake through a very wet spot without getting it stuck. When right in the middle of the demonstration, he disappeared, equipment and all, into the deep, swampy mud, leaving his hat floating.

He came up uttering the shrill, yelping screams that gave him his name.

During the six or seven weeks my boys are on the ranch, they might go into Elko, sixty miles away, once or twice, usually to catch a picture or see a baseball game.

Elko has quite a town team. It's financed by Red Ellis of the Stockmans Hotel. I don't think it's ever been beaten on its home grounds. The team is plenty good enough in its own right, but it gets a certain amount of help from the altitude. When teams come from San Francisco, at sea level, to Elko's six thousand five hundred foot altitude, they can't judge fly balls. All an Elko hitter has to do is get a ball up and it's apt to be some kind of a hit because in high altitude a ball goes much further and it's difficult for a sea-level player to judge its flight. The altitude also does tricky things to hitting. But the Elko team practice hitting and fielding every day and they're used to these conditions.

There's good hunting for boys at the ranch. They can shoot badger, raccoon, possum, skunk, and an occasional mountain lion that passes through. If they're riding the range they're apt to see grouse and sagehen and twenty or thirty deer of an afternoon. There's lots of pickings for them after dinner or during their lunch period if they happen to be close enough.

The place is infested with rabbits and gophers to such an extent they're quite a nuisance. In the evening before dark, the boys will go out in the jeep pick-up, and two or three of them will stand in the back with twenty-twos and they'll drive up and down the dirt roads popping away at varmints.

Like all working buckaroos, each boy has a string of six horses he rides. This is necessary, for when they're working with cattle they're generally in the saddle by seven o'clock. They skip lunch and they seldom get back before five or five-thirty. They work in pretty rough country and with such a day a horse takes a beating. It takes a horse a couple of days to get over it. For that reason mounts are rotated.

A couple of years ago a horse show and riding contest was held at Hayden Lake for youngsters. There were more than a hundred entries. I tried to get Linny to enter because he's not very big and I thought his smallness would lend him appeal as a contestant. He nixed the idea, but Denny went for it instead. He borrowed a horse and some tack from a pal, worked the horse about a week, found out on what basis the events were judged and entered all of them.

I'd forgotten about it until one day when I was out on the links he came by with a cup as big as a juke box. The competition had been scored on horsemanship, form, the way they handled their tack and gear, how they saddled. And Denny had won the over-all championship.

Denny does all of the flying mounts the cowboys use in pictures. And he's a good hand with a rope and he works cattle intelligently.

I notice that the boys are reluctant to spend those ranch-earned checks. Phil still has the first one he ever earned. He deposited it in the bank five or six years ago, as well as his succeeding checks. Dennis is more profligate—or generous. He lends his money to his brothers and to his teen-age friends. He always winds up broke at the end of his month at Hayden. That's his nature, I guess. Even having worked hard for the money doesn't seem to impress its value upon him.

Five or six years ago, when Linny first took up golf, I bought a set of clubs for him suitable for a kid his size. He was careless with them and lost most of them before the season was over. A year or two later I bought him a set of ladies' golf clubs, which happen to be a good size for a boy of twelve. He took no more care of these than he did his first set.

Last year he wanted a set of man-sized clubs, but instead of buying them for him, I commandeered his ranch paycheck, cashed it, bought the clubs he wanted and gave them to him. He hasn't mislaid any of these. He watches over them and protects them conscientiously.

It's hard to beat Elko's climate in spring, summer, and fall. Because of the altitude, you can stand outside bareheaded during the summer and feel the heat soak pleasantly into your bones. In the shade or after five or six o'clock in the evening, it's pretty cool even in July and August. You need a jacket and there's sleeping under blankets twelve months a year. Early fall is a lovely season there with its cool, clear days and frosty, sparkling nights.

The winters, however, are real rough. The thermometer plummets down to twenty-five or thirty degrees below zero. Sometimes stays there for ten days or two weeks at a time. But it's simply amazing how much cold white-faced cows can take. As long as you get a little hay into their bellies, they can withstand the most freezing blasts. Last winter I went out on horseback to look at some heifers when it was down to about fifteen or sixteen below. I had on long underwear and all the jackets and scarves I could carry. Even so, I had to give up after an hour or two. I was congealed to the marrow, but not those heifers. They were kicking and playing in the snowdrifts while a blizzard beat against their backs.

Once, at the opening of fishing season when we rode high up into the mountains to try a creek, we found that six or seven head of cattle had wintered up there in a big draw, at an elevation of about eighty-five hundred feet. It must have been much colder up there than it was at the ranch. They were feeling gaunt—they call it "gant" in Elko County—but they all were alive. They must have survived by browsing on leaves and digging under snow to get at the bunch grass. At least they'd been smart enough to stay where they were when winter came instead of traveling. If they had, they would have perished in the deep drifts.

We get very deep snow up there. When Dixie and I left the house in winter time to visit a neighbor, even if he lived only five or six miles away, we were cautioned to phone as soon as we arrived and let our people know we'd arrived. If they didn't hear from us within an hour or two, they'd send out an expedition to dig us out.

Once, when Dixie and I were ready to leave, it took us all day with a bulldozer to open a road from the ranch buildings to the main highway, three or four miles away. Then we went to bed, but in the morning, when we got up, we couldn't find the road. It had all drifted over again. But we finally got out. I had a broadcast to do in San Francisco, and I barely made it.

Amusing things happen up there on our party telephone line. One day Mrs. Eacret asked Johnny Eacret to get some soap flakes in Elko and he called her from Elko and told her that her favorite store didn't have soap flakes. A strange voice interposed to say, "Try the A.&P." Things get pretty lonely on the far-flung ranches and it's not unusual for some of the cooks or the ladies of the house to listen in for a few hours. I've heard them say it's better than soap opera. "More real like. Besides, our radio reception is very poor."

As far as I'm concerned, I don't begrudge them any entertainment they get out of my calls. They must hear some very broadening conversation when Phil Harris, Bill Morrow, Bill Frawley or some of my uninhibited companions call me long distance.

Elko County has done a lot for me, and it's done more for my sons, but looking at the proposition more cold-bloodedly, it's the best investment I ever made. I've been able to improve the ranch to a point where there's none finer in the county for its size. Its extent is considerable, but it's not a vast place, because much of its acreage is unusable. It's a functioning cow-and-calf operation with nothing dudey about it.

It sometimes seems to me that most of the good handy-men still left in the country have gravitated to our section of Nevada. You can hire a buckaroo for one hundred and thirty-five dollars a month who can ride, brand, fix fence, irrigate, feed cattle, be an amateur veterinarian, drive any kind of mechanical equipment, or fix any kind of mechanical equipment. He does everything that needs to be done around a ranch and never complains, although his hours are from seven in the morning until seven at night. And after that he may have some other chores, like butchering or moving cattle.

Long ago the twins told me they wanted to go into the ranching business. And in the seven or eight years they've been at Elko working under John Eacret they've acquired a knowledge of the practical operation of such a place. Our cow boss, Jim McDermott, has been at it some forty-odd years, and he's taught the twin Crosbys the ABC's of proper cattle handling. They're taught not to work them too fast when it's hot or push them around too much when they've new calves at their sides, and they know how to mother calves and how to handle bulls. Now they're attending the State College of Washington, where they're studying animal husbandry, ranch economics, and ranch management. They'll need all of that lore they can pack into their noggins to keep abreast of the competition in the years ahead.

To give the boys their due, they work conscientiously during their period at Elko. I sometimes think their inspiration comes from their admiration for "Chunky" Grabil, the foreman. He's one of the strongest and best set up men I've ever seen, and hardly a day goes by but what they don't come in with some fabulous tale of his physical feats. Also, he knows every gold-bricking caper and he can jump them out in stentorian tones if he catches them taking an unscheduled five.

But they're not unhappy when they head for Hayden Lake

at the summer's end, to water-ski, golf, swim, beach-party and do the other things youngsters do at lake resorts in the summer time.

There are, however, relaxing interludes at the ranch. A pleasant one comes along each year during the summer. Chet Samson, an instructor at Grosse Pointe High School, outside of Detroit, takes sixty Grosse Pointe High graduates on an annual cross-country tour. They travel in a fleet of station wagons. Our ranch is one of the stops they make. We've allotted a camping ground for them up one of our streams and we go up there and have a barbecue and a little entertainment with them after dinner. My sons look forward eagerly to this visit. It's the one break they get in their long stay. And of course, the prospect of meeting vacation-taking Eastern chicks is a break worthy of anticipation.

The Detroit girls select one of their number as the most popular girl of the tour and name her Miss Sleeping Bag of 1950, or whatever year it happens to be.

We have a lot of beaver on our ranch. The Government sends men around to trap them and those trappers give the rancher a portion of the pelts. I always give Miss Sleeping Bag one of those beaver pelts to take home with her, as a souvenir of the Grosse Pointe visitation.

It's quite an event. Chet Samson tells me they look forward to it. I know we do.

One of Elko's most interesting citizens was Dobey Doc. I say "was" because having exhausted the possibilities of Elko, Dobey has sought greater glory and wider fields for his talents in Las Vegas. Dobey Doc wears bib overalls, always freshly laundered, a black string tie and a wide-brimmed Stetson. He calls all women Honey Chile and all men Sonny Boy. His silver tongue could charm the butcher birds out of the quakin' aspens.

Dobey Doc is an opportunist of the first water. One of his most famous coups occurred during the war when the Air Force established an air base at Wendover, Utah, not far from Elko. Dobey Doc went down to see the man in charge of the kitchen operation. There would be about thirty or forty thousand men producing left-overs so there would be a considerable slosh of garbage. He asked him what he planned to do with the garbage and the fellow said he hadn't made any plans. "If you deliver it in Elko, I'll take care of it for you," Dobey said.

When the man said, "Okay," Dobey Doc leased ground, had it fenced in and bought some hogs. For the remainder of the war the Army delivered garbage to Dobey Doc free and Dobey Doc raised hogs and sold them back to the Army at Wendover at a very clever price.

Dobey was also a great antique collector. He spent much of his time driving about Nevada visiting old mining towns and deserted villages and picking up furniture and other items from the few residents who still remained in those places. He had a warehouse in Elko where he kept these things and it was filled with such Americana as old furniture, dishes, and other household equipment which had been brought West by wagon train by the first settlers.

When Sophie Tucker played at Newt Crumley's Commercial Hotel, she met Dobey Doc and, hearing about his treasure trove, she evinced a desire to see his hoard. Dobey Doc showed it to her but he made no move toward presenting any of his antiques to her as a present.

As they were about to leave, Sophie could restrain herself no longer. "Dobey," she said, "aren't you going to give me one of these things?"

"Why sure," said Doc, pointing into a corner, "take that anvil there if you want to."

E VEN WITH SUCH VISITATIONS as the one from the ice cream merchant-turned-song writer and the brief but action-packed call from Pants Donnegan, the ranch at Elko and our home at Hayden Lake are oases of enjoyment in a hurly-burly world. Dixie knew that during the rest of the year our sons plan and dream of nothing except their vacation at Hayden Lake, and last August, even though she was desperately ill, she insisted that we go up there without her. When I consulted her doctors about this, they told me, "If you don't go, she'll fret because you're hanging about here, and she'll feel worse if you stay. The best thing for you is to go."

That's why I went. It's also why I went to Paris last summer to make a picture called *Little Boy Lost*. She demanded that I go, and once more her doctors said, "You'd better do it. Every day you're here, she'll think you're staying because of her and it'll make her uncomfortable."

She was that way always. She never wanted me to do anything because of her that interfered with my work. And it worked both ways. I never asked anything of her that she didn't want to do. As long as it was right, fair, and honest, we did what we pleased. When I went anywhere, it was because she wanted me to go. It was the same with her. If she wanted to go anywhere, she packed up and went. Neither of us went on the theory that marriage is a trap. We married because we fell in love, and we refused to let a family and homes turn our love into a cage. We never had any real arguments about the time I spent away from home. She knew that since I was in show business I had to go lots of places other men don't go—unless they happen to be soldiers or sailors or traveling salesmen. That seemed difficult—if not impossible—for many people to understand.

I hope to keep this section about Dixie simple, honest, and straightforward. She would have liked it that way. That was the way she was herself. Any mawkish sentimentality about her would have made her wince. She would have had more than one salty comment about it if I'd slopped over about her while she was still around to hear it.

Dixie not only collected my records, she kept every letter I ever wrote to her. Primarily this was a sentimental expression on her part but it also had its practical side. Once, when she took a trip, she was able to plan her entire itinerary by referring to my old letters. From them she was able to list the points of interest she should visit, the restaurants she would enjoy, even classifying them as to price—expensive, moderate, cheap—and the people she should seek—and avoid. For instance, one of my warnings went: "Paramount man in this city very charming. He will be delighted to show you around. Avoid his wife. Big gabber."

In the summer of 1950 Dixie went East to visit friends who have a summer home in West End, New Jersey. She stipulated only one thing. No pictures. Her privacy was respected, and although the whole town knew that she was visiting in West End, no one intruded. Knowing her fondness for good tennis, I'd arranged for tickets for her to the Nationals at the West Side Tennis Club in Forest Hills, New York. That was the first year that those great Aussies, Sedgman and McGregor, came over to trounce the Americans and take the Davis Cup home. Dixie was anxious to see them, and she made the trip to Long Island, even though it was sixty miles away. But distance and time never deterred her once she made up her mind to do something.

It was oppressively and stickily hot, and Dixie wore a smart tweed sport suit and hat to match with a pert feather in it. If she had been more familiar with August temperatures in the vicinity of New York she would have worn a cool print. But she wasn't, and half-way through the matches she was so uncomfortable that she looked around for relief and spied the marquee reserved for the press and club officials. Although not given to begging favors, the heat was too much for her and she asked her friends to see if it couldn't be arranged for her to sit under the cooler canopy.

The girl in charge of the tickets was named Muriel. She graciously changed the tickets, and Dixie and her friends saw the rest of the matches in comfort. That was late in August. Four months later, on Christmas day, the phone rang in the New York apartment belonging to the friends who had accompanied Dixie to the tennis matches. It was Muriel and she was too excited for words.

"What do you think happened this morning . . . not the day before or the day after, but Christmas morning?" she asked. "The postman delivered a small box to my house and it was a string of pearls from Mrs. Crosby! Just think of her remembering me for one little favor I did for her at the matches last August. What a lady."

When I've had to be abroad or on tour, working, I've got letters, most of them anonymous, from people taking me to task because I didn't spend more time with Dixie. They pictured her as lonely and forgotten. That was not true.

Dixie had a host of friends and she never lost one of them, although some of her attachments went back twenty-five years. She remembered the birthdays of scores of them and sent them gifts. It was a year-round job for her. Christmas was an even bigger production. In October she took over a whole room, stocked it with a table and rolls of wrapping paper, tinsel, holly, cards, and paste, and set up an Operation Xmas.

She not only shopped endlessly herself, she pressed her friends and her secretary into service as shoppers. Her gift-wrapping went on from nine in the morning until dinner time, with time out for tea and sandwiches for those who came to help her. A week or two before Christmas the Crosbys went into the local delivery business. In addition, a lot of Dixie's packages had to be mailed all over the world, for she had friends in England, France, Hawaii, and South America. I've never seen packages wrapped the way she wrapped them. With the colors she employed, the silver balls, the holly and the other ornaments, they were things of beauty. It was a shame to open them. For our Christmas at home she insisted on a big tree. It had to be tall enough to reach from floor to the ceiling. Sometimes it was touch and go whether she'd lop off a few feet of tree or call for the wreckers to cut a hole in our roof.

Our house was a singing house during the holidays. Although the boys are getting big for it now, we used to go out—the five of us—singing Christmas carols around the neighborhood. Those we serenaded asked us in for refreshments, and there were cookies for the youngsters, and a few shiny coins for all of us. I declared myself in on this spendable loot, too, to keep our caroling fivesome a real team and all of us on the same basis. If we called at the right time, when the bowl was flowing, and the cup of cheer was in hand, we'd do pretty good and come away with three or four dollars from a single house. My supporting choristers watched me like hawks to make sure I split the take five ways.

Because of something which happened during one of our caroling sessions, I'm afraid that my sons regard their Uncle Everett as a pinchpenny. We reached Everett's place last, after a successful evening. Our neighbors and their guests had been in an exceptionally expansive mood and had done handsomely for us. But during the early part of the evening Everett had been bothered by groups who had come to carol, but who had remained to be obstreperous. They had broken some of his furniture and his yuletide spirit was curdled.

When we appeared, he came to the door yelling, "Get out! I don't want any more of you scalawags!" but when he saw who it was, he let us in and we sang some songs for him. He has a famous stock of liquors under lock and key, but he just let me look at it. He gave me a carbonated soft drink instead.

When we left he placed four dimes in my sons' hands. Their faces fell and they went back to our car speechless. Then, as we drove along, Linny piped up, "We'd have done better with Jack Benny." That was a few years ago, but I don't think that my offspring have got over it yet.

I miss Dixie especially at Christmastime. She was shy, but she wasn't shy as far as her sons were concerned, nor was she diffident with me. We had our spats—as who doesn't over a span of twenty-odd years?—but they were never anything serious. I can't recall that we ever had any real down-to-the-mat arguments that ended with one of us stalking out.

The last special family reunion we had was Dixie's surprise birthday party for me in 1952. It was less than two months later that Dixie was so desperately ill that she required the surgery from which she never rallied.

No one could give a party with a more elegant touch than Dixie. She planned this surprise for me with loving care, because it was the first time in several years that I was able to be home on my birthday. The invitations read:

You are cordially invited to attend
A Surprise
Birthday Dinner
for
Bing Crosby
on Friday evening, May 2, 1952
BLACK TIE
(That'll surprise him!)

For days before the event, as soon as I left for the studio mornings, Dixie proceeded with her secret plans. She carefully picked over her guest list, making sure that all our old friends were invited and that all the people I especially liked would be on hand. She consulted with her beloved "Aunt Mary," the colored caterer who knew exactly how to carry out the plans for Dixie's parties. And she made all the arrangements for Gary, Phil and Denny to fly down from their respective schools on Friday, May 2, so that they could arrive home without my knowing it, just in time to don their black ties for the big celebration.

When I left for the studio that morning, all was as usual. Linny was getting ready for school, Dixie was at breakfast, the rest of the household bustling about their usual tasks.

When I got home at seven that evening, the Crosby manse had been transformed into a veritable tropical garden. A great marquee stretched from the back patio to the far end of the lawn. There were tables under the marquee, each bearing candles in a red and white tropical floral centerpiece. Palm trees had been temporarily planted around the patio, which had been made into a huge dance floor. At the far end of the garden was a bandstand with Les Brown and full orchestra aboard, playing "Happy Birthday to You."

As I stepped into the foyer, this was the sight that greeted me, along with about one hundred seventy-five guests, who had come to wish me well. As Dixie came up to me and put her arms around me, I am not ashamed to admit that my eyes were swimming.

I don't plan to talk about my grief at losing her. I believe that grief is the most private emotion a human being can have, and I'm going to keep mine that way. But in the years that lie ahead I'm going to sorely miss her love, her steadfast and constructive support. She was the most completely honest person I've ever known, and as the last events in her life demonstrated, one of the most courageous. Two weeks before her death, she took daily transfusions to build up her strength so she could come to the station and meet the train which brought me home. And she was there, just as she'd always been: beautifully dressed, gay, and smiling. I don't ever want anything more in life than the memory of all she did for me.

I NEED NO CRYSTAL BALL to tell me that television looms big in my future, as it does in the future of any entertainer. The principal reason I haven't had a go at it is that radio, recordings, picture-making and the other businesses in which I'm involved take up so much of my time and mean so many trips away from home that the time to do it right just isn't available. Then, too, there are a lot of things I like to do aside from business, like golfing, and fishing, and hunting, and if I did TV, when would I so indulge myself?

TV is here to stay, and it will be here when I get ready to go into it. There's a question in my mind as to what TV format would be best for me. I'm investigating the possibility of a filmed half-hour show, employing motion-picture techniques the way a big studio films a short subject. But the expense would be tremendous. It might cost so much to make that it wouldn't be practical. I'm not sure I could find a sponsor who could get up the large bundle of coin such a show would cost. But given the right format, television doesn't frighten me. I should be able to get by, doing what I've done in pictures, in camp shows, and in vaudeville—entertain.

I do think this: anybody who goes into TV should be sparing in how much work he does. No entertainer who's in everyone's home once a week can survive very long. His welcome can't be stretched that far. If a new motion picture of mine were released each week for fifty-two weeks—or even for thirty-nine weeks—I soon wouldn't have many friends coming to the theaters to see me. And they'd drop the flap on me at home, too. They'd weary of my mannerisms, my voice, my face.

Three years ago the price for my complete radio package was twenty-seven thousand five hundred dollars a broadcast. This included my salary of seven thousand five hundred dollars a week. For my 1951–52 radio broadcasting season I made a package deal with General Electric at sixteen thousand dollars a week. This same contract stipulates that so long as I'm doing a radio show for G.E. I will not do a TV show of my own—except for General Electric. I have no agreement on price with G.E., but there are indications that a big show on television would be worth up to fifty thousand per week.

In view of this, it may be cause for wonderment on the part of some that I don't succumb to the lure. Naturally, I am toying with the idea—who wouldn't at such prices?—but I'm content to take my time. After all, I'm doing reasonably well now, and I don't have to work at all if I don't want to. The reason I don't quit is that I've stayed in the entertainment business so long I've become a squirrel on a treadmill. I can see no end to my road, so I can't jump off.

I've heard many people, particularly people in show business, say that they wouldn't know what to do with themselves if they stopped. I'd know what to do. There are so many things I'd like to do that I wouldn't be bored for ten or fifteen years at least. If I did call it a day as a performer, I could take an active interest in the TV-film-producing venture I'm backing. Or I could gorge myself on fishing and hunting.

A number of interviewers have asked me, "What has been your most thrilling moment? What has given you the biggest kick?" I didn't think that the readers of fan magazines would get any emotional lift out of my answer if I leveled with them. For the truth is that I've found my most exciting moments in field-and-stream sports. I hope no one will think I'm boasting when I say I've done every kind of hunting there is to be done in this part of the world. I've hunted bear and moose, caribou, mountain sheep and goat, deer and elk in Canada. I've shot ducks, pheasants, quail, grouse, sagehens, partridge—practically everything that flies or there's an open season on. And I've enjoyed every minute of every hunting trip I've ever made.

I've fished the Cascapedia River for Atlantic salmon. I've fished in Puget Sound and on Vancouver Island for the tyee and the king salmon, and the colorful, fighting coho. I've fished in Idaho, Nevada, California, Arizona, Oregon, and in Washington. I'm a member of the Catalina Island Tuna Club and I've caught marlin, broadbill, tuna, albacore, and yellow-tail. I've fished off the coast of Mexico and every other place where rumor has reported the fishing good.

But my personal nomination for the greatest thrill of them all is to fish a good trout stream—a stream with plenty of room in which to throw a dry fly. When the conditions are right—the hatch is rising, the fly's working perfectly—you cast upstream and your fly floats lightly down on the current, and then you see a boil under the fly, a gleaming body in the sun, and your reel sings out. One such experience pays off for the longest and most arduous trip.

The coho salmon is a great fish. He's spectacular, he fights on top, and he's a jumping fool. The Atlantic salmon—*le beau saumon*—is a great fish, with a spectacular fighting ability. I've fought marlins which have earned my respect and tuna whose doggedness I admired. But for sheer excitement, the rainbow trout is the king of them all. Or at least it seems that way to me. Since I feel so strongly about the pleasures of the gun and the rod, it may seem odd that I don't call it a day and devote more time to my Nimroding and Izaak Waltoning.

Jack O'Melveny says that the real reason I don't quit is that I love to sing too much. He knows that I love show business, the people you meet in it and the excitement of it. I love music; I love working with fine orchestras and with clever and talented people at making pictures; but actually, I'd be much happier if I weren't doing it. I'm not a great actor—I'll never be one

330

—and I'm never going to create anything of lasting importance. So, no matter what I've done to date or no matter what I'm likely to do, there's little promise of great artistic satisfaction in it. With the exception of a phonograph record or two, I don't think I've ever done anything really worthwhile.

I always look at the "rushes," the previous day's work, after lunch. I dare not do so before lunch. My appetite would be ruined.

Almost anybody in pictures has that kind of reaction. You always look lousy to yourself up there on the screen. You're either over-acting or under-acting, doing nothing, or doing the wrong thing. And you always think, "If I had that to do over again, I'd do it differently."

The only reason I go to my rushes is because I generally make comedies and I have to see if there's any way I can extract a running gag from something I've already done or there may be some gag I've used that I'll want to be careful not to use again.

For that matter, I've been in several pictures I've never seen. I didn't feel they were much good when they were being made, and I didn't force myself to look at them when they were finished. I'll amend this by saying that there are a couple of pictures I'm proud of, not because of anything I did in them but because I was proud to be associated with those enterprises.

Looking back over the years since I first broke out of the Palouse country around Spokane, I recall some outstanding things in show business, things which made lasting impressions on me. These things excited me at the time and I still haven't forgotten them. I recall going to see a show called *Calico Days*, in 1928 in Chicago. It had an all-Negro cast. A tall, handsome Negress walked out in "one." Her face was wreathed in a warm, ingratiating smile. Her eyes sparkled as she sang, "Dinah." Her name: Ethel Waters.

When I was emceeing the Paramount stage show in the early 1930's, there was an act I introduced. Then I'd stand in the wings and watch them every show, five times a day during their two-week engagement. There were about twenty violins in the string section of the orchestra and they played *"Toujours l'amour"* as the two attractive people—he in white tie and tails and she in a lovely evening gown—moved gracefully about the stage while I stood bewitched. Their names were Veloz and Yolanda.

Then there was the great team of Buck and Bubbles, particularly the dancing member of the team, Bubbles. He was considered by Fred Astaire (and many others) to be the greatest soft shoe, buck and wing, or tap dancer who ever lived. At every performance we had visiting dancers in the wings, who had dropped in from other vaudeville circuits or motion picture presentation houses, who came over to watch and learn. People like Eleanor Powell and Hal Le Roy. Five times a day, seven days a week, Bubbles never danced the same routine twice, but always an inspired improvisation. Later he went on to play "Sportin' Life" in *Porgy and Bess.*

I remember the first time I sat in the Whiteman Band and heard it play George Gershwin's "Rhapsody in Blue." And when I heard the great Glenn Miller band in England during the war. In my opinion that was the greatest all-purpose band ever put together. And I remember Benny Goodman's first band, which was likewise an immortal group. And the great Jean Goldkette orchestra when they played at the Greystone Ballroom in Detroit. And Roger Wolfe Kahn's orchestra of All-Stars.

Other blinding highlights were seeing Mary Martin in *South Pacific,* and Ethel Merman in *Annie Get Your Gun.* These two performances are in a photo-finish for the greatest I've ever watched on the musical-comedy stage.

High on my personal list of memorable moments are the great duets of Joe Venuti and Eddie Lang when they recorded together and when they played a specialty performance.

I could list a jillion acts from vaudeville that I religiously made it a point to catch, and I still remember fondly acts like Williams and Woofus, and Roy Cummings of the Avon Comedy Four, and the Marx Brothers.

Turning to memorable moments in a more classical tradition, I can get real dreamy when I hear a fine orchestra play the "Intermezzo" from *Cavalleria Rusticana*. Any reasonably good bass-baritone can move me with a rendering of "Ol' Man River," particularly if he doesn't duck the highs and lows. I can listen with genuine (if uncomprehending) pleasure to any good orchestra playing Debussy or Ravel. Puccini I feel wrote some of the greatest melodies of all time. I'm playing infield for most of Wagner's music, and except for the "Toccata and Fugue" Bach eludes me, as do Brahms, Beethoven, and Mozart, although they have written some things that give me pleasure.

Bear in mind that I pose as no expert. This is merely the way these things strike me, and affect my untutored taste. I can listen to any good contralto sing anything and like it. Although I appreciate the technique of sopranos, they don't thrill me much because I'm always conscious that it's the employment of such technique that makes them great.

When all is said and done, my favorite music is Dixieland music. I can get up in the morning after a restless night, feeling blue and depressed, put on some of those good Decca LP's featuring Eddie Condon's band or Red Nichols or Louis Armstrong—or any solid practitioner of the cult, for that matter—and after half an hour of this music I'm picked up and ready to go again. I guess what I've disclosed reveals me as a fellow without much class.

But those are the things I have enjoyed and enjoy now.

As far as my story is concerned, I guess that's just about it.

Comes now the expression I picked up from director Lloyd Bacon, "This is *aloha* on the steel guitar." It means "This is the end." Bacon brought the saying with him from Honolulu, where *aloha* is a way of saying good-bye. It's the last thing you hear when you leave that port.

About five-thirty at the studio, when I'm growing weary and the director says, "How about one more scene?" I say, "O.K., but after that it's *aloha* on the steel guitar." So I'm saying it now.

A

Academy of Motion Picture Arts and Sciences, 38, 162, 182
"Adeste Fideles," 141
Agua Caliente (Mexico), 105
Albert, Colonel Charles S., 76-77
Albertson, Frankie, 45
Ambassador East Hotel (Chicago), 278
American Handicap, 236
American Society of Composers, Authors, and Publishers, 286
Andrews Sisters, 140
Aquacade, New York World's Fair, 226-227
Aqueduct Race Track, 238
Arcadia, California, 231
Armstrong, Louis, 140-141, 238, 333
Arnheim, Gus, 96, 103, 104, 108
Astaire, Fred, 156, 173, 292-293, 332
Auditorium Theater (Spokane), 65
Auer, Mischa, 177
Avon Comedy Four, 50, 332

B

Babcock, Chester
  see Van Heusen, Jimmy
Bacon, Lloyd, 333
Bailey, Mildred, 50, 75, 77, 79
Bailey's Music Company, 75
Bakersfield, California, 78-79
Balaski, Lester, 236-237
Baldwin, Hank ("Bandit"), 221-225

Baltimore, Maryland, 114-115, 234
Bampton, Rose, 151
Bargy, Roy, 50, 86
Barrancosa, 236
Barris, Harry, 42, 92-97, 103-107, 140
Barrymore, Ethel, 183-186
Barrymore, John, 183
Barrymore, Lionel, 183
Bay Meadows Race Track, 233, 248
Beery, Wallace, 107, 120
Beiderbecke, Bix, 50, 85, 87-89, 93, 258
Beldame Handicap, 236
Bell, Art, 193
Bellarmine Academy, 303
The Bells of St. Mary's, 177
Belmont Park Race Track, 236, 238
Belvedere Hotel (New York), 86-87
Benny, Jack, 153
Bergman, Ingrid, 177
Berkeley, California, 81-82
Berlin, Irving, 78, 142, 279-280
Bernie, Ben, 47
Beverly Hills, California, 122, 261, 301
Beverly Hills Hotel, 168
Biltmore Hotel (Los Angeles), 83
Big Broadcast, The, 115, 122
Big George, 313
Boone Avenue gang, 62
Bing, Rudolph, 274
Bing-Lin stable, 234
Bing's Bucket, 39
Bing's Things, 254
"Bingville Bugle," 57
Birth date, 55

335

Birthday party, 325-326
Birth of the Blues, The, 172
Black Forest, 232-234
Blackstone Valley Handicap, 234-235
Blondell, Joan, 177
Blue, Ben, 201
Bogart, Humphrey, 187
Boles, John, 101, 102
Bolsheviks, The, 71
Boomer, Roy, 74
Boston, Massachusetts, 272
Boswell, Connee, 238
Boswell Sisters, 140
Boulevard Theater (Los Angeles), 80
Boyington, C. J., 62-63
Bradley, Colonel E. R., 232, 246-247
Bradley, General Omar, 294-295
Bradley, Truman, 212
Brandstatter, Eddie, 103
British Amateur Golf Tournament,
    210, 268
Brewster, Edmund (ancestor), 53
Brook, Clive, 134
Brooklyn Dodgers, 278
Brooks, Shelton, 96
Brown Derby (Hollywood), 167
Brown, Francis, 195
Brown, Les, 326
Brown, Nacio Herb, 118
Brussels, Belgium, 273-275
Brox Sisters, The Three, 101
Brunswick Record Corporation, 139
Buck and Bubbles, 332
Burke, Johnny, 34, 135, 138, 162-171
Burns and Allen, 115, 125
Burr, Henry, 56
Butler, Dave, 124, 177-180
Butler, Frank, 157
Butler Hotel (Seattle), 78
Butte, Montana, 38
Butterworth, Charlie, 238-239

C

Calcutta Pool, 193, 195
Callahan, Pinky, 71
Calloway, Cab, 94
Camden, New Jersey, 86
Cantor, Eddie, 50

Capitol Theater (New York), 115,
    116, 156
Capitol Theater (San Francisco), 80
Capra, Frank, 181-182
Carlisle, Mary, 174
Carmel, California, 303, 304
Carmichael, Hoagy, 88, 182
Carps, Jack, 109
Carroll, Carroll, 150
Carroll, Madeleine, 180-181
Catalina Island, 126-128
Catalina Island Tuna Club, 330
Cavanaugh, Jimmy, 93
Celebrities' Golf Tournament, 296
Chaliapin, Feodor, 151
Challis, Bill, 86
Charlie Dale's (nightclub), 75
Chapman, Jack, 72
Chasen's (restaurant), 156
Cherbourg, France, 267, 293
Chesterfield cigarettes, 150
Chicago, 43, 44, 45, 48, 83, 93, 99,
    140, 271, 277, 288, 331
Chicago Cubs, 277
Church of the Good Shepherd, 122
Cincinnati, Ohio, 95, 258
Ciro's (Hollywood), 164
Clark, Jack, 34
Clarke, Don, 83
Clemmer Theater (Spokane), 74, 76
Cleveland, Ohio, 84
Clifford, Gordon, 104
Coconut Grove (Los Angeles), 103-
    105, 107, 111, 115, 148, 162, 208
Coffee Dan's (Los Angeles), 208
Cohen, Manny, 174-175
Cole, Nat King, 52
Coleman, George, 215-217, 264
College Humor, 116, 164
College Inn (Chicago), 45
Colman, Ronald, 131
Colonna, Jerry, 201-204, 238
Columbia Broadcasting System, 107-
    108, 111, 270
Columbo, Russ, 103, 114
Columbus, Ohio, 95
Commercial Hotel (Elko), 313, 320
Como, Perry, 114
Condon, Eddie, 333
Confessions of a Co-ed, 115

Cooper, Gary, 38, 42, 116, 132
Corkery, Father, 188
Cotton Club (Culver City), 140
Cotton Club (New York City), 94
Cottrell, Jimmy, 62, 175-181
Cowboy and the Lady, The, 79
Cremo cigars, 111-112
Crosby, Bob (brother), 57, 131, 132
Crosby, Dennis (son), 130, 271, 299-305, 307-309, 314-319, 324-326
Crosby, Dixie Lee (wife), 45-49, 58-59, 103, 107, 116, 121, 130-131, 134, 136, 162, 164, 166, 187, 271-272, 299, 300, 302, 303, 304, 308, 317, 321-327
Crosby Enterprises, 133, 254, 273
Crosby, Everett (brother), 57, 77, 79, 101, 107-109, 110, 112, 118, 131, 133, 254, 324-325
Crosby, Gary Evan (son), 116, 280, 298-305, 306, 307-309, 314-319, 324-326
Crosby, Harry (father), 52-53, 54, 55, 56, 57, 63, 131-133, 242
Crosby, Kate Harrigan (mother), 51, 52-53, 54, 55, 56, 57, 60, 61-63, 75, 77, 131-134, 241, 242
Crosby, Larry (brother), 57, 62, 77, 131, 141-142, 306
Crosby, Lindsay (son), 40, 41-42, 197, 299-304, 307-309, 314-319, 324-326
Crosby, Lloyd (cousin), 64
Crosby, Mary Rose (sister), 57, 61, 131, 133
Crosby, Nathaniel (great-grandfather), 53-54
Crosby, Philip (son), 299-304, 307-309, 314-319, 324-326
Crosby, Ted (brother), 57, 65
Crumley, Newt, 264, 320
Cuhl, Cal, 150
Culpepper, Edward, *see* Pepper, Jack
Culver City, California, 140
Cummings, Roy, 332
Cypress Point Club, 190-197

D

Dallas, Texas, 201-204
Davies, Marion, 118-121, 168, 261

"Day You Came Along, The," 117
Dean, Barney, 34, 35, 158-162
Decca Records, Incorporated, 139-140, 253, 254, 333
Del Mar Race Track, 35, 237-238, 239-242
Demaret, Jimmy, 191-192, 197, 213-215
De Mille, Cecil B., 136
Derham, Mike, 71
De Sylva, Buddy, 37, 93, 124, 145
Devine, Andy, 174
Di Maggio, Joe, 273
Dirty Six, The, 71
Dishman, Washington, 73
Dixieland Jazz Band, 72
Dobey Doc, 319-320
Doctor Rhythm, 174
Doheny, Pat, 254
Don Bingo, 236
Don Mike, 236
Donoso, Ruperto, 235
Donovan, John, 273-275
Dorsey, Jimmy, 50, 89, 93, 140
Dorsey, Tommy, 50, 93, 140
Dreamboat, 242-245
Dudley, Ed, 197
Duffield, Marshall, 245-246
Dunne, Artie, 114-115

E

Eacret, Johnny, 317, 318
Eacret, Mrs., 311, 317
Ebbets Field, Brooklyn, 278
Edwards, Gus, 96
Eisenhower, General Dwight D., 295-297
Elko County, Nevada, 41, 67, 91, 214-215, 264, 285, 287, 289, 301, 306, 309-321
Elko, Nevada, 285, 287, 289, 312-313, 314, 317, 319-320
Ellington, Duke, 94, 140
Ellis, Red, 314
Ellis Island, 258
Elman, Mischa, 279-280
El Paso, Texas, 201
Emperor's Waltz, The, 160, 215
Empire City Race Track, 238

Etolia II, 236
Everyman's Club, 64, 65

F

Fairbanks, Douglas, Sr., 115
Fanchon and Marco circuit, 79
Farley, Max, 50
Fields, W. C., 155-156
Fields, Benny, 148
Fight On, 245-246
Fitzgerald, Barry, 37, 38, 156, 188, 189
Flippen, Jay C., 201
Fontainebleau, France, 296
Forest Hills, New York, 322
Fox Studio, 45, 46, 121
Fradkin and Tarradasch, 158
Frank, Abe, 105, 107, 110-111, 121
Frawley, William, 317
Freed, Arthur, 80, 118
Friday, Pat, 164-165
Frisco, Joe, 247-252
Fulton, Jack, 86

G

Gallagher, Skeets, 117
Gallico, Paul, 268
Galt, Colonel, 295
Gargan, Leslie, 306
Gargan, William, 271, 306
Garron, Tubby, 143-146
Gaylord, Charlie, 86
General Electric Corporation, 329
George Olsen's Club, 92
Gennet records, 88
Gibson, Dick, 167
Gilmartin, Father, 65
Gilmore, Father, 71
Ginsberg, Henry, 145
Glasgow, Scotland, 292-293
Going Hollywood, 118-120
Going My Way, 35-38, 186-189, 255
Goldkette, Jean, 332
Goldstein, Leonard, 103
Gonzaga High School, 63, 64-65, 68-70, 71-72, 134, 303
Gonzaga University, 38-40, 60, 65, 72-74, 123, 134, 163, 188, 284

Goodman, Benny, 173, 332
Goodwin, Bill, 167-168
Gorman, Ross, 78
Gottler, Archie, 96
Grabil, "Chunky," 318
Grainger, Percy, 151
Granada Theater (San Francisco), 205
Grauman's Chinese Theater (Los Angeles), 38
Graves, Charles, 228
Great Northern Railway Company, 76-77
Green, Harry, 117
Greer, Jimmie, 104
Greystone Ballroom (Detroit), 332
Griffith Park Golf Course, 205-210
Grofé, Ferde, 86
Grosse Pointe High School, 319
Guinan, Tommy, 257-258

H

Halley, Matt, 284-285
Harrigan, Annie (aunt), 54
Harrigan, Ambrose (uncle), 54
Harrigan, Dennis (grandfather), 33, 54
Harrigan, Ed (uncle), 54
Harrigan, Frank (uncle), 54
Harrigan, George (uncle), 54-55, 61
Harrigan, Katherine (grandmother), 33, 54
Harrigan, Will (uncle), 54
Harriman, Tennessee, 45
Harrington, Pat, 201
Harris, Phil, 211-212, 317
Hartman, Don, 157-158
Hass, Buddy, 234
Hay, Peter, 192
Hayden Lake, Idaho, 285, 301, 302, 315, 318-319, 321
Hayden, Sterling, 180-181
Hayton, Lennie, 86
Heafner, Clayton, 196
Hearst, William Randolph, 118, 120
Heaton, Jimmy, 72, 76
Heidt, Horace, 307
Held, Otto, 65-66
Here Comes the Groom, 181

Index

Herman, Woody, 140
Hicks, Milt, 211-212
Hobart family, 57
Hobart, Valentine, 57
Hoelle, Bill, 192
Hoffman, Biff, 195-196
Hogan, Ben, 91, 198-200, 213-215, 223
Hogan, Society Kid, 271, 273, 275
Holiday Inn, 173
Hollywood, 46, 47, 79, 97, 99, 101, 103, 115, 116-117, 131, 135, 159, 162, 163, 164, 169, 170, 175, 247, 251, 256
Hollywood Park Race Track, 235-236, 238, 239
"Home on the Range," 150
Hope, Bob, 69, 115, 123, 148, 153, 156-161, 166, 168, 179-180, ♦187, 192, 197-204, 227-229, 231, 235, 238, 241, 253, 254, 266, 272
Howard, Charles, 232, 234, 239, 240
Howard, Eugene, 65
Howard, Lindsay, 116, 234-240
Howard, Willie, 65
Hyers, Frankie, 201

I

Idaho, 284-285
"Ile de France," 290
Inland Brewery, 55, 63, 65, 131
"I Surrender, Dear," 104, 106, 108, 203

J

Jackson, Chevalier, M.D., 112
Jamaica Race Track, 238
Jasper National Park, Canada, 160, 215
Jasper Park Invitational Golf Tournament, 215-216
Jesmer's Bakery, 53
Jesuits Order, 63, 68-69, 72, 186, 298
Johnson, Albert, 231-232, 236, 245, 246-247
Johnson, Spike, 75
Johnson, Tod, 253
Jolson, Al, 50, 65, 143, 153-154

Jordan, Louis, 140
Juicy Seven, The, 72
Just for You, 183-184, 287
Justin, Sidney, 109
"Just One More Chance," 106, 108

K

Kahn, Roger Wolfe, 332
Kapp, Jack, 139-140, 141-142, 253
Keaton, Buster, 238
Keene, Dick, 121-122
Keith-Orpheum Circuit, 94-97
Kemp, Hal, 262-263
Kennelly, Father, 70
Kenny, General George, 59
Khan, Aly, 273
KHJ (radio station), 256
Kibbee, Guy, 265-266
King, Charlie, 256-257
King of Jazz, The, 97-99, 102
Klamath Falls, Oregon, 78
Klein, Manny, 111
Kraft Music Hall, 150-151, 164, 262
Kruger, Stubby, 226, 227

L

Laemmle, Carl Jr., 97
Laemmle, Carl Sr., 97
Lakeside Golf Course, 117, 122, 156, 212, 213, 220, 229
Lamour, Dorothy, 121, 272-273
Lang, Eddie, 89-92, 111, 261, 332
Lane, Eastwood, 87
Lareida's Dance Pavilion (Dishman, Washington), 73, 76
Lee, Dixie, *see* Crosby, Dixie Lee
Lee, Peggy, 138-139,
Lehmann, Lotte, 151
Leib, Muriel, 323
Lemmon, Gladys, 62
Levant, Oscar, 175-177
Ligaroti, 235-236, 239-240
Lillie, Bea, 93, 174
Lindy, Leo, 278-279
Little Boy Lost, 103, 124, 182, 321
Little, Lawson, 194-196, 197
Livingston, Fred, 89
Lobero Theater (Santa Barbara), 82

Index

Logan Avenue gang, 62
Lombard, Carole, 125-129
London, Dan, 273
London, England, 177, 210, 229-230, 268, 291, 292, 305
Los Angeles, California, 40, 42, 43, 44, 45, 50, 62, 77; 78, 79, 80, 81, 82, 83, 84, 100, 102, 103, 104, 155, 177, 205, 214, 251, 256, 273, 296
Louis, Joe, 184
Loyola University (Los Angeles), 123
Lyman, Abe, 79, 103
Lyman, Mike, 79
Lynch, Joseph, M.D., 57, 71
Lynn, Leo, 134-136

M

McCarey, Leo, 35-38, 188-189
McDermott, Jim, 318
McDonnell, Jim, 158-159
McGinnis, Al, 264
McGregor, Kenneth, 322
McHugh, Frank, 37, 189
McKinney's Cotton Pickers, 72
McLarnin, Jimmy, 275-276
McLean, Jack, 205-210
McSpaden, Jug, 197
MacDowell, Edward, 87
MacGregor, Chummy, 89
Madam La Zonga, 236
Majestic Theater, 80
Malneck, Mattie, 92, 93
Manone, Wingy, 172-173, 238
Marciano, Rocky, 184
Marco, 79-80
Martin, Mary, 172, 173, 332
Marx, Groucho, 153, 271, 276-279
Marx Brothers, 332
Mason-Dixon Orchestra, 43
Mayer, Ray, 79
Mazarro, Salvatore, see Lang, Eddie
Medford, Oregon, 78
Memphis Five, The, 72
Mercer, Johnny, 182
Merman, Ethel, 125, 332
Metro-Goldwyn-Mayer, 159
Metropole Hotel (Brussels), 274-275
Metropolitan Theater, see Paramount Theater

Metz, France, 293
Meyers, Vic, 72
Michelmans, Hen, 291
Midge, 236-237
Miller, Glenn, 291, 332
Million Dollar Theater (Los Angeles), 42
Mills Brothers, The, 115, 140
Minute Maid Orange Juice Distribution, 192
Mississippi, 46, 125, 155
"Mississippi Mud," 93
Mr. Music, 147
Monaco, Jimmy, 236
Moncrief, Monty, 254
Monterey, California, 194
Monterey Peninsula Country Club, 190-197
Montmartre Café (Los Angeles), 45, 103
Morin, Les, M.D., 41
Morrisey Music Hall Revue, The, 80-82
Morrisey, Will, 80
Morrow, Bill, 154, 253, 262, 266-275, 281-282, 317
Morse, Jack, 186-187
Mound City Blues Blowers, 80
Munnings, Sir Alfred, 161-162
Murray, Ken, 238
Musicaladers, 72-76, 77
Myers, Johnny, 273

N

Nancy, France, 293
Narragansett Race Track, 234-235
Nashville, Tennessee, 95
National Tennis Championships, 322-323
Nelson, Byron, 197, 198-200
Newkirk, Newton, 57
New London, Connecticut, 272
New Orleans, 45, 172, 197-198
New York City, 33, 43, 44, 84, 86-88, 91, 92-95, 98-99, 108, 110-114, 115, 132, 156, 169, 200, 226-227, 246, 265, 272, 278-279, 280, 296
Nichols, Red, 333

Niven, David, 229
Novis, Donald, 104

O

Oakie, Jack, 46, 117-118
Oakland, California, 209
Oblath's Restaurant, 132
O'Brien, Father, 71-72
O'Brien, Pat, 238-239
O'Keefe, Dennis, 254
Oldham, Johnny, 313
Old Gold cigarettes, 97, 256
"Old Ox Road, The," 116
Oliver, Ed, 191
Oliver, "King," 87, 140
Olney, 235
Olson, Nancy, 147
O'Melveny, John, 109, 253, 308, 330
Ontario, Canada, 54
Oom Paul, 245
Orange Grove Theater (Los Angeles), 80
Oscar Award, *see* Academy of Motion Picture Arts and Sciences
O'Sullivan, Denis, 56

P

Paley, William, 108, 110, 111
Palmer, Ford, 245-246
Palm Springs, California, 168, 188-189
Palo Alto, California, 298-299
Paramount-Publix, Inc., 82, 159, 205
Paramount Studios, 36-37, 46, 109-110, 115, 118, 122, 124, 132, 133, 136, 145, 156, 157-158, 175, 187, 227
Paramount Theater (Los Angeles), 42, 82, 205
Paramount Theater (New York), 84-85, 112, 113-114, 331-332
Paris, France, 124-125, 151, 182-183, 264, 267-269, 282-284, 293, 321
Paris-Louvre, The (San Francisco), 250
Partington, Jack, 82
Patterson, Bessie, 164
Patton, General George R., 211
Pebble Beach (California), 42, 135, 215, 273, 300, 303, 304

Pebble Beach Golf Club, 190-197, 303
Peers, Donald, 228-229
Pekin, The (Spokane), 74
Penna, Toney, 197
Pepper and Salt, 200
Pepper, Jack, 200-204
Perella, Harry, 50
Perlberg, Bill, 103, 182
Philadelphia, Pennsylvania, 86, 89, 91
Philco Corporation, 152
Piatigorsky, Gregor, 151
Pimlico Race Track, 234
Pingatore, Mike, 50
Pittsburgh Pirates, 255, 277, 278, 301-302
Playground, Tommy Guinan's, 257-258
Plaza Hotel (Brussels), 274
Pleasanton Fair Grounds, 233
Pocantico Hills, 33-35
Polesie, Herb, 57-58, 175, 236
Polesie, Midge, 236, 237
Pongo, 313
Poor Clare Order, 51
Pope Pius XII, 186
Porter, Bob, 71
Portland, Oregon, 54, 65, 75, 78, 102, 104, 213
Powell, Jack, 177-179
Preceptor, 234-235
Pressman, Joel, M.D., 271-272
Prince of Luxemburg, 210-211
Pritchard, Bob, 72, 76
Pritchard, Clare, 72, 76
Professional Golfers Association of America, 283
Professional Golfers Association Tournament, 213
Pullman, Washington, 73

Q

"Queen Elizabeth," 279
Quicksell, Howdy, 89
Quigley, Bill, 237-238, 240

R

Raft, George, 122
Ragland, Rags, 34

Rancho Santa Fe, California, 237, 239, 265
Ray, Harry, 123
Ray, Ted, 228-229
Reaching for the Moon, 115
Reis, Les, 114-115
Rhythm Boys, The, 42, 45, 72, 92-97, 101, 103-107, 115
Rhythm on the River, 173, 175
Rice, Grantland, 265
Rich, Freddie, 111
Richardson, Speck, 239-240
Rinker, Al, 42, 43, 44, 50, 72, 74, 75, 76, 77-86, 92-97, 103-107, 140, 204-210
Rinker, Mildred, *see* Bailey, Mildred
Rinker, Miles, 72, 76
Ritz Carlton Hotel (Boston), 169
Roach, Hal, 231
Road to Bali, The, 157
Road to Morocco, The, 69, 124, 179-180
Road to Rio, The, 273
Road to Singapore, The, 156
Road to Zanzibar, The, 168
Rockefeller, Winthrop, 33-35, 280
Rockford, Illinois, 96
Rogell, Al, 180-181
Rogers, Will, 120, 149-150
Romanoff's (restaurant), 183-184
Roosevelt, Eleanor, 277
Roosevelt Hotel (Hollywood), 100
Rose, Billy, 227
Roseland Ballroom, 87
Ruggles, Wesley, 268
Ruskin, Simon L., M.D., 112-113
Ryan, Jim, 121-122

S

St. Andrews, England, 210
St. Catherine Hotel (Catalina Island), 126-128
St. Francis Hotel (San Francisco), 273
St. Louis, Missouri, 95
St. Louis Browns, 255
Saint Mère Eglise, France, 295
St. Valentine's Day Massacre, 99
Samson, Chet, 319

"Sam's Song," 300-301
San Antonio Golf Tournament, 219
San Diego, California, 102
San Fernando Valley, 57, 116-117
San Francisco, 50, 78, 80, 81, 195, 205, 209, 231, 233, 250, 273, 286, 317
San Jose, California, 209, 303
San Juan Capistrano Handicap, 244
Santa Anita Race Track, 231, 233, 235, 237, 238, 242-244, 248
Santa Barbara, California, 82
Santa Monica, California, 130-131
Saratoga Race Track, 232, 238
Saratoga Springs, New York, 149-150
Savoy and Brennan, 50, 65
Schertzinger, Victor, 157
Scott, Cyril, 87
Scott, Ralph, 41
Screamin' Shortie, 314
Screen Actors Guild, 135
Seabiscuit, 232, 239-240, 303
Seagle, Oscar, 56
Seaton, George, 182
Seattle, Washington, 55, 65, 72, 78, 102, 103, 104
Sebastian, Frank, 140
Sedgman, Frank, 322
Seminole Golf Club, 223-224
Sennett, Mack, 105-107
Service, Robert W., 68
Shaeffer, Harvey, 217-227, 242-245, 265
Sharp, Father, 38-39, 303
Shaw, Artie, 111
Shay, Dorothy, 35
Shelley, Dave, 168
She Loves Me Not, 121, 122-123
Sherman Hotel (Chicago), 45
Sherry-Netherland Hotel (New York City), 34
Sholderer family, 66-67
Sholderer, Walter, 66
Shurr, Dr., 169-171
"Silent Night," 141-142
Silvers, Phil, 34, 238, 239
Silvers, Sid, 159
"Simple Melody, A," 279-280, 300
Sinatra, Frank, 103
Sinclair, Harry, 246-247

Smith, Kate, 115
Snead, Sammy, 223
Souders, Jackie, 78
Sousa, John Philip, 56
Southern California Golf Association, 209
Sparks, Ned, 117
Spokane Ideal Laundry, 60
Spokane, Washington, 40, 42, 50, 51, 55-56, 57, 62, 65, 66, 67, 72, 73, 74, 75, 77, 78, 83, 84, 119, 131, 175, 187, 331
Spokesman-Review, 63-64
Stafford, Mr., 79
Stanford University, California, 298-299
Stanley Theater (Philadelphia), 86
Star Simon, 242
Stevens, Arnold, M.D., 137-139
Stevens, Risë, 151, 189
Stillwater, Minnesota, 54
Sterling, Ford, 107, 117
Street Singer, The, 115
Stockmans Hotel (Elko), 314
Surburban Handicap, 236
Sunset Handicap, 235-236
Swede's, The (Los Angeles), 79

T

Tacoma, Washington, 54, 55, 104
Tarleton, Nel, 275-276
Tarrytown, New York, 34
Taurog, Norman, 129
Teagarden, Jack, 141, 172
Television, 328-329
Temple Golf Club, Maidenhead, 228-229
"Temptation," 120
Tent, The (Los Angeles), 79
Texas Open Golf Tournament, 198-200
"Thanks," 117
Thomas, Danny, 138-139
Thomas, Lou, 212
Tivoli Theater (Chicago), 43, 44, 83-84, 93
Togo, 57-58
Toluca Lake, 116-117, 156
Too Much Harmony, 117

Trotter, John Scott, 238, 253, 262-264, 271
Tucker, Sophie, 320
Turf Club (Del Mar), 238
Twenty-Second Agricultural District of San Diego County, California, 237

U

Universal Pictures, 97, 99, 177
University of San Francisco, 39
University of California, 81-82, 100
University of Southern California, 80, 100, 164
University of Washington, 78, 137

V

Vagrancy, 236
Vallee, Rudy, 103, 114, 148
Vancouver Hotel (Vancouver), 59, 281-282
Vancouver, British Columbia, 281
Vanderbilt, Alfred, 280
Van Heusen, Jimmy, 34, 168-171
Vanity Handicap, 236
Varian and Mayer, 79
Veloz and Yolanda, 332
Venuti, Joe, 50, 91, 111, 173, 253, 255-262, 332
Versailles, France, 295-296
Victory Caravan tour, 277
Vocco, Rocco, 242

W

Walker, Jimmy, 93
Walla Walla, Washington, 44
Walsh, Raoul, 118-121
Waring, Fred, 73
Washington, D. C., 288, 296
Washington State College, 73, 76, 318
Waters, Ethel, 94, 331
Waxahachie, 202-204
Webster School, 57, 59-60, 61, 62, 63
Weiss, Sam, 301
Weissmuller, Johnny, 226-227
Wenatchee, Washington, 64

Index

We're Not Dressing, 125-129, 130
West End, New Jersey, 322
Westmore, Wally, 124-125
West Side Tennis Club, 322-323
Weyerhaeuser Timber Company, 64
Wheeler Ridge, California, 79
"When the Blue of the Night," 142, 203
"White Christmas," 142, 293-294
Whiteman Club (New York City), 93
Whiteman, Loyce, 103
Whiteman, Paul (Pops), 42-44, 45, 50, 72, 82-87, 89, 92-102, 103, 112, 172, 255-257, 259-261, 306, 332
Whitney, Jock, 231, 280
Wiedoeft, Rudy, 78

Wild Horse Charley, 313
Williams and Woofus, 332
Wing, Toby, 117
Wolfe, Georgie, 239-240
Wolverines, 87-88
Woodbury soap, 150
World's Fair, New York, 226-227
Wyatt, Grandpa (father-in-law), 306
Wyatt, Wilma Winifred, *see* Crosby, Dixie Lee

Y

Yakima, Washington, 64
Yates, Ducky, 265-266
Young, "Skin," 42-43, 86